ESSAYS IN THE
ECONOMIC AND SOCIAL HISTORY
OF TUDOR AND STUART ENGLAND

ESSAYS IN THE ECONOMIC AND SOCIAL HISTORY OF TUDOR AND STUART ENGLAND

IN HONOUR OF

R. H. TAWNEY

*Professor Emeritus of Economic History
in the University of London*

EDITED BY

F. J. FISHER

*330.942
F533
40004*

CAMBRIDGE
AT THE UNIVERSITY PRESS
1961

Printed in Holland

DEDICATION

These essays are respectfully presented to Professor R. H. Tawney
on the occasion of his eightieth birthday
and as a tribute to the work
of one of the great historians of Tudor and Stuart England,
by some of those
who owe much to his inspiration and guidance.

CONTRIBUTORS

F. J. Fisher, *Professor of Economic History in the University of London, London School of Economics*

Christopher Hill, *Fellow and Tutor in Modern History, Balliol College, Oxford*

Maurice Beresford, *Professor of Economic History in the University of Leeds*

Joan Thirsk, *Senior Research Fellow in English Agrarian History, University of Leicester*

Lawrence Stone, *Fellow of Wadham College, Oxford*

Ralph Davis, *Lecturer in Economic History, University of Hull*

Robert Ashton, *Lecturer in Economic History, University of Nottingham*

G. E. Aylmer, *Lecturer in History, University of Manchester*

D. H. Pennington, *Senior Lecturer in History, University of Manchester*

D. C. Coleman, *Reader in Economic History in the University of London, London School of Economics*

CONTENTS

TAWNEY'S CENTURY

'THE century which separates the Dissolution of the Monasteries from the Great Rebellion may almost be defined...as "Tawney's century".[1] So wrote Professor Trevor-Roper, and many will think his definition a happy one. Yet it is doubtful whether all will accept his reason for offering it—i.e. that Tawney has reinterpreted that century in terms of a rising gentry drawing their strength from new agricultural techniques and a declining aristocracy weakened by economic conservatism and fashionable extravagance—or share his fear that such an interpretation is in danger of becoming a new orthodoxy. Unanimity is scarcely a characteristic of those whose work owes most to Tawney's influence, and Tawney himself has made the appropriate comment upon the fragility of historical orthodoxies—'all flesh is grass and historians wither quicker than most.' His influence has been exercised through more varied channels and at a more profound level. A great teacher has the gift of attracting men of sufficient calibre to be able critically to test his suggestions in the light of the empirical evidence which they unearth, to modify where necessary the views which he originally inspired, and to carry investigations beyond the point at which he himself left them. He shapes the course of scholarship not only through his own, inevitably provisional, conclusions but also—and perhaps mainly—through his capacity to suggest the questions that are most worthwhile exploring. It is by operating through both these channels that Tawney has made the pre-Civil War period his own. Much of what has recently been written about that period is Tawney modified and amplified in the light of further research. And even those who reject his views most vigorously find themselves answering, rather than ignoring, the questions which he has raised. In the last

[1] H. R. Trevor-Roper, *The Gentry, 1540–1640.* (1953), p. 1.

resort, his influence lies in his flair for suggesting to the twentieth century what of interest is to be found in the sixteenth and seventeenth and, as Burkhardt pointed out, what any age finds interesting in its past is the very marrow of history.

The reasons why the twentieth century should be interested in the economic history of the sixteenth and seventeenth are no doubt various, but one is suggested by Sir Theodore Gregory's shrewd description of that part of the world which it is now fashionable to call underdeveloped:[1]

'There may be a fringe of plantation-cultivation and some large-scale industrial and mining enterprise, but there is also a mass of peasant cultivators... and an indigenous industry organised not on the basis of power-driven machinery but on the basis of the human hand. Finance is provided by the "money-lender" not by a commercial bank; life flows in a traditional pattern. Birth rates are high and so is mortality, production *per capita* is low and the struggle for existence is hard... It is a familiar pattern and the danger is of over-simplification. There is the temptation to suppose that because the technical way of life in many parts of the world is traditional, therefore the populations who live that life are simple, unsophisticated souls, unaffected by the economic calculus, unaware of the pull of the more or less, the greater or the smaller gain. Nothing could well be more mistaken. I venture to think... that it is not in those parts of the world... that self interest and the profit motive are tempered by considerations of the public good.'

Those words might well constitute a description of the England of which Tawney is the great expositor, for the late sixteenth and early seventeenth centuries constitute perhaps the last period in English history in which economic appetites were remarkably vigorous but in which economic expansion was still slow.

Of the vigour of economic appetites under the later Tudors and early Stuarts there can be little doubt. Both contemporary comment and contemporary behaviour testify to it, and Weber's attempt to

[1] Sir Theodore Gregory, 'The Problems of the Under-developed World', *Lloyds Bank Review*, Oct. 1948 pp. 39-40.

identify a capitalist ethic distinct from the simple desire for economic gain appears increasingly unconvincing as more about individual capitalists becomes known. The slowness of economic growth must, in the absence of statistics, be more open to question. Clearly, it was not an age of stagnation. The growth of population was undoubtedly accompanied by some expansion of the national income. As a result of the developments in foreign trade and of the growth of London there was a widening of the range as well as an increase in the volume of the goods and services available for consumption. Yet the steep and prolonged rise in agricultural prices may reasonably be interpreted to mean that agricultural production was slow to expand. For what they are worth, the Customs figures suggest that for much of the period exports were sluggish. The persistence of high interest rates may well mean that the rate of capital accumulation was slow. The lag of wages behind prices, the contemporary concern about pauperism, and the mounting fear of over-population all suggest that the growing labour force was absorbed into employment only with difficulty; and it is perhaps significant that the second quarter of the seventeenth century, when the upward swing of agricultural prices began to flatten out and real wage rates began to rise, was also a time when disease and emigration were probably combining to check the rate of population growth. With respect to such an economy, the task of the historian is less that of demonstrating the expansive force of economic ambition than that of examining the impediments which contained it, less that of proclaiming its successes than that of recording the strains and stresses to which it gave rise.

In primary production, the obstacles to expansion lay mainly in the field of supply and arose largely from the limitations of contemporary techniques. In fishing, it is true, men seem to have found it easier to catch herrings than to sell them; but elsewhere the difficulty lay in raising output rather than in disposing of it. The story of mining was one of a growing struggle with the problems of drainage and ventilation as deposits near the surface became exhausted. That of agriculture was largely one of the increasing difficulties with which men wrested an adequate supply of commodities from the soil. At first sight, that difficulty may seem surprising since the labour force

3

was growing and land was, by modern standards, still plentiful. But much of that land was infertile; much was waterlogged; many areas were still thinly peopled; yields were generally low; and the demands upon the soil were many. For in the sixteenth and seventeenth centuries, as in the Middle Ages, men looked to the land not only for their food but also for their drink, for their fuel, and for such basic industrial materials as timber, wool, hides, skins and tallow. It was called upon to provide, not only the horses which maintained the internal system of transport, but also the fodder by which those horses were themselves maintained. And much land was still required to satisfy the appetite of the king and upper classes for the chase. Under such circumstances economic and demographic expansion tended to place upon the land a strain that, in later ages and under different circumstances, they were to place upon the balance of payments. In the course of time, the combined pressure of these competing uses was to be relieved in a variety of ways. For both political and economic reasons the hunting rights of the king and his subjects were to be curtailed. The pressure of the demand for fuel was to be eased by the substitution of coal for wood, by the concentration of the major fuel-using industries in those regions where fuel was most abundant, and by the importation of iron smelted abroad. The pressure of the demand for timber was to be eased by the greater use of brick in building and by the growth of substantial imports from Scandinavia and the Baltic. Improvements in water transport were to bring with them economies in horse power. English pastures were to be supplemented by those of Ireland, Wales and Scotland, which sent increasing quantities of wool and livestock into the English market. And as the pressure of these competing claims was eased, the efficiency of land use was to be raised by the introduction of turnips and the artificial grasses to raise the fertility of the lighter soils and to improve the country's grasslands. But those developments belonged to the seventeenth century rather than to the sixteenth, and to the later years of that century rather than to the earlier. It was not until the later years of Charles II that the flow of produce from the land was to become so great as to inflict upon men the horrors of plenty. Bacon looked back on the reign of Elizabeth as a critical period during which

England had become dangerously dependent on foreign grain, and both the course of prices and the literary evidence suggest that, despite land reclamation and the increased use of lime, marl and leys, the pressure upon the land continued to mount at least until the reign of Charles I.

Given these competing demands upon land, it was inevitable that the question of land use should become a major issue. Should men be allowed to change the use of their land—and in particular to convert arable to pasture—as considerations of profit prompted them? Should the forest rights of the king and the hunting grounds of his greater subjects, compatible though they were with both rough grazing and the production of wood and timber, be swept away to permit an extension of arable and improved pasture? Above all, should rights of common grazing—a relatively inefficient form of land use—be preserved in the interests of social stability or be suppressed in the interests of productivity? In large measure, no doubt, those questions were resolved by the forces of the market. Men converted their land from arable to pasture, or from pasture to arable, as prices dictated. More than one landowner converted his chase or his park into farms. Enclosure—i.e. the suppression of common grazing rights—by agreement was a feature of the age. But as the pressure upon land mounted, the question of its use became increasingly a political one. Despite growing criticism in the Commons and the ranks of the landlords, the Crown clung to the Tudor policy of forbidding the conversion of arable to pasture save where that conversion ministered to the improvement of arable farming itself. The Crown clung to its forest rights, partly for reasons of prestige and partly, perhaps, because the surrender value of those rights tended to increase with time. Although enclosure by agreement was legal, the difficulties of obtaining agreement were sometimes such as to produce demands that agreement should be dispensed with. As one Jacobean, probably an M.P., argued, 'the difficultys attending inclosures lye only in the preposterous wills of perverse men who may, and will not, understand reason nor entertain a benefit offered them; and it is therefore not fit that matters of publick good should rest on the consultation and determination as such as afore resolve wilfully to withstand it, not knowing truly what they oppose.'[1] But the political climate was not yet favourable to enclosure by compulsion.

In secondary production, by contrast, the obstacles to expansion seem to have lain in the field of demand rather than in that of supply. Technical difficulties, it is true, existed. As in mining and agriculture, men's impotence in the face of wind and weather tended to make employment irregular. Changes in their relative scarcities raised the problems of substituting coal for wood as an industrial fuel and long wool for short in the manufacture of textiles. In some industries English methods were poor by comparison with those of the Continent, and skilled immigrants were required to repair the deficiency. But these problems were either solved or remained comparatively unimportant in the century before the Civil War. Both the course of prices and the literary evidence suggest that, although secondary producers may have found it difficult actually to reduce their costs, they did not find it difficult to increase their output at current prices. In most industries, the main factor of production was labour and labour was both plentiful and cheap. It was easy enough to set more men and women on work; the problem, as many a poor law officer found, was to dispose of their output. The situation was, in short, one that is often found in countries in which the agricultural sector is large but agricultural productivity is low. High food prices meant that the industrial worker had little to spare for the purchase of manufactured goods, but the low output which made those prices high also limited the purchasing power of many agriculturalists. The labourer and cottager, irregularly employed and miserably paid, were poor customers. The small husbandmen, most of whose petty surpluses might be swallowed up in rent, were little better. Prosperity was largely confined to the landlords and more substantial farmers, and although their purchases of manufactured goods were no doubt considerable they were hardly enough to ensure a high level of industrial output. Much of their wealth went on personal services; much on building; much on luxuries and imports. Industrial activity was, moreover, further discouraged by the fact that the bulk of the population lived scattered in small communities with the result that

[1] J. St. John *Observations on the Land Revenue of the Crown* (1787), Appendix III.

6

much production was for local markets too small to encourage any high degree of specialisation. One of the most striking features that emerges from the probate inventories of the time is the extent to which the more prosperous artisans tended to diversify their interests instead of ploughing back their profits into their basic activity.

The effects of that situation on thought and policy are obvious enough. On the one hand, there was a series of attempts to check the production of industrial goods—or at least to restrict the number of industrial workers. The commercial crisis of 1551 was followed by a series of measures designed to prevent any repetition of the mushrooming of textile production that had characterised the preceding boom. Although it is possible that the Statute of Artificers was primarily designed to ensure an adequate supply of cheap agricultural labour—in a letter to Sir Thomas Smith, Cecil described it as 'a very good law agreed upon for indifferent allowance of servants' wages in husbandry'[1]—in its final form it placed serious restrictions on the flow of labour into industry. And although there is no evidence that the government, either central or local, took positive steps to enforce those restrictions, Mrs. Gay Davies has shown that common informers were sufficiently active to make them of some significance. Moreover, in the late sixteenth and early seventeenth centuries, many of the corporate towns reconstructed their gild systems and tightened up their bye-laws in an effort to ensure full employment for their citizens by suppressing the enterprise of those who did not share their freedom. On the other hand, men increasingly looked to the manipulation of foreign trade to solve the problems of industry. The curtailment of manufactured imports would create and stimulate the production of native substitutes for them; new markets overseas could make good the deficiencies of the market at home. Unfortunately, the circumstances of the time tended to favour the growth of imports rather than that of exports.

From the later middle ages until the eighteenth century, England's major export consisted of woollen textiles; no other English product —and certainly no other English manufacture—was in great demand abroad. In the late fifteenth and early sixteenth centuries Eng-

[1] Conyers Read, *Mr. Secretary Cecil and Queen Elizabeth*, (1959), p. 274.

land had enjoyed important competitive advantages in the production of the heavier fabrics suitable for the climate of north, central and eastern Europe and exports of those fabrics had risen substantially, with the consequence that more labour had found employment in the textile industry and that more land had been put down to grass. By the middle of the sixteenth century, however, that rise was virtually over. During the next hundred years such exports, for a complex variety of reasons admirably discussed by Dr. Supple, were to fluctuate around a trend that rose scarcely at all and by the reign of Charles I was undoubtedly falling.[1] By that reign, it is true, the trade in heavy woollens was being significantly and increasingly supplemented by a trade in the lighter and cheaper fabrics known as the new draperies. But under the early Stuarts those draperies were still very new, and for most of the century before the Civil War English industry can have received but little direct stimulus from expanding exports. Admittedly, that century was a time of great mercantile activity and saw the creation of great mercantile fortunes. But the aim and effect of much of that activity was less to increase the volume of English trade than to transfer that trade to English hands. Under the later Tudors, tariff changes and the cancellation of the privileges of the Hansards gave native merchants a predominant position in the shipment of goods from England. Under the early Stuarts, and to some extent even before, those goods were increasingly being shipped, not to some cross-channel entrepot, but to more distant regions whither they had previously been taken by Continental middlemen, and imports were more frequently being obtained in or near their countries of origin. By the reign of Charles I, moreover, a re-export trade in Asiatic and colonial produce was beginning to appear and Englishmen were carrying goods between foreign ports without ever bringing them to England itself. Thus commercial expansion took the form, not only of a slowly increasing export of native commodities, but also of a rapidly increasing export of commercial and shipping services. This export of services enriched the merchants, added to the national income, and led to a growth of imports. But

[1] B. E. Supple, *Commercial Crisis and Change in England, 1600-1642*, (1959). pp. 136-49.

its effects on industry were essentially indirect and ambivalent. Greater imports of raw materials such as wool, silk and cotton no doubt gave some stimulus to English manufactures: but greater imports of consumer goods must have had a contrary effect.

Modern experience suggests that economies in which the competition between alternative uses for land is keen and in which industry is sluggish are likely to see the development of two phenomena. There is likely to be a vigorous struggle for the occupancy and ownership of land; and ambitious young men are likely to seek in the professions the wealth that is not abundantly available in the business world. Tudor and Stuart England was characterised by both. 'Do not', wrote Winstanley, 'all strive to enjoy the Land? The Gentry strive for Land, the Clergy strive for Land, the Common people strive for Land; and Buying and selling is an Art whereby people endeavour to cheat one another of the Land.'[1] At the bottom of the social ladder there was a growing competition for agricultural holdings, a competition that was reflected in a steep rise of rents and entry fines. In the middle of the sixteenth century it had been usual to attribute that rise to the avarice of landlords, but by that century's end the more percipient observers saw that it had its roots in the struggle of tenant against tenant. Even from remote Pembrokeshire it was reported that whereas 'in tymes past... fewe sought leases for most commonly the Landlord rather made suite for a good tenante to take his lande then the tenant to the Landlord... and as for fynes yt was not a thinge knowne among them a hundred yeares past... nowe the poore tenants that lyved well in that golden world ys taughte to singe unto his Lord a newe songe... the worlde ys so altered with ye poore tenants that he standeth so in bodylie feare of his greedy neighbour, that ii or iii yeares eare his lease end he must bowe to his Lord for a newe Lease and must pinche yt out many yeares before to heape money together.'[2] Nor was that struggle surprising. It was the result, partly of the growth in population, but partly of the state of agricultural technique. A man's ability to profit from the rise in agricultural

---

[1] Quoted in Christopher Hill, *Puritanism and Revolution*, (1958), p. 153.
[2] G. Owen, *The Description of Pembrokeshire*, Cymmrodorian Society Record Series, (1892-7), Part I, p. 190.

prices obviously depended on his having a worthwhile surplus for sale; and since the limited range of knowledge at his disposal made if difficult to obtain that surplus by more intensive cultivation there was an obvious temptation to seek it by enlarging his farm. In practice, no doubt, the tendency thus to create larger farms was kept in check. But it was often kept in check by competing offers from desperate smallholders driven to offer rents greater than their agricultural output really justified.

Further up the social scale, there was a parallel competition for estates. 'For what purpose', wrote Sir Richard Weston, 'do soldiers, scholars, lawyers, merchants and men of all occupations and trades toil and labour with great affection but to get money, and with that money when they have gotten it but to purchase land?' Such men competed to purchase, not only manors, but also freeholds, copyholds and even long leaseholds. For, as an investment, land offered the attraction of relative safety combined with the prospect of a rising income. And, as a consumer-good, an estate, with the amenities and status that accompanied it, was among the most seductive that the age could offer.

The history of the professions in the sixteenth and seventeenth centuries has yet to be written, but at least its main outlines are becoming clear. As C. S. Lewis has pointed out, those centuries saw education move up the social scale. Grammar schools multiplied and the more successful among them significantly changed their social complexion. The universities not only expanded but were gradually converted into congeries of boarding schools for the sons of gentlemen. Increasingly, the Inns of Court served as finishing schools for men who had no intention of devoting themselves to the law. That growing demand for education may, in part, have reflected a growing demand for culture. But contemporary comment leaves no room for doubt but that education was looked upon mainly as an avenue leading, through the professions, to influence and affluence. For that reason, some were to argue that it should be denied to the sons of the lower orders and Bacon was to warn of the dangers of educating more persons than the market could absorb.

Both the vigorous demand for land and the enthusiasm for a

professional career may legitimately be held to reflect the relative unattractiveness of the alternative employments for capital and skill. In that sense, they appear as results of the slowness of economic growth. Yet in economic affairs cause and effect are not always clearly distinct, and the diversion of so many resources into those two channels may also be seen as one reason why that growth was, in fact, so slow. With respect to the demand for land the case is clear enough. The purchase of an estate did not necessarily mean any increase in the amount of real capital invested in agriculture; a rising rent roll might well represent the results of inflation and hard bargaining rather than of any growth in real output; the briskness of the land market was partly the result of a process whereby the savings of the professional and mercantile classes were used to finance the expenditure on consumption of those from whom they bought. It is difficult to believe that, in an age when capital accumulation was slow and the rate of interest was high, such was, from the point of view of the community, the most beneficial use to which savings could be put. Those contemporaries who attributed the growing commercial supremacy of the Dutch partly to the fact that, whereas English mercantile fortunes were often transmuted into land, the fortunes of the Dutch were retained in trade, did so with some justice.

With respect to the professions, the case is perhaps more tenuous. Professional services are an integral part of the national income; their growth in volume and quality no doubt made England richer; it would be ludicrous to dismiss the works of Shakespeare as products of the mis-allocation of economic resources. Yet two points may, perhaps, be made. The first is that, if contemporaries are to be believed, there was not always a close relationship between rewards obtained and the services rendered, and some men achieved wealth without adding much to the public welfare. The second is that, whatever was to be the case in later periods, in Tudor and Stuart England success in the professions depended on qualities very similar to those required for success in business. On the acquisitiveness and business capacity of lawyers it is needless to comment, for they were long to remain a feature of English life. According to at least one contemporary, medical men showed similar qualities; and the fact that Barbon, Petty and Hugh Chamberlayne, three of the biggest speculators of the later seventeenth century, were all doctors certainly suggests some affinity between medicine and money-making. As the Church became poorer, financial success within it came often to depend upon the discreet purchase of benefices, the operation of those benefices by means of dependent wage labour supplied by an ecclesiastical proletariat, and the astute exploitation of any real estate that such benefices carried with them. Many public offices, it is clear, were treated less as contractual obligations than as a species of property that could be bought, leased and mortgaged and that yielded its fruits in the form of fees and perquisites which it was the incumbents' responsibility to maximise. Even University teaching, sometimes regarded as the last resort of the unwordly, showed some of the same characteristics. 'I am credibly informed', wrote Burleigh, 'that thorowe the great stipendes of tutors and the little paines they doe take in the instructinge and well governinge of their puples, not onely the poorer sorte are not able to maintaine their children at the universitie; and the ritcher be so corrupte with libertie and remissness so that the tutor is more afrayed to displease his puple thorowe the desire of great gaine, the which he haithe by his tutorage, then the puple is of his tutor.'[1] The professions, it would seem, were absorbing talents that the business world might well have used.

The vigorous demand for land and the scramble for professional employment are, it has been suggested, found in many under-developed economies. But in Tudor and Stuart England they were encouraged, not only by the nature of the economy, but also by the contemporary system of public finance. As John Aylmer pointed out to his fellow-countrymen, that system was essentially one of light taxation.[2]

'Now compare them (i.e. the Germans) with thee: and thou shalt see howe happye thou arte. They eate hearbes: and thou Beefe

---

[1] J. B. Mullinger, *The University of Cambridge*, (1884), Vol. II, p. 398.
[2] Quoted in Geo. Orwell and Reginald Reynolds, *British Pamphleteers*, (1958), Vol. I, p. 31.

and Mutton. Thei rotes: and thou butter, chese and egges. Thei drinck commonly water: and thou good ale and beare. Thei go from the market with a sallet: and thou with good fleshe fill thy wallet. They lightlye never see anye sea fish: and thou has they belly full of it. They paye till theire bones rattle in their skin: and thou layest up for thy sonne and heir. Thou are twise or thrise in thy lifetime called uppon to healpe thy Countrye with a sub-sidie or contribution: and they daily pay and never cease. Thou livest like a Lorde, and they like dogges... Oh if thou knewest thou Englishe man in what welth thou livest and in how plentifull a Countrye: Thou wouldst vii times of the day fall flat on thy face before God, and geve him thanks, that thou wart born an English man, and not a french pezant, nor an Italyan, nor Almane.'

The attractions of light taxation are never difficult to perceive. But when it is accompanied by heavy government expenditure such attractions are apt to be delusive, since the alternative methods of financing that expenditure may well prove more burdensome. Such, it may be argued, was the position that obtained by the end of the sixteenth century. By that time the Crown was relying to a significant extent on the sale of privileges, which tended to restrict economic activity; on the creation and sale of offices, which drew more labour and enterprise into the performance of unnecessary professional duties; and upon land sales that tended to absorb the country's savings. There can be little doubt that one reason for the attractiveness of land as an investment was that royal sales kept its price lower than it would otherwise have been. It may well be significant that, as the sale of royal lands declined, the rate of interest tended to fall and men turned more of their attention to land drainage, land reclamation, and colonisation.

If it be granted that, in the century before the Civil War, circum-stances raised the questions of land use, land ownership, land occu-pancy, foreign trade, public office and public finance to the status of major issues, it is easy enough to see why the century may aptly be described as Tawney's. For each of these questions has been illuminated both by his own writings and by the work of those whom he has taught. Nor is that all. History is concerned, not only with men's behaviour, but also with their beliefs; and men's changing beliefs with respect to individual ambition, business enterprise, and economic innovation provide economic history with one of its most important themes. After the Restoration, those forces were to be increasingly sanctified by both theory and experience. But before that happy event neither theory nor experience offered them much support. The view that the golden age lay in the past, that men were living in a senile universe, that all change was the equivalent of biological decay was repeatedly advanced in the later sixteenth century and was expounded at length by Goodman in the reign of James I. Nor do Hakewill's attacks on that argument seem to have had much immediate effect. And Goodman found no difficulty in supporting his pessimism with appeals to contemporary economic experience. For at a time of rising food prices, low wages and growing pauperism it was easier to demonstrate that many men were becoming rich by methods which made others poor than to show that there was any increase in total wealth. Under such circumstance, the economic appetites inevitably became objects of suspicion and controversy, and the most perceptive accounts of contemporary attitudes to them are still those contained in the famous introduction to Wilson's *Discourse on Usury* and in *Religion and the Rise of Capitalism.* In the history of social thought, as well as in the history of economic practice, Tawney has made the late sixteenth and early seventeenth centuries his own.

PROTESTANTISM AND THE RISE OF CAPITALISM

'If... the motive is generosity or to give to the Church, and
if any prize is really incidental—and the main motive is fellow-
ship and giving to the work of Christ—then that would seem to be
right. It is a question of taking it back into the conscience of each
person and examining the motive in that way.'

The Rt. Rev. G. F. ALLEN, Bishop of Derby, on the lawfulness
of using football pools, raffles and games and chance to raise funds
for the Church (*The Times*, November 9, 1959).

I

IT is over 30 years since historical thinking in this country was
stimulated by the publication of Professor Tawney's *Religion and
the Rise of Capitalism*. Most historians would now accept the
existence of some connection between protestantism and the rise of
capitalism, though Professor Trevor-Roper is a conspicuous exception. But there is little agreement on the nature of the connection.
Seventeenth-century protestants themselves emphasized the fact that
godly artisans had been the backbone of the Reformation, and that
protestantism in its turn had proved to be good for trade and industry; and they were right on both points. Nevertheless there are still
untidinesses at the edge of the thesis. The object of this article is to try
to clear away some of them, by developing hints given by Professor
Tawney himself.[1]

One criticism, levelled especially against Weber, is that he made
inadequate chronological distinctions, illustrating the causal influence
of protestantism in moulding "the capitalist spirit" by quotations
from 17th century writers; even Professor Tawney relies largely on
Baxter and Bunyan in his discussions of English Puritanism. Another

[1] R. H. Tawney, *Religion and the Rise of Capitalism* (Penguin ed.), pp. 101-3.

criticism is that some of the countries in which Calvinism developed in its classical form (Scotland, Hungary) were economically backward; many aristocratic supporters of, for instance, the French Huguenots, were not at all bourgeois in origin or outlook. A third criticism is that Weber and Tawney emphasised points of doctrine which would not have seemed central either to the reformers or to their critics. Protestant teachings on usury, callings, treatment of the poor, and so forth, were peripheral: granting that individual protestants contributed to the rise of a capitalist ethic by what they said on these subjects, it still has not been shown that protestantism as such is associated, either as cause or effect or both, with the rise of capitalism. If connections are to be established, they must be sought in the central doctrines of the reformers, those which most sharply differentiated them from their Roman Catholic contemporaries. And then we have to face a fourth objection in the fact that the reformers thought they found their doctrines in the New Testament and St. Augustine. Are we to regard these writings as emanations of the capitalist spirit? If not, why not?[1]

II

The central doctrine of protestantism is justification by faith. The central target of the reformers' attack was justification by works. We must begin here.

When protestants criticised the doctrine of justification by works, they were not saying that charitable works should not be performed. They were attacking the purely formal routine actions by which many Roman Catholic theologians taught that merit could be acquired—telling of beads, saying of paternosters, giving of candles. Luther distinguished between 'two kinds of works: those done for others, which are the right kind; ... and those done for ourselves,

[1] By 'the capitalist spirit' I mean something more specific than a love of money, which can be found in earlier ages. I mean an ethos which, within the framework of a market economy, emphasizes productive industry, frugality and accumulation, as good in themselves. On this definition, banks and usury are not central to the problem, since they existed before the rise of capitalism. (See R. H. Hilton, 'Capitalism—What's in a name?', *Past and Present*, No. 1).

which are of smaller value'. 'We wear and consume our bodies with watching, fasting and labour, but we neglect charity, which is the only lady and mistress of works. ... Paul not only teacheth good works, but also condemneth fantastical and superstitious works.'[1] 'Fixed holidays and fasts, fraternities, pilgrimages, worship of saints, rosaries, monasticism and such-like' were the 'childish and unnecessary works' which the Confession of Augsburg denounced in 1530 as having been exclusively emphasised by popular Roman Catholic preachers. Tyndale, Foxe and other early English reformers delighted to draw up lists of these superstitious works, by which, they did not fail to point out, the church invariably drew money from the pockets of the faithful.[2]

These 'extern matters and ceremonial observations, nothing conducing to any spiritual purpose' were what the reformers had most of all in mind when they denounced 'works'. In discussions between protestants and papists in England in 1559, the former singled out for criticism the sermon on Candlemas Day, in which 'there is also a history of a woman which never did good deed, but only that she had continually kept a candle before our lady', in return for which Mary saved her from hell. 'What occasion of dissolute life and sin may be ministered to simple people by these and an infinite number of such like fables, it is easy to perceive.'[3] The protestant objection was to mechanical actions in which the heart was not involved.

Where 'good works' in the wider sense were concerned—acts of mercy or charity—a protestant thought that *what* a man did was less important than the spirit in which he did it. Justification by works

---

[1] Ed. B. L. Woolf, *Reformation Writings of Martin Luther*, II, p. 110; cf. pp. 121-3, 293; Luther, *Commentary on Galatians* (English translation, 1807), II, p. 216; cf. pp. 148, 270. In discussing theology, I have by preference quoted Luther, since he initiated the protestant break-through, and Calvin only secondly: for my concern here is with the *theological* distinction between protestantism and catholicism. I do not wish to imply that Lutheranism, as it came to exist in Germany and Scandinavia, contributed significantly to the capitalist spirit.

[2] William Tyndale, *An Answer to Sir Thomas More's Dialogue* (Parker Soc., 1850), pp. 202-; 3 J. Foxe, *The Acts and Monuments* (4th ed., n.d., ed. J. Pratt), I, pp. xxii-iii, 61, 74-6, 85-6.

[3] Ed. E. Cardwell, *A History of Conferences* (1840), p. 90.

led to a formal righteousness: by performing a round of good works, one bought oneself off from the consequences of sin. Grace came through the sacraments, through the miracle of the mass. Penance was imposed by the priest: it could be performed without true inner penitence. But protestants thought the effectiveness of the sacraments depended on the moral state of the recipient. Man was justified by faith alone: by turning towards God with the full consciousness of his moral being. He was saved not by his own righteousness, not by his own efforts, but by the righteousness of Christ imputed to the favoured few whom God had chosen. Once a protestant had acquired this sense of unity and close personal relationship with God, his attitude towards the world, to sin and to repentance was transformed. The goodness of an action depended not on what that action was (the pagan philosophers had attained to moral virtue) but on the conviction, the love of God, which inspired it. 'Christ is eaten with the heart', said Cranmer in debate before Protector Somerset. 'Only good men can eat Christ's body.'

On Luther's visit to Rome, as he climbed Pilate's stairs on hands and knees, repeating a paternoster on each stair and kissing it, he wondered if this really did release souls from Purgatory. From Erasmus's Greek Testament he learnt that 'penentential agite' meant not 'do penance' but 'be penitent'. This he described as a 'glowing' discovery. In his consciousness of sin, Luther had come to hate the God whose commandments he could not keep: until his outlook was transformed by the Pauline sentence 'the just shall live by faith'. Henceforth, for him, external ceremonial, outward actions, were contrasted with internal conviction, a change of heart. God ceased to be an enemy to be propitiated: works flowed from grace, but man was not justified by them. He had been justified long before, or else his works were worthless. A good man made a good work, not a good work a good man. Faith was 'nothing else but the truth of the heart.'[1]

This insistence that each believer should look inward to his own heart contributed to give protestantism its fundamentally individualist bias. Papal doctrine since the 14th century had postulated a common

[1] Luther, *Galatians*, I, p. 250; cf. II, pp. 299-300.

store of grace, accumulated in the first instance by Christ, and added to by the merits of saints, martyrs and all who performed more good works than were necessary for their own salvation. Monks and chantry priests, by dedicating their whole lives to religious exercises, built up a superfluity of 'works'. 'This treasure', said the Bull Unigenitus in 1343, 'is... entrusted to be healthfully dispersed through blessed Peter, bearer of heaven's keys, and his successors as vicars on earth... to them that are truly penitent and have confessed.' Individuals could draw on this treasury of grace only through the mediacy of priests, whose authority came through the hierarchy from the Pope. Indulgences, sold by papal permission, were cheques drawn on the treasury of merits: they could shorten time in Purgatory, for the dead as well as for the living. Thus good works were bought and sold, said Luther.[1]

Justification by works, then, did not mean that an individual could save himself: it meant that he could be saved through the Church. Hence the power of the clergy. Compulsory confession, imposition of penance on the whole population—the majority of whom were illiterate—together with the possibility of withholding absolution, gave priests a terrifying power. Obedience to the Church was an obligatory part of the virtue of humility. 'If she [the Church] shall have defined anything to be black which to our eyes appears to be white', said St. Ignatius, 'we ought in like manner to pronounce it to be black.' Protestants would inculcate such blind faith in no earthly institution or man, but only in God; and fortunately God's pronouncements were more subject to argument than those of the Church. Even the Bible was checked by what the Spirit of God wrote in the believer's heart.[2]

Justification by works meant that salvation out of communion with the Church was unthinkable. For the reformers, the direct relationship of the soul to God was what mattered: the priest, the Church as an institution, were quite secondary. So from the very

[1] Luther, *Reformation Writings*, II, p. 214.
[2] Loyola, *Spiritual Exercises*, part ii, No. 13; Luther, *Galatians*, I, p. 284; Tyndale, *Answer to More*, pp. 51; Jean Calvin, *Institutes of the Christian Religion* (trans. H. Beveridge, 1949), I, pp. 72-5.

beginning the protestant revolt against the Roman Church was from the nature of its theology an individualist revolt. That of course was not how Luther and his contemporaries saw it. They began by criticising specific abuses—sale of indulgences, commutation of penance. But even when they went on to attack confession and monasticism, their starting-point remained the same: a rejection of outward ceremonial enacted without a change of heart. Here is Luther on monasticism:

'Hitherto it hath been the chief holiness and righteousness... [for a man] to run into monasteries, to put on monkish apparel, to be shaven, to wear a hempen girdle, to give himself to fasting and prayer, to be clothed with hair-cloth, to lie in woollen garments, to observe an austere manner of living, and in fine, to take upon him monkish holiness and religion; and thus, resting in a show of good works, we knew not but we were holy from top to toe, having regard only to works and the body and not to the heart, where we were full of hatred, fear and incredulity, troubled with an evil conscience, knowing almost nothing rightly of God. ... But there is another righteousness which God esteemeth and accepteth, which also we must consider; it consists not in a grey garment, nor in a black or white cowl, but in a pure conscience. ... When the heart is pure, the house is unto it as the field, and the field as the house; the market is as much esteemed as the monastery; and on the contrary, neither remaineth unto me any work, place or garment which I count profane; for all things are alike unto me, after that holiness hath fully possessed my heart.'[1]

Luther thus ended the dual morality, not merely by bringing the ascetic out into the world, but by telling him that his standards were all wrong. Monastic routine could be imposed only on men and women who did not know the direct relationship to God which Luther had experienced and taught. Once the heart was changed, it would leap beyond the formal confines of monastic restrictions into Christian liberty. 'He that bideth in the world, as the monks call it', wrote Tyndale, 'hath more faith than the cloisterer: for he

---

[1] Luther, *Thirty-four Sermons* (Dublin, 1747), pp. 76-7.

hangeth on God in all things.'[1] For Christians no action can be casual or perfunctory: the most trivial detail of our daily life should be performed to the glory of God, should be irradiated with a conscious co-operation with God's purposes. This was not originally to sanctify the life of all laymen: on the contrary, Luther held that the world belonged to the devil. But the true Christian could live in the devil's world without being of it, because of his saving faith.[2]

But my motives, my intentions, the spirit in which I perform an action, are within my control. Philosophically, protestant theologians believed that the inclination of one's will towards God came from outside, from God; practically, as moralists, they emphasized the careful scrutiny of motives, the conscious attempt to see that one's will was tuned in to the divine harmonies. 'Impenitence is the unpardonable sin', declared Luther, for whom faith was 'the most difficult of all works'. Faith without a desire of repentance is as worthless as repentance without faith, wrote Calvin. No priest can search the secrets of my heart.[3] 'Is there any angel', asked the Homily Concerning Prayer, 'any virgin, any patriarch or prophet among the dead, that can understand or know the reason of the heart?' The question expected the answer No. I, and I alone, can know whether the illuminating contact with God has been established. If it has not, all the priests and all the ceremonies in the world will not establish it. Compulsory confession cuts across the individual's direct relation to God; it is 'both tyrannical [to the sinner] and insulting to God, who, in binding consciences to his Word, would have them free from human rule.'[4] For the godly, morality should be self-imposed: unquestioning obedience to the priest was a positive hindrance.

Protestants thus had a new measuring-rod. Duties, Calvin declared, are estimated not by actions but by motives. 'There is nothing which God more abominates than when men endeavour to cloak themselves

[1] Tyndale, *Doctrinal Treatises* (Parker Soc., 1848), p. 280.
[2] N. O. Brown, *Life against Death*, chapter XIV, *passim*. The Cathari, who also thought the world was the devil's, drew the conclusion that what happened there was a matter of indifference: trade and usury were therefore permissible.
[3] Luther, *The Bondage of the Will* (1823), p. 23; *Reformation Writings*, I, p. 259; Calvin, *Institutes*, I, p. 29.
[4] Calvin, *Institutes*, I, p. 555.

by substituting signs and external appearance for integrity of heart.'
To wear mourning apparel from mere social convention, without
feeling real grief, was evil and hypocritical. Scholastic sophists,
Calvin continued, 'talk much of contrition and attrition, torment the
soul with many scruples, and involve it in great trouble and anxiety;
but when they seem to have deeply wounded the heart, they cure all
its bitterness with a slight sprinkling of ceremonies.' 'There is nothing
which gives men greater confidence and licence in sinning than the
idea that after making confession to priests they can wipe their lips
and say, I have not done it.'[1]

Bishop Fisher regretted that he was not left time enough between
condemnation and execution to perform so many good works as
he believed to be necessary to salvation. Such good works no doubt
included frequent repetition of the Lord's Prayer. Luther prided himself on having freed people from this mechanical repetition of the
paternoster in the gabbling manner which has given the word
'patter' to the language. 'Neither words nor singing (if used in
prayer)', said Calvin, 'avail one iota with God, unless they proceed
from deep feeling in the heart.'[2] The Preface to the First Prayer Book
of Edward VI complained that when men attended services in Latin
'they understood not, so that they have heard with their ears only:
and their hearts, spirit and mind have not been edified thereby.'

Ceremonies are of value only in so far as they contribute to this
edification of the believer, help him to understand the act of worship
he is taking part in. Hence Bible and Prayer Book in the vernacular;
emphasis on preaching rather than on prayer and sacraments; music
must edify and not distract—hence metrical psalms and hostility to
organs, polyphony and choristers, dislike of images and gaudy
churches. All these sprang from the same concern with turning the
heart of the worshipper towards God. The same principle opened the
way to many of the heresies of later radical protestantism. The
attack on set prayers, the desire of laymen to pray and preach, are

---

[1] Calvin, *Institutes*, II, pp. 75, 465; I, pp. 534, 551; cf. II, p. 101, and Foxe,
op. cit., I, p. 77.
[2] Calvin, *Institutes*, II, p. 180.

natural extensions of Lutheran principles.[1] So was adult baptism.[2] So was Milton's demand for divorce where religious temperaments were incompatible.[3] Laud's attempt to revive ceremonies flew in the face of this long tradition. 'The matter is not great which way we turn our faces, so the heart stand right.' Ralegh had written in a phrase he later made famous at his execution. The chapel of Emmanuel College, its former Master told Laud, was 'consecrated by faith and a good conscience', and so did not need the ceremony of episcopal consecration.[4] Many came to think tithes and the Sabbath mere ceremonies. And, since no one can judge the heart of another, we have in Luther's teaching the germ of the most subversive of all heresies, religious toleration, horrified though Luther would have been at the thought.[5]

It took time for such conclusions to be drawn. But in a society where custom and tradition counted for so much, this insistence that a well-considered strong conviction overrode everything else had a great liberating force. We see more clearly by the light of grace than by the light of nature, Travers told Hooker. We must, of course, take care that our inner light is not darkness. 'Beware of thy good intent, good mind, good affection or zeal, as they call it', Tyndale warned. 'Labour for knowledge, that thou mayest know God's will.' So inquiry, searching the Scriptures, was stimulated. The godly man looked beyond ceremonies and sacraments to the thing signified, 'and will not serve visible things', for that was idolatry.[6] As soon as protestantism established churches, it had itself to face the dissidence of

[1] Luther, *Reformation Writings*, I, p. 314; Tyndale, *Doctrinal Treatises*, pp. 118-19; *Expositions of Scripture* (Parker Soc., 1849), pp. 80-1.

[2] Luther, *Reformation Writings*, I, p. 255.

[3] Contrast Professor Boxer's agreeable account of a Jesuit who turned protestant and married twice. He subsequently pleaded to the Inquisition that the ceremonies, being protestant, were invalid, and so he had been guilty only of 'a sin of the flesh'. His plea was accepted (C. R. Boxer, *Salvador de Sá and the Struggle for Brazil, 1602-86*, pp. 197-8).

[4] Sir Walter Ralegh, *History of the World* (1820), I, p. 78; H. R. Trevor-Roper, *Archbishop Laud*, p. 209.

[5] Luther, *Reformation Writings*, I, p. 180.

[6] R. Hooker, *Of the Laws of Ecclesiastical Polity* (Everyman ed.), I, p. xiii; Tyndale, *Doctrinal Treatises*, pp. 105, 362; *Answer to More*, pp. 6-7.

dissent. The Calvinist discipline was one method of curbing the exuberant consciences of laymen, rather more doctrinally satisfactory than Luther's reliance on the secular arm. The Anglican *via media* left room for men to have it both ways. 'There is no religion where there are no ceremonies', said Archbishop Bancroft. 'The more ceremonies, the less truth', said the Puritan Greenham.[1]

Luther had started more than he knew when he laid it down that the heart decides for itself. 'A man can form his own rule and judge for himself about mortifying his body.' 'Neither pope, nor bishop, nor any one else, has the right to impose so much as a single syllable of obligation upon a Christian man without his own consent, ... for we are free from all things.' This Christian freedom makes us 'kings and priests with power over all things.'[2] The important thing is not that Luther made such remarks, though that mattered; but that they flowed from the logic of his theological position. 'To have faith', added Calvin, 'is... to possess some certainty and complete security of mind, to have whereon to rest and fix your foot.'[3] That is what protestantism gave to the 16th century man of scruple, tormented by a sense of his own sinfulness: an inner calm and self-confidence, intermittent perhaps, but firmly based on moments of elation which, once experienced, marked a man off in his own eyes from his fellows. (Hence the importance of the doctrine that the elect could never wholly fall from grace.) The tension between hyper-consciousness of natural sinfulness and the permanent possibility of God's grace expressed itself in exuberant efforts to do good works, which had nothing in common with formal righteousness. 'We teach', Thomas Taylor declared, 'that only Doers shall be saved, and by their doing though not for their doing. The profession of religion is no such gentlemanlike life or trade, whose rents come in by their

[1] R. G. Usher, *The Reconstruction of the English Church*, II, p. 124; R. Greenham, *Workes* (1612), p. 653.

[2] Luther, *Reformation Writings*, I, pp. 370, 268, 270. The Puritan representatives at the Hampton Court Conference in 1604 were supplied in advance with arguments against the ceremonial observances they objected to. 'Whatsoever is not contained in the Word is burdensome to the conscience of Christians, who are set at liberty by Christ' (*Montague MSS.*, Historical MSS. Commission, p. 37).

[3] Calvin, *Institutes*, II, p. 70.

stewards, whether they sleep or wake, work or play.' The godly look often into their account books and cast up their reckonings. 'But a bankrupt has no heart to this business.'[1] For 'the Papal doctrine of doubting of God's love cuts the sinews of endeavour'.[2]

III

Luther was always very unwilling to apply this principle outside the purely religious sphere; yet its extension was inevitable. All action should rest on faith, he told the city of Nuremberg, when it was worried about the lawfulness of resisting the Emperor. Action taken in faith might be good 'even though it were an error and a sin'. 'To steal, rob and murder', Tyndale thought, 'are holy, when God commandeth them.' *Pecca fortiter*: sin may not be sin after all if the heart believes strongly enough that it is commanded by God. And only the individual can decide this. He is therefore placed under a tremendous obligation to make sure that his heart is properly informed. But in the last resort conscience is the supreme court, from which there is no appeal.[3] Bishop Hall found it difficult to determine 'whether it be worse to do a lawful action with doubting or an evil with resolution', since that which in itself is good is made evil by doubt. Oliver Cromwell was sure he should not accept the crown in May 1657 'because at the best I should do it doubtingly. And certainly what is so done is not of faith', and consequently is 'sin to him that doth it'.[4]

The danger of antinomianism always lurked behind Lutheranism and Calvinism. 'Whatsoever thou shalt observe upon liberty and of love, is godly', said Luther; 'but if thou observe anything of necessity, it is ungodly.' 'If you have the true kind of Christian love and faith, everything you do is of service. We may all please ourselves what we do.' Calvin agreed that, with safeguards, 'the consciences of

---

[1] Thomas Taylor, *Works* (1653), pp. 166-7.
[2] Richard Sibbes, *The Saints Cordials* (1629), p. 92.
[3] Tyndale, *Doctrinal Treatises*, p. 407; Sibbes, *The Saints Cordials*, pp. 41-2.
[4] J. Hall, *Works* (1625), p. 93; W. C. Abbott, *Writings and Speeches of Oliver Cromwell*, IV, p. 513.

believers may rise above the Law, and may forget the whole right-eousness of the Law.' 'The elect, having the Law written in their hearts, and loving it in their spirits', declared Tyndale, 'sin there never; but without, in the flesh.' 'If an adultery could be committed in the faith', Luther reflected, 'it would no longer be a sin.' Barely a century later Laurence Clarkson acted on the principle that with God adultery and marriage are but one, 'and that one holy, just and good as God.'[1]

But the antinomians were a fringe, and can be disregarded for our purpose. What matters is the main stream of protestant thought. Luther and Calvin set men free from forms and ceremonies, and even from the law. It is essential to understand the release and relief which protestantism brought to ordinary men and women if we are to obtain any insight into the astonishing rapidity with which it spread. The political consequences of looking into the heart, of making integrity of intention the test, are clear. 'If we deposed the said Queen Regent rather of malice and perverted envy than for the preservation of the commonwealth', said Knox, then God would prevail against us even if she deserved her fate.[2] But revolutions made with the right motives are godly. In October 1647 the members of the Army Council sought God in prayer before reporting to one another the inclination of their hearts towards Charles I. Ceremonies are the form of worship laid down by public authority. This authority is held to be inferior to the voice of God speaking within the pure heart. Strafford observed to Laud, of the Puritans, that 'The very genius of that nation of people leads them always to oppose, as well civilly as ecclesiastically, all that ever authority ordains for them.'[3]

Protestantism then was infinitely more flexible than catholicism. Catholicism had the iron framework of the hierarchy, headed by the pope. It had the machinery of confession, penance and absolution, and of church courts and excommunication, not to mention the

---

[1] Luther, *Thirty-Four Sermons*, p. 281; *Reformation Writings*, II, pp. 115-16; Calvin, *Institutes*, II, p. 683; Tyndale, *Answer to More*, p. 114; Clarkson, *A Single Eye* (1650).
[2] J. Knox, *History of the Reformation* (1832), p. 162.
[3] Quoted by Tawney, *Religion and the Rise of Capitalism*, p. 213.

Inquisition, with which to enforce traditional standards of orthodoxy. Protestantism lacked many of these barriers to change of moral attitudes. Some of the institutions and codes of the past were retained in the Lutheran countries and in the Anglican church. Efforts were made to erect new disciplinary institutions and codes in countries where Calvinism triumphed. Desperate attempts were made to compile a protestant casuistry. But the guides to godliness, the plain man's pathways to heaven, the practices of piety, were perforce addressed to the consciences of lay heads of households. The ministers may have helped such men to discipline and educate their families and employees. But the Roman Church was able slowly to adapt its standards to the modern world through a controlled casuistry guiding a separate priestly caste, which wielded the power of confession and absolution. Protestant ministers had to tag along behind what seemed right to the consciences of the leading laymen in their congregations.

It is here, through its central theological attitude, that protestantism made its great contribution to the rise of capitalism. What mattered was not that Calvin was a trifle less strict than the canonists in his approach to usury. What mattered was that protestantism appealed, as mediaeval heresy had done, to artisans and small merchants, whom it helped to trust the dictates of their own hearts as their standard of conduct. The elect were those who felt themselves to be the elect. What was astonishing was that so many people had at the same time the same miraculous experience of conversion: thanks to God's direct intervention, grace made them free. It would indeed be inexplicable if we could not see that the psychological states leading up to conversion were the effects of a social crisis which hit many unprivileged small producers in the same sort of way. There was no salvation in the old priestly magic, because that no longer gave them any sense of control over the world of economic fluctuations in which they now had to live. Only an assertive selfconfidence could do this, and that was so novel that it must seem to come arbitrarily from outside.

> *'Take me to you, imprison me, for I*
> *Except you enthrall me, never shall be free,*
> *Nor ever chaste, except you ravish me.'*[1]

[1] John Donne, *Complete Poetry and Selected Prose* (Nonesuch ed.), p. 285.

The social situation set large numbers of men and women seeking answers to similar problems. As, thanks to a Luther, a Calvin, a Zwingli, groups of men realised that 'the object of [Christ's] struggle was to raise up those who were lying prostrate',[1] this in its turn redoubled their confidence. They were the elect, not only because they felt they were, but also because other people, good people, recognized that they were; and shared their views. So, once the religion of the heart spread (and the printing press, that technical triumph of the urban craftsmen, gave it a great advantage over mediaeval heresies) Lutheranism, and still more Calvinism, was a magnificent bond of unity and strength. Once touched with grace, the small group of the elect felt themselves to be unique, differentiated from the mass of mankind. Lack of numbers ceased to matter: if God was with them, who would be against them? So their numbers grew.

In the last resort, what comes out of the conscience of a man bears some relation to what goes into it: to the social environment in which he lives. Absolute individualism of conscience, paradoxically, means that society has a greater influence on conduct. So protestantism spread as a negative reaction to institutions and practices which large numbers of men and women felt to be abuses. But, for the same social reason, the positive forms which the protest took tended to vary from region to region, and in the same region from class to class. Belatedly, Calvinism tried by organization to impose homogeneity. But once the pamphlets and sermons had encouraged wide discussion of theology and church government, it proved as impossible to maintain unity as it was among English Puritans after 1640 or within the French Tiers Etat after 1789. Unity existed only so long as there was an enemy to be overthrown. After that the voice of God said different things to different people. So the earnest minority which found the eternal decrees and the rule of the godly not unacceptable was challenged by those descendants of the mediaeval heretics who were prepared to contemplate the possibility of all men being saved: who wanted to be freed from the rule of new presbyter no less than of old priest.

From their different points of view both Hooker and Perkins

[1] Calvin, *Institutes,* I, p. 445.

showed themselves aware of this social background. Perkins asked how we should judge what is the measure of wealth which the master of a family may with good conscience seek. His reply was: not by the affection of covetous men, but by 'the common judgment and practice of the most godly, frugal and wise men with whom we live.'[1] Hooker wrote ironically that 'whosoever shall anger the meanest and simplest artisan *which carrieth a good mind,* by not removing out of the Church such rites and ceremonies as displease him, "better he were drowned in the bottom of the sea".'[2] Fulke Greville well expressed this sense of permanent criticism in protestantism, its ability to interpret even the Bible, when he made his chorus of priests conclude *Mustapha* with the words:

> *'Yet when each of us in his own heart looks*
> *He finds the God there far unlike his books.'*[3]

For the protestant conscience there were no absolutes, no accepted infallibilities, though each sect as it arose tried to establish them. But there was no final court of appeal, not even the Bible. Even yesterday's conscience might be repudiated to-day. The religious radicals inherited from the mediaeval heretics the concept of the Everlasting Gospel, written in men's hearts; more respectable Puritans evolved the doctrine of progressive revelation: both allowed moral standards to be modified as society changed.

IV

When the business man of 16th and 17th century Geneva, Amsterdam or London looked into his inmost heart, he found that God had planted there a deep respect for the principle of private property. The more sophisticated might express this in the 17th century by saying that respect for property was a fundamental law, or part of the law of nature (or reason): but it was easier, and more likely to overbear opposition, to say with Colonel Rainborough in the Putney

---

[1] W. Perkins, *Workes*, I, p. 769.
[2] Hooker, *Of the Laws of Ecclesiastical Polity* (Everyman ed.), I, p. 406. My italics.
[3] Ed. G. Bullough, *Poems and Dramas of Fulke Greville*, II, p. 137.

Debates that God had commanded 'Thou shalt not steal'. Such men felt quite genuinely and strongly that their economic practices, though they might conflict with the traditional law of the old church, were not offensive to God. On the contrary: they glorified God. For here the protestant theologians had sold the pass, by their fundamental distinction between formal and charitable works, and by making the individual heart the ultimate arbiter.

The elect, Luther had said, must perform good works to help their neighbour, the community, the commonwealth, humanity; this prevents the doctrine of justification by faith giving 'licence and free liberty to everyone to do what he will.' Men serve God in their callings, however vile, because they serve their neighbour. 'A cobbler, a smith, a farmer, each has the work and office of his task, and yet they are all alike consecrated priests and bishops, and every one by means of his own work or office must benefit and serve every other, that in this way many kinds of work be done for the bodily and spiritual welfare of the community.'[1] In his doctrine of usury Calvin always insisted that men must consider the good of the commonwealth before their own gain. It all depends on the attitude with which we go about our work. George Herbert derived directly from Luther when he wrote that labour was dignified or degrading according to the spirit in which it was done.

> '*A servant with this clause*
> *Makes drudgery divine;*
> *Who sweeps a room, as for thy laws,*
> *Makes that and the action fine*'.[2]

The enthusiasm with which English Puritan preachers took up this point shows that it met a real need. It was very arguable that productive economic activity in the 16th and 17th centuries was a charitable good work in Luther's sense. The protestants' emphasis on hard work,

---

[1] *Thirty-four Sermons*, p. 215 and *passim*; cf. *Reformation Writings*, I, pp. 375-6; II, pp. 110-11, 121; Tyndale, *Doctrinal Treatises*, pp. 100-2; *Expositions*, pp. 125-6; *Answer to More*, p. 173.

[2] Cf. *Thirty-four Sermons*, p. 211; *Reformation Writings*, I, p. 276; J. Dod and R. Clever, *A Plain and Familiar Exposition of the Ten Commandments* (19th ed., 1662), p. 190.

which linked their reprobation of idle monks with their reprobation
of idle beggars, sprang from the economic circumstances of the time
as reflected in the thinking of bourgeois laymen. When Francis Bacon
suggested that the age-old problem of poverty might at last be soluble
if the resources of the community, including its labour, were ration-
ally utilized, he was only developing an idea which he might have
received from his very Puritan mother.[1] The ambiguity of the word
charity helped. The law without charity was nothing worth. Fuller
said that Edward VI's charity was no less demonstrated in his foundation of Bridewell for the punishment of sturdy beggars than of St.
Thomas's Hospital for relief of the poor. Perkins thought the Poor
Law of 1597 was 'in substance the very law of God.'[2] Professor Jordan's remarkable book on philanthropy in England shows how in the
16th and early 17th centuries sober and rational calculation of what
was of advantage to the community replaced the mediaeval ideal of
indiscriminate alms-giving. The latter created beggars, and was self-
regarding anyway; true charity was to encourage self-help in the
deserving.

The preachers, and still more their congregations, might well be
genuinely convinced in their hearts that industry was a good work,
for the 'common good', for 'the use and profit of mankind'; that
negligence in business harms the public state.[3] It is a duty to God
and the commonwealth to use your talents, said John Preston.
Provided you do not make gain your godliness, provided you do not
seek riches but accept them as the blessing of God if they happen to
come—then you may lawfully take care to increase your estate.
'Ask thyself then', said Thomas Taylor, 'what good doth my life to
church, to commonwealth, to family, to men?'[4] It was in fact the

[1] See my essay on 'William Perkins and the Poor', in *Puritanism and Revolution,*
p. 234; and a communication by V. G. Kiernan in *Past and Present* No. 3,
esp. pp. 49-51.
[2] T. Fuller, *The Holy State* (1648), p. 144; Perkins, *Workes,* I, p. 755.
[3] Dod and Clever, *A Plaine and Familiar Exposition of the Proverbs of Salomon,*
(1612), Chapter IX, pp. 65-6; Chapter XVIII, pp. 10-11; cf. Chapter XIII,
pp. 70-3.
[4] J. Preston, *Sinnes Overthrow* (4th ed., 1641), pp. 254-9; T. Taylor, *A Commentary Upon the Epistle of St. Paul to Titus* (1658), p. 183.

labour of generations of God-fearing Puritans that made England the leading industrial nation in the world—God, as His manner is, helping those who helped themselves.

Through this emphasis on the inner conviction which inspired actions, bourgeois lay society could impose its own standards. 'God's children look to the spiritual use of those things which the worldlings use carnally', said Greenham. The actions of the Scribes and Pharisees 'were good in themselves, and for others', said Sibbes; 'but the end of them was naught, and therefore both they and their works are condemned.' 'Man may with good conscience', Perkins thought, 'desire and seek for goods necessary, whether for nature or for his person, according to the former rules: but he may not desire and seek for goods more than necessary, for if he doth, he sinneth.' ('The former rules' include the convenient provision that 'those goods without which a man's estate, condition and dignity... cannot be preserved' are necessary.[1]) The preachers attempted to spiritualize what men were doing away, by telling them to do it for the right reasons. One may suspect that their congregations paid more attention to the general permission than to the careful qualifications with which it was hedged around. 'They are very hot for the Gospel', said Thomas Adams of such laymen; 'they love the Gospel: who but they? Not because they believe it, but because they feel it: the wealth, peace, liberty that ariseth by it.'[2]

Men are too ready to accuse Puritans of covetousness, observed William Gouge: we should be very cautious about this, since we cannot read the hearts of others, or know all the extenuating circumstances. 'Covetousness doth especially consist in the inward desire of a man, which is best known to himself... Observe the inward wishes of thine heart. If they be especially for the things of this world, they argue a covetous disposition.' 'When therefore thou thinkest of sparing', Dod and Clever advised, 'let not the greedy desire of gathering draw thee to it, but conscience of well using that which God hath lent thee.' 'Seek riches not for themselves but for God',

[1] Greenham, *Workes*, p. 20; Sibbes, *The Returning Backslider* (1639), pp. 451-2; Perkins, *Workes*, II, p. 125.
[2] T. Adams, *Workes* (1630), p. 389.

was Thomas Taylor's simpler formulation.[1] 'We teach you not to cast away the bag, but covetousness', Thomas Adams reassured his City congregation. 'O ye rich citizens', announced Joseph Hall, 'we tell you from Him, whose title is Rich in Mercy, that ye may be at once rich and holy.' When ministers went as far as that, we can imagine the simplifications and self-deceptions of laymen. The Presbyterian preachers, Hobbes noted two generations later, 'did never inveigh against the lucrative vices of men of trade or handicraft.'[2]

The Puritans tried to spiritualize economic processes. God instituted the market and exchange, Dod and Clever assured their large public. 'He would have commerce and traffic to proceed from love', and He favours a fair bargainer. Greenham made unrepining acceptance of the market price evidence 'that thine heart is rightly affected, both to God and to the brethren.'[3] Emphasis on the motive of the heart is the key to the preachers' distinction between 'biting' usury and legitimate commercial transactions,[4] no less than to their distinction between indiscriminate alms-giving and relief of the deserving poor, and to the protestant doctrine of the calling. All stem from the theology of justification by faith. Did adventurers sail to North America, 'to seek new worlds for gold, for praise, for glory'? 'If the same proceed of ambition or avarice', they were warned in 1583, 'it cometh not of God', and will not prosper. But if men are impelled by zeal for the honour of God, by compassion for the 'poor infidels captured by the devil', as well as by desire to relieve the poor of England and advance the interest of their honest and well-affected countrymen, then 'so sacred an intention' gives them the right 'to prosecute effectively the full possession of those so ample and pleasant

[1] W. Gouge, *A Commentary on the Whole Epistle to the Hebrews* (1866-7), III, pp. 293-5; cf. Greenham, *Workes*, p. 784; Dod and Clever, *A godly forme of household government* (2nd. ed., 1614), Sig. E. 6v-7; T. Taylor, *Works* (1653), p. 477.
[2] Adams, *Workes*, p. 862; J. Hall, *Works* (1808), V, pp. 103-4; T. Hobbes, *Works*, VI, pp. 194-5.
[3] Dod and Clever, *Proverbs*, XI, pp. 2-3; XX, p. 132; Greenham, *Workes*, p. 620.
[4] Cf. Bullinger, *Decades* (Parker Soc., 1849-52), III, pp. 41-2. Roman Catholic casuistry, on the other hand, by its emphasis on the formal and external, made release from the sin of usury depend to some extent on methods of accountancy (H. M. Robertson, *Aspects of the Rise of Economic Individualism*, p. 164).

countries.' 'If we first seek the kingdom of God', wrote Hakluyt with divine simplicity and prophetic accuracy, 'all other things will be given unto us.'[1]

This emphasis on the religious motive for colonization was often repeated. Historians looking only at the result have regarded it as gratuitous hypocrisy. Those who have tried to penetrate the hearts of the colonizers have seen it as a seriously-held intention, which for some reason was never carried out.[2] It was rather, I suggest, a necessary part of the thought-processes of men whose protestant training made secular pursuits possible only if entered into with the right motive. But the example of colonization shows how easily emphasis on godly motive could become a cloak for economic calculation. Protestants, said a preacher at Paul's Cross in 1581, are freed from the tyranny of the law upon the conscience. Hence we are prone to carnality, since 'we live to ourselves.'[3] Zeal-of-the-Land Busy, when asked about the lawfulness of eating a Bartholomew pig at the Fair, reflected that 'The place is not much, not very much, so it be eaten with a reformed mouth, with sobriety and humbleness'. The sin of Ignorance, Bunyan recorded 60 years later, was that he thought all problems of salvation were answered by saying 'My heart tells me so'.

V

Doctrines emphasizing the motives of the heart, allowing social pressures to influence individual conduct more freely, flourish especially, it may be suggested, in periods of rapid social change, and among those persons most exposed to its effects. Christianity arose in such a period; St. Augustine, on whose theology the reformers drew so heavily, also lived in an age when old standards were breaking down; and he too stressed inner motive rather than external action. 'When it is plain to him what he should do and to what he should aspire, even

[1] R Hakluyt, *Principal Navigations* (Everyman ed.), VI, pp. 3-4; *Divers Voyages* (1582), Dedication to Sir Philip Sidney.
[2] Perry Miller, *Errand into the Wilderness*, pp. 99-140.
[3] M. Maclure, *The Paul's Cross Sermons, 1534-1642* (1958), p. 126.

then, unless he feel delight and love therein, he does not perform his duty.' 'If they said that any works of mercy may obtain pardon even for the greatest and most habitual sins, they would be guilty of much absurdity: for so might the richest man for his 10d. a day have a daily quittance for all his fornications, homicides, and other sins whatsoever.'[1] There appears to be a permanent tendency for established churches to revert to ceremonial, and for opposition groups to stress the internal element. In the Middle Ages, after the Church had become institutionalized, those who laid the strongest emphasis on the intention, the purity of heart of ordinary lay Christians, were the heretics—Massalians, Paulicians, Bogomils, Albigensians, Lollards, to whom radical protestants from Foxe to Lilburne looked back for the true Christian line of descent. This age-old protest acquired a new significance as educated townsmen, trained by their mode of life in rational calculation and independent thinking, began to challenge the clerical monopoly of education and to assert their own standards of morality. The protestant emphasis on the heart helped to dissolve the hard crust of custom, tradition and authority.[2]

To summarize the argument, then:—The appeal to inner conviction, and the rejection of the routine of ceremonies through which the priesthood imposed its authority, could have liberating effects in any society. The hold over men's minds of an established doctrinal system had to be broken before the political and social order sanctified by those doctrines could be challenged. The appeal to the heart was common to early Christianity and many mediaeval heresies. Its most obvious effects were negative. But, positively, it facilitated the evolution of more flexible doctrines. Since opposition to the Roman Church in 16th and 17th century Europe drew its main strength

---

[1] Augustine, *De Spiritu et Litera*, 5; *The City of God* (Everyman ed.), II, p. 353. Cf. Samuel Butler's shrewd observation, 'The Stoical necessity and Presbyterian predestination are the same' (*Characters and Passages from Notebooks*, 1908, p. 279).
[2] The failure of full-scale capitalism to develop in 14th century Florence may be connected with lack of a thorough-going heresy to unite its citizens against the Church. The heretical possibilities in the early Franciscan movement were tamed by the Papacy: the big bourgeoisie who came to rule Florence needed the Papacy, for this and for economic reasons (Hilton, 'Capitalism—What's in a Name?', *Past and Present*, No. 1).

from the big cities, protestantism could be developed in ways which favoured the rise of capitalism. But there is nothing in protestantism which leads automatically to capitalism: its importance was rather that it undermined obstacles which the more rigid institutions and ceremonies of catholicism imposed. The reformation mobilized masses of men against the Roman Church and the political authorities which protected it. Initial support for protestantism and especially Calvinism came from the educated minority, largely urban, which thought seriously about problems of church and state. But doctrines evolved by and for the middle class could appeal to other dissatisfied elements in the population, like the gentry of Hungary and Scotland, or the plebeians of the Dutch towns. By the same token, protestant churches were established—in Scandinavia, in central Europe—which made only slight and incidental contributions to the development of capitalism.

The protestant revolt melted down the iron ideological framework which held society in its ancient mould. Where capitalism already existed, it had henceforth freer scope. But men did not become capitalists because they were protestants, nor protestants because they were capitalists. In a society already becoming capitalist, protestantism facilitated the triumph of the new values. There was no inherent theological reason for the protestant emphasis on frugality, hard work, accumulation; but that emphasis was a natural consequence of the religion of the heart in a society where capitalist industry was developing. It was, if we like, a rationalization; but it flowed naturally from protestant theology, whose main significance, for our present purposes, is that in any given society it enabled religion to be moulded by those who dominated in that society.

'All external things [are] subject to our liberty', declared Calvin, 'provided the nature of that liberty approves itself to our minds as before God.' But Christian liberty was for the elect only. Professor Brown has argued that later Puritan attempts to spiritualize the market were the opposite of Luther's view that the world was given over to the devil.[1] Yet the transformation was due at least as much to the victories of the protestant outlook in the world as to an aban-

[1] Calvin, *Institutes*, II, p. 135; Brown, *Life against Death*, Chapter XIV, *passim*.

donment of its theology. When true religion had triumphed, the godly could hardly surrender the world so cheerfully to the devil. In a society run by protestants the ungodly must be disciplined; and the duty of performing good works for one's neighbour became a duty to the community. Hence the overwhelming emphasis of later Puritanism on the religious duties of industry, thrift and accumulation. As the bourgeois virtues triumphed, so the society of largely self-employed small producers was transformed into a society of domestic- and wage-workers, who could be profitably employed only by those who owned capital. In this society the few who climbed the social ladder did so at the expense of their neighbours. So the thought of the fortunate upper ranks came to stress more and more the vices and follies of the poor. Later Calvinism in England became harsher and more hypocritical, because of changes in society which it had helped to bring about.

Professors Haller and Jordan have stressed the importance of the Calvinist discipline and organization in giving a sense of status and self-respect to the unprivileged; and have suggested that Calvinism's spread, and its success in building revolutionary parties, owed more to this than to its theology. But the emphasis on motive also helped the theology to flourish among earnest, sincere and responsible men in any sort of environment; and the discipline, ideally designed for preserving the domination of a small nucleus, was adaptable to almost any form of revolt. The appeal of Calvinism in the 16th and 17th centuries was no more limited to the urban middle class than that of Marxism has been limited to the urban working class in our own day. In Scotland Calvinism became the bond of union between those who wished to be free of France and the French court, as well as of exploitation by the international Church. It was led by quite different social groups from those which dominated English Puritanism. The ministers were almost its only intellectuals. Because the Kirk headed a movement for national independence, Calvinism drove far deeper roots than it did in England, where capitalism and the class divisions which accompanied it were much more developed. So in England, within little more than a century of the Reformation, Calvinists had led a successful revolution but had failed to monopilize state power because they could not hold together the diverse groups which had helped to make the revolution: whereas in Scotland Presbyterianism became a popular religion in the same sense as Catholicism did in Ireland, and in a way that Anglicanism never did in England. There were 'nationalist' elements also in the Calvinism of Transylvania and the Netherlands.

So the fact that strong political feelings, of any kind, could express themselves, and be shared, through the emphasis on the heart, helps to explain the existence of sincere Calvinists among the aristocracy and gentry—themselves experiencing social crisis—in many countries from Hungary to France. But we should not be naive about this. Calvin deliberately set out to win the support of the high aristocracy in France; and the latter no doubt saw the use for themselves of a tightly-disciplined, wealthy and dedicated urban organization.[1] The godly in England also had few scruples about casting out devils with Beelzebub, in the shape of the Dukes of Northumberland or Buckingham, the Earls of Leicester or Essex.

An age of ignorance is an age of ceremony, Dr. Johnson correctly observed.[2] The victory of protestantism helped to end the animistic magical universe, and undermined the traditional popular conception of religion as propitiation. Henceforth God and the individual soul stood face to face. The sense of sin remained, became indeed more overwhelming, because sin had to be grappled with alone. But the sense of sin was now also a sense of potential freedom. No magician or priest or saint could help, but God could. His promises were free and sure. The Puritan remained terribly conscious of his own sinful nature, even whilst he tried, by careful scrutiny of motive, to identify his will with the will of God. 'It does not need modern psychology to enable us to appreciate that the more bitter the internal struggle, the more complete was the assumption of identification with the Will of God in external activities.'[3] The simultaneous conviction of depravity and righteousness does not make the most attractive characters

[1] R. M. Kingdom, *Geneva and the Coming of the Wars of Religion in France, 1555-1563*, p. 56 and *passim*.
[2] Samuel Johnson, *A Journey to the Western Islands*, Raasay.
[3] John Marlowe, *The Puritan Tradition in England* (1956), p. 133.

in the world; but it gave a vital stimulus to productive effort in countries where capitalism was developing, at a time when industry was small-scale, handicraft, unrationalized. Successful mediaeval business men died with feelings of guilt and left money to the Church to be put to unproductive uses. Successful protestant business men were no longer ashamed of their productive activities whilst alive, and at death left money to help others to imitate them. None were more industrious than those who had abandoned the concept of a work of supererogation.

> *'Not the labours of my hands*
> *Can fulfil Thy law's demands.'*

The paradox of protestantism is that it eternally strives to fulfil a law which it knows to be unfulfillable. The paradox of capitalism is that production and accumulation become objects in themselves, losing sight of the end of consumption: just as the man whom Hobbes abstracted from this society sought power after power, ending only in death. Hobbist man is what capitalist man would have been if he had ceased to worry about his motives. At worst the preachers clothed his nakedness in a fig-leaf of hypocrisy; at best they humanized some industrial relations and directed energy towards public service as well as private profit.

HABITATION VERSUS IMPROVEMENT: THE DEBATE ON ENCLOSURE BY AGREEMENT

'Depopulation hath cast a slander on Inclosure, which because often done with it, people suspect it cannot bee done without it.'
PSEUDOMISUS, *Considerations Concerning Common Fields* (1654), p. 39.

THIS essay attempts an examination of the period between the Tudor statutes, which sought to preserve tillage and houses of husbandry, and the Hanoverian statutes which offered the majority of proprietors in a village who wanted enclosure a means whereby they could override the conservative minority who were averse to Improvement. It is the period of Enclosure by Agreement.

Enclosure as such has never been illegal in England but in the sixteenth century there were many Acts of Parliament and much governmental action which looked coolly on the results of certain enclosures, particularly those which changed land-use or brought a diminution in householders.

Nor has there ever been a time when the statutes allowed general enclosure without conditions. The Enclosure Acts of the eighteenth and early nineteenth centuries were not a blanket approval but a long series of local Acts permitting local proposals; even when in 1845 the scrutiny of the few remaining enclosure proposals was delegated to Civil Servants each case had still to be taken on its merits.[1] What of the period before even local Enclosure Acts were available to those who could afford them?

Ideally, one ought to be able to chronicle the stages by which official opinion, the practice of the courts and the votes of the legis-

[1] The first truly General Enclosure Act of 1836 demanded the agreement of the majority of proprietors; the General Act of 1845 set up permanent Commissioners in London.

lature moved from the suspicion and hostility shown by the Acts[1] of 1597 to the benevolent neutrality of the Hanoverian Enclosure Acts. Because there are no full records of Parliamentary debates and votes in the seventeenth century there are only brief occasions scattered through the period when anything like the mind of Parliament can be discerned. The records of the law courts at Westminster and in the provinces are much fuller but their bulk is an equally formidable obstacle to historical judgements since they have been so little calendared and indexed. But even if a coherent account of the encloser-at-law could someday be written it would be hopeless to look for coherence in official policy or unanimity in the voice of the legislature.

Men took up different stances towards enclosure because the issue raised fundamental tests of social attitude. The enclosure debate of the sixteenth century, as the author of *The Agrarian Problem* and *Religion and the Rise of Capitalism* taught us, passed beyond a contest between those who wore the badge of corn and those who wore the badge of sheep. There were heavy overtones of social approval in the very roll of the word 'husbandman' and they were times when 'grazier', like 'brogger', seemed to be simply a translation of the Mammon of Unrighteousness. The long debates produced a clash of voices because the fundamental issue of the common weal and private profit was one on which men were not unanimous.[2]

Some aspects of the transition from suspicion of enclosure to neutrality or approval are indeed illuminated by regarding it as one stage in the triumph of self-love over social: but it is only a partial illumination. It is also necessary to see the transition in other lights. This essay will consider approval of enclosure agreements successively as: a refutation of the slander summarised in the quotation at the head; a concession to the realities of variety in local agrarian practice; an aspect of faith in the market mechanism and a distrust of regulation; finally, a search for an administrative device whereby enclosure could be 'Regulated'.

---

[1] 39 Eliz. I cc 1 and 2.

[2] Contemporary *Notes* on the two Acts of 1597 set 'a trifling abridgement to gentlemen' against 'the misery of the people and the decay of the nation's strength': *Hist. Mss. Comm. Salisbury*, xiv (1923), p. 27.

I

The most formidable obstacle to any shift in public opinion towards tolerating enclosure by agreement was the slander which the pamphlet by Pseudomisus sought to refute. Once upon a time enclosure had brought depopulation: was not that the effect, if not the aim, of all enclosures? In November 1597 it was this conjunction of enclosure, conversion of tillage to grass and decay of households which animated the speech by Bacon and initiated the two statutes which mark the final attempt to legislate for the status quo. Although two bills were needed to cover the issues, the reformers' purpose was single. One member noted the ears of the sheepmasters hanging at the door of the Commons but others could have remarked the ghosts from deserted villages haunting the Parliament chamber; and although some critics feared that the sheepmasters had wrung too many concessions in the course of the bill's passage it was these ghosts who triumphed.[1]

When the villagers of Croft, Leicestershire, objected to the terms of an enclosure agreement in 1632 their complaint was summed up in these words: 'the ayme and ends tend to a generall Inclosure and consequently to a Depopulation'.[2]

It was this chain of 'consequently' which had to be broken before enclosure by agreement could become possible, but it was natural in a Leicestershire village encircled by deserted villages that the consequence seemed inevitable. It was not long afterwards that Sir William Dugdale, on the other side of Watling Street, rode from country house to country house collecting for his *History of Warwickshire* and managed to identify most of the deserted village sites of that county without recourse to air photographs. The debate was being carried on in a countryside whose scars seemed fresh.[3]

[1] J. E. Neale, *Elizabeth I and her Parliaments, 1584-1601* (1957) pp. 337-351 and sources there cited.

[2] Public Record Office (hereafter, P.R.O.), P.C.2/41 f. 506: 6 April 1632; the enclosure agreement dated from 1629.

[3] *The Antiquities of Warwickshire* was published in 1656 and Dugdale seems to have drawn his own maps, on which depopulated places are indicated by a symbol: P. D. A. Harvey and H. Thorpe, *The Printed Maps of Warwickshire* (1959), p. 15.

The protagonists of enclosure had therefore to advocate a 'Regulated Enclosure' with some arbiter to leash the over-greedy:

'to prevent depopulation under some grievous penalty and to leave the decay of tillage at more liberty.'[1]

It was necessary to find a way of marrying Improvement and Habitation and this policy was advocated by the author of *A Consideration*, aroused by the anti-enclosure rising of 1607 and the government commissions of enquiry:

'By redressinge the fault of Depopulation and Leaveinge encloseinge and convertinge arbitrable... the poore man shalbe satisfied in his ende; Habitation; and the gentleman not Hindered in his desier; Improvement'[2]

John Norden, a public advocate of enclosure for Improvement, nevertheless regarded depopulating enclosure as

'the bane of a commonwealth, an apparent badge of Atheisme and an argument of waspish ambition or woolvish emulation.'[3]

The fears of depopulating enclosure were an unconscionable long time in dying. They appear in private comment as well as in public pamphleteering. In 1668 the tithe collector at Pickering, Yorkshire, criticised a local enclosure proposal—

'I should think the Chancery should hinder inclosure because it will make a greate depopulation, above 150 families will be undone.'[4]

Two years after Pseudomisus' pamphlet, John Moore's *Scripture Word Against Inclosure* showed a Leicestershire parson still appealing to the ghosts from the deserted villages:

'They say there may be an inclosure without decay of Tillage of Depopulation... They would not have a Spade called a Spade'.

The core of his opponent's case was this:

To inveigh against Inclosure in generall as if it were the proper cause or occasion of depopulation and decay of tillage is not ratio-

[1] *Hist. Mss. Comm. Hastings*, iv (1947), p. 323 (undated but 1613-23).

[2] British Museum (hereafter, B.M.), Cott. Mss. Titus CII f. 165; FIV f. 319; Lans. Mss. 487 f. 21; printed in W. Cunningham, *Growth of British Industry and Commerce*, iii (1917), pp. 898-9.

[3] John Norden, *Surveiors Dialogue* (1607), p. 224.

[4] Yorks. Arch. Soc. Mss. DD32, Marshall to Osborne, July 1668. I am indebted to Mr. A. Harris for this reference.

nall; and that to hinder all Inclosure for the future is neither a necessary nor a sufficient means to prevent or to reforme those evils'.[1]

These two pamphleteers came from Leicestershire and made the air thick with local village names, the deserted villages convincing Moore that he was right: and the villages which had survived an enclosure by agreement comforting his opponent's case. But it is significant that the village names cited by Moore were predominantly old desertions, and if fears of depopulating enclosure seem to have faded to nothing by the end of the seventeenth century it could only have come about by a genuine absence of new depopulations. In debate, evanescent words and actions could be explained away and glossed over but newly decayed villages would have been impossible to refute.

II

If the opposition to enclosure was partially disarmed by fewer and fewer deserted villages, what of the traditional suspicion of conversion of tillage to pasture, even conversion which stopped far short of a depopulation? Had not one statute of 1597 made it an offence to decay a house of husbandry? And had not the other revived the practice of putting

'land having once been tilled into a perpetual bondage and servitude of being for ever tilled?'[2]

The increasing toleration of a changing land-use was a most important aid to the toleration of enclosure by agreement. The more liberal attitude towards conversion from corn to grass sometimes derived from a general liberal sentiment approving the right of individuals to decide what to do with their own property; this aspect is well known and can be summed up in Raleigh's words in 1601:

'I do not like the constraining of them to use their Grounds at our

---

[1] Moore, rector of Knaptoft, published his first pamphlet in 1656. The opposing quotation is from [J. Lee, parson of Catthorpe], *A Vindication of the Considerations etc.* (1656), p. 17.

[2] *Hist. Mss. Comm. Salisbury*, vii (1899), p. 542.

wills but rather let every man use his Ground to that which it is most fit for, and therein use his own Discretion.'[1]

But a toleration of conversion also arose from a belief in the virtues of local agricultural specialisation, and, like many contemporary statements on free trading, the advocacy stemmed not from theory but from practical interest and self-interest. Indeed, Raleigh's next sentence went straight from the study to the field.

'I know land which if it had beene unplowed (which it now is because of the Statutes of Tillage) would have been good pasture for Beasts,' and he was prepared to see the principle of local agricultural specialisation developed as between England and the continent. He almost preached comparative advantage. For that microcosm of a continent, the English counties, the same view had been put in the Tillage debates of 1597 when it had been successfully argued that the statute ought not to embrace Shropshire[2] since that county's soils made it fittest to be grass and the 'Dayrie house to the whole Realme'; for had not the same Providence arranged that the soil of neighbouring Herefordshire made that county 'the Barne'?

It is the progress of this sentiment of local specialisation which we must now examine, and the victory of the sentiment in Stuart England rested on very substantial advances even under the Tudors. There never had in fact been a complete bondage and servitude of being for ever tilled. On paper the Acts of 1489 and 1515 might read that way, but in enforcement the Crown was weak. When the Act of 1536 gave strength to enforcement it also admitted the principle of local limitation; fourteen counties only were affected by it: roughly, the Midlands and the Isle of Wight (which had set the pace by having its own Act in 1488).[3] The Tillage Bill of 1597 came from the Commons already limited to 25 counties and the Lords added a proviso[4] exempting land converted from tillage to grass within two

[1] H. Townshend, *Historical Collections* (1680), p. 188.

[2] A. F. Pollard and Marjorie Blatcher, 'Hayward Townshend's Journals', *Bull. Inst. Hist. Res.*, xii (1935), p. 16: 17 Dec. 1597.

[3] For the legislation and prosecutions before 1597 see M. Beresford, *The Lost Villages of England* (1954), pp. 102-33.

[4] House of Lords Mss., engrossed Acts, 39 Eliz. I, c. 2; the counties exemption is in the hand of the Commons clerk on the parchment Bill, while the Watling

miles of Watling Street all along its course from the end of the Chiltern downs at Dunstable to Chester, a local concession in the interest of finding fodder for the drovers' herds on their journey south; there is a suggestion that Huntingdonshire had been left out of earlier Acts for the same local reason.[1] The Houses of Husbandry Act had no local exemptions but the provision for the exempt counties in the Tillage bill converted one M.P. (in his own confession) from Saul to Paul. An M.P. who did not see the light on the road to Damascus was the member for Ludlow borough who wanted Shropshire in the bill; the county members cried him down.[2]

Some recognition that local circumstances might make conversion not always a sin against the common weal can also be seen in the limited areas where enforcement of the Acts of 1489, 1515 and 1536 took place; and the Act of 1556 which appointed a Commission with permanent clerks to enforce the existing agrarian legislation gave the Commission express latitude:

'they may use theyr discretions in temporing and qualifeing. . . In some places of this Realme yt ys not necessary the purview of this Estatute extende and bee fully executed.'[3]

Local husbandry practices were accepted also in the Act of 1536 which gave the Crown until the day of reconversion half the profits of land illegally converted to grass. But the reconversion was qualified:

'. . . from pasture into tillage agayn, according to the nature of the soyle and course of Husbandrye used in the Countrey where any such Landes doe lie.'[4]

The Tillage Act of 1597 likewise recognised that in some districts grass replaced tillage not permanently but as part of convertible husbandry.[5] 'The course of husbandrye used in that parte' is a Lords'

Street proviso is in the paper format which the Commons were insisting on for Lords' amendments at this time (Sir. S. D'Ewes, *Journals of all the Parliaments 1680*), pp. 535 and 576-7.

[1] B. M. Lans. Mss. 487 f. 219: proposal to include the London to Berwick road.
[2] Pollard and Blatcher, *art. cit.*, pp. 15-6.
[3] 2 & 3 Ph. and Mary c. 2.
[4] 27 Henry VIII c. 22.
[5] A 'politic' clause: *Hist. Mss. Comm. Salisbury*, vii (1899) pp. 541-3.

revision of the original Bill[1] which had had simply 'custome'. The same Act also continued the tradition of the Act of 1563 in not penalising the conversion of land to grass when it fed a man's own horses, draught oxen or domestic kine. In 1597 it was safe to decay tillage in one place if equivalent areas of grass were ploughed up elsewhere on the estate. This flexibility was approved by the villagers of Eagle (Lincs.) in 1656. Like the villagers of Croft they looked around at their neighbours' example but saw no deserted villages after enclosure:

> 'most of the land now tilled is more proper for grass, and that moor ground now eaten as common is fitter for corn as if proved by experience amongst our next neighbours.'[2]

Durham witnesses in a case of 1608 deposed that the enclosure of the common moor of Gainford had increased tillage,[3] and an advocate of the enclosure of Sedgemoor urged that more and not fewer employment opportunities would result.[4]

Local variations in soil were increasingly argued as a defence by those prosecuted for conversion in the 1630's. Thus Sir Thomas Burton of Frisby, Leicestershire, ordered by the Privy Council in 1631 to sow two yardlands of enclosed land with corn, protested

> 'the soile is a cold claie and not so fitt for Corne as grasse.'[5]

It is not surprising that the odd little Act of 1608 which may claim to be the first English pro-enclosure Act permitted some enclosure by agreement in six Herefordshire parishes on exactly these grounds:

> 'they doe differ in the manner of their Husbandrie from many partes of the said Countie and other Counties in the Realme.'[6]

At the other extreme there were local circumstances which made the northern Border counties vulnerable to the old type of depopul-

---

[1] see f.n. 4 p. 45, above.

[2] quoted in *Lincs. Notes and Queries*, x, p. 248.

[3] P.R.O., E. 178/3749.

[4] Adam Moore, *An Apologie for His Majesties Royall Intention*: B.M. Add. Mss. 48111 (Yelverton Mss.). He was probably identical with the author of *Bread for the Poor* (1653) wherein common fields were declared a 'common prostitute'.

[5] P.R.O., S.P. 16/187 no. 80; other defences of this kind in Joan Thirsk, *English Peasant Farming* (1957), pp. 166-7 and 184-5.

[6] 4 Jas. I c. 11.

ating enclosure at the very end of the sixteenth century. Since the
mid-century there had been concern about the decay of husbandmen
here.[1] There is the well-known letter from the Dean of Durham
pleading for the inclusion of the northern counties in the Tillage
Act of 1597:

> 'Of all places those most needed to be looked to. The depopulations
> are not, as supposed, by the enemy but private men have dispeopled
> whole villages.'[2]

Northumberland was added to the bill during the Commons debates[3]
and the Lords added Pembroke: but Northumberland was not
protected for long. In 1601 it was agreed to continue the Tillage
Acts but Northumberland was excluded from their provisions.[4]

III

It might be argued that these statutory recognitions of variety in
local practice amounted to official toleration of a Regulated Enclosure,
if only silently. This point of view is strengthened by examining the
machinery by which statutes were enforced. The Act of 1556 admitted that agrarian legislation need not be 'fully executed' and, as in
much Tudor legislation, a general prohibition was a prelude to
personal exemptions. The dog wagged its tail for a bone while it
barked.

Some bought royal pardons, such as that the encloser of Cotesbach
received from James I at the instance of a courtier.[5] For others, the

---

[1] e.g. surveys of 1584: S.P. 15/28 ff. 232-74.

[2] *Cal. S.P. Dom. 1595-7*, p. 347.

[3] It cannot have been a Lords' addition, *pace* J. E. Neale, *op. cit.*, p. 345, for
Lords' amendments had to be on paper (see f.n. 4 p. 45 above) and 'Northumberland' is interlineated in the parchment Act, House of Lords Mss; 'Pembroke',
however, is on the paper sheet of amendments.

[4] 43 Eliz. I. c. 9 s. 2; the exemption was urged on the grounds that the plague
had swept away whole villages locally: D'Ewes, *op. cit.*, p 674

[5] P R.O., C. 66/1618 no. 22; in 1601 a Mr. Dormer sought to have his licence
endorsed by Act: the Commons agreed by a majority of 43 but the proviso is
not in the Act, 43 Eliz. I c. 9. Other pardons and dispensations to individuals are:
C. 66/1020 mm. 29-30 (1566, following the Bucks. Enclosure Commission,
E. 178/424;) C. 66/1013 and 1024; C. 66/1787 (1608); and C. 66/2452 no. 46
(1628).

Commissions to Compound and the legal underworld of the common informer gave opportunities to enclose and convert for anyone who could afford to pay. In its most open form the payment was a composition for fines after a confession of past sins. In its most covert form it was a payment to a blackmailing informer in order to seal his lips. The royal revenue benefited a little and the legal middlemen a great deal.

The prerogative powers of suspending and dispensing contributed in a double way to the eventual toleration of enclosure by agreement. In so far as they allowed local and personal circumstances to be taken into account they helped to weaken an unqualified opposition to all enclosure and all change in land use. But their most powerful educative force was one which their originators could hardly have intended: abuse of these powers in the hands of the common informer and their use as a means of non-Parliamentary revenue-raising considerably discredited the principle of restriction by statute or Privy Council.[1] Coke welcomed the repeal of much agrarian legislation in 1624 as

'unnecessary statutes unfit for this time. . . snares that might have lien heavy upon the subject.'[2]

The process of discredit (by which shields had become snares) can be seen even before the debates of 1621. In 1597 some feared that the Tillage Laws would simply open the doors to dishonest informers but the official view was that genuine informers would operate; of the informers-by-patent the Queen, it was said,

'naturally likes them as little as monopolies or concealments;'[3]
the private common informer in the provinces would be encouraged to act by 'love of justice or faction or emulation.'
an ill-assorted trinity of incentives. In February 1618 a Commission of judges and others was appointed to grant exemptions from the Tillage Acts.

[1] M.W. Beresford, 'The Common Informer, the Penal Statutes and Economic Regulation', *Ec. Hist. Rev.*, 2nd ser., x (1957), pp 221-38. Informers operated chiefly in Exchequer (E 159) but see also e.g. K.B. 27/1429 (1611, Mich.), mm. 'Rooper' nos. 114, 116, 146 for cases before King's Bench.
[2] Sir. E. Coke, *The Third Part of the Institutes* (1644), pp. 191-4.
[3] *Hist. Mss. Comm. Salisbury*, xiv (1923), pp. 27 and 37.

'The rigor of the statutes may be mitigated according to these present tymes and occasions. . . Lands which have heretofore bene used in tillage for corne and grayne have of late tymes out of their tryall and experience had of the unaptness and unfruitfulnes thereof for tillage bene turned from tillage into pasture for the mayntenaunce and keepinge of cattell whereby they have in some sorte incurred the penalties of the lawes.'[1]

From these technical offences only the informer had wrung benefit: 'no benifitt redounded to the common wealth nor profitt unto Ourselves but secretly and under hand benifitt made to and by the Informers more to the molestation of our subjects than any to the reformation that the lawes intended.'

A document headed 'Motives and Reasons of the Commissioners for Pardons for Decay of Tillage' claimed that two thousand informations had been thwarted by the Commission's dispensations,[2] and in March 1620 a similar patent was issued to the judges, learned counsel and others. This second patent was revoked in 1621 at a time when the repeal of the tillage laws seemed imminent,[3] but the first patent may be 'Mr. Edward Ramsey's patent' which the Commons debated[4] but did not condemn in November 1640.

The revival of anti-depopulation Commissions during Charles I's period of non-Parliamentary government displayed a familiar mixture of paternalism and pickpocketry. A few oppressors of the poor and would-be depopulators were no doubt penalised or deterred but the victims seem to have been mostly landowners who had enclosed by agreement and infringed the Acts of 1597 (unrepealed in 1624) by some small diminution of the area of tillage or the number of farm-houses.[5] A convenient list of the victims is set out in a document which begins

[1] C. 66/2134 m.1d; C. 66/2150 no. 17.

[2] B. M. Harl. Mss. 7616 f. 6; 7614; f. 127.

[3] *Commons Journal*, i, p. 573; S.P. 14/187/94: the patent concerned parks and warrens for which compositions had been allowed also by a patent of 19 May 1615: Hist. Mss. Comm., *3rd. Rep. App.* (1871), p. 15.

[4] S.P. 16/472 ff. 16-7: 23 Nov. 1640.

[5] The commissioners' allegations and the victims' estate records must be compared where possible: as in M. E. Finch, *Five Northants. Families* (Northants. Record Society, xx, 1956) pp. 158-63.

in 1635 and ends in the Easter term of 1640 with prosecutions which were annulled when Parliament at last met and the Commissions were condemned.[1] It was remembered in Laud's impeachment that 'he did a little too much countenance the Commission for Depopulations.'[2]

The patents show the Commission in its dual role. In March and April 1635 the Commissions were appointed to enquire into depopulations since 1588 in Lincoln, Somerset and Wiltshire.[3] But in May the tone charged:

'patent to release and determine all offences concerninge depopulations and converting arable land to pasture within this Realme and also to compound with Fynes with such offenders as the Commissioners shall thinke fitt to be pardoned.'

In September 1637 another patent for fines and pardons gave the Commissioners discretion in deciding how much reconversion and rebuilding be demanded of one of these repentant sinners: one such pardon was that to William Boughton for offences in Warwickshire, granted on July 12, 1639. After the payment

'his Majestie doth dispence with him for the continuance of the same houses and lands.'

Thus by 1640 conciliar action to maintain tillage had been discredited by the company it kept; but even if it was unlikely that any law would be passed to enforce enclosers to maintain the area of tillage, Parliament had not yet expressed any positive approval of enclosure and had taken no steps to facilitate a Regulated Enclosure. It is ironical that in a period very conscious of Parliamentary sovereignty it was not Parliament but the courts of Chancery and Exchequer which provided the eventual means of lawful Regulation; when Parliament began to approve local Enclosure Bills in the eighteenth century more than a hundred years had elapsed since its solitary approval of the Herefordshire enclosure agreements in

---

[1] C212/20; one proposal of 1631 suggested rebuilding St. Paul's from the depopulation fines for Leics., Lincs. and Northants: S.P. 16/187/95.

[2] S.P. 16/499 no. 10 also censured the Privy Council's committee on depopulations.

[3] All these patents occur in the papers of Lord Keeper Coventry: Birm. Ref. Library Mss. 604190, arranged by date.

1608; and many of the early Hanoverian enclosure Acts were simply Parliamentary approval of existing agreements registered already in Chancery or Exchequer.

Section V of this essay will discuss the facilities which developed in Chancery and Exchequer but, first of all, the missed opportunities in Parliament deserve comment.

IV

It has not been noticed hitherto that a permissive clause was deleted from the Bill which formed the basis of 39 Eliz. c. 1 'Against the Decaying of Towns and Houses of Husbandry'. The bill caused a long debate in the Commons Committee and when it reached the Upper House the Lords produced 31 written objections to it. The bill was re-written and re-titled after a conference of the two Houses and the final version which came down to the Commons for re-consideration was very different.[1] In form, it was made up of one large and one very small membrane in the hand of the Lords' Clerk (clauses I-IV of the printed Act) stitched to another large membrane, in the hand of the Commons' Clerk, containing clauses V onwards. Clause VI allowed exchange of land between lord and tenant or tenant and tenant 'for the more better and commodious occupyinge of husbandrye' when deficiencies in the acreage of land going with a farm had been made up from the surplus of another farm with more than the statutory minimum. At the end of clause VI, but struck out, is an even more liberal permission which can still be read underneath the cancellation.

[1] D'Ewes, *op. cit.*, pp. 537 and 542: 14 and 26 Jan. 1598. The Lords changed the title of the Act from 'for the Increase of People' to 'Against the Decaying of Towns etc.' The original bill is in House of Lords Mss., 15 December 1597. This Bill and the Tillage Bill reached the Lords together on 17 Dec. (*Lords Journal*, ii, p. 212). The Tillage Bill passed all its stages in both Houses by 23 Jan. but the Decaying of Towns took until 8 February, the eve of the royal assent, to pass the Commons in its revised form. Despite this it was numbered c. 1 and the Tillage Bill c. 2. The preambles to the original 'Increase' Bill and the Act are worth comparing; originally there was a rhetorical flourish akin to that which survived in c. 2, a Baconian ring.

'It shalbe lawfull for anie tenant of anie howse of husbandry with
the consent of the Lord of that soyle and of such other Lord as
hath Common or interest therein from tyme to tyme hereafter,
to inclose into severaltie the landes whiche shalbe put or belong
unto his howse of husbandry or any parte thereof.'[1]

The provenance of this part of the document is uncertain. Although
in the hand of the Commons' bills of that session it is not a relic of
the original bill, for that document survives elsewhere. It does however form part of the new bill which went from the Lords after the
Conference, for it bears the order *soit bailee aux Commons:* perhaps
it is the acceptable residue of a draft which the Commons brought to
the Conference?

In this Parliament of 1597-8 there were two other attempts to
give freedom to enclose but they do not seem to relate to this deleted clause. On 20 January 1598, in the midst of the discussions between the two Houses over this bill, it is recorded that the Commons
rejected

'a bill for the most Commodious usage of Lands dispersed in the
Common Fields.'

but no more is known of it than its title. When the revised Husbandry
Bill arrived from the Lords there was a last minute attempt to amend
it on 30 January

'that a Man maie inclose soe much Lands as himself listeth soe it be
for the mayntenance of his house.'

but it was defeated as

'a gapp to Lett more Sheepe in.'[2]

Alongside this abortive permission to enclose by agreement may
be set the single Act of 4 James I c. 11, a timid authority to six Herefordshire parishes to enclose one third of their commons by agreement.

---

[1] House of Lords Mss. engrossed Acts. The Commons hand has a strong left
slope on the flourishing small 'd' and will be found in the engrossed cc. 2 and
4-7 of the session The Lords hand is quite different and will be found on the
paper amendments (see f.n. 4 p. 45 above), on the provisos sewn to the Commons
Bills by the Lords (e.g. c. 6). All c 8 (Deprivation of bishops) is in this hand: it
was one of the bills which originated in the Lords (*L.J.*, ii. pp. 198-200).
[2] Pollard and Blatcher, *art. cit.*, p. 22 from BM. . Stowe Mss. 362 f. 17b; D'Ewes,
op. cit., p. 584.

The Act had no immediate successors but the psychological climate of 1607 and 1608 was not very tolerant of the word 'enclosure', over which blood had been freshly spilt in the agrarian riots.

A plan for a general permission to enclose was put to James I by John Shotbolt in his 'Verie necessary considerations for the Weale Publique'. (The document[1] is undated but this may be the Shotbolt who obtained a patent for a road-repairing machine in May 1619). He felt that public opinion had become less hostile

> 'the vulgar or common sorte of people... might nowe bee per-suaded and make a generall Triall of the contrary course, that is freely and willingly to assent to a speedy and generall Inclosure in all partes of the Kingdome and bee humble Suitors to his Majestie not onely to yeild his Royall assent thereunto or to tollerate the same but rather to endeavour by all means possible to sett so good a business in hand for soe generall Inriching to all sortes and every particular.'

Shotbolt declared himself an enemy of depopulation:

> 'most Unchristianlike it tooke not alone ye Bread from ye Mouths but ye Mouths from ye Bread.'

For him, enclosure was not the first step towards a change in land-use but a means to more efficient arable production. The glebe would gain by being consolidated, and the king might act as a model land-lord and set an example by allowing a general enclosure on the royal estates.

In essence Shotbolt's plan was for

> 'a mutuall consent for a generall Exchaunge (not altering either tenure or title but place along)'

and perhaps as early as 1623 Adam Moore's *Bread for the Poor*[2] urged a Grand Committee in each county for 'just proceeding' in an agreed enclosure.

An abortive bill of 1621 for the improving and better ordering of Commons was based on the idea of local Commissions and may have been connected with Shotbolt's project although it did not embrace

---

[1] B.M. Royal Mss. 18A/XXV; a project dated 27 March 1610 was also for a general enclosure: S.P. 14/120/10.

[2] Published 1653 but 'penned thirty years since'.

enclosure of open field land.[1] In 1621 the Commons was neutral
between the liberal and the conservative policies for it also rejected
a Depopulation Bill,[2] and had the King not ended the session abruptly
the Acts of 1489, 1515, 1536 and 1563 would have been repealed.[3]

The author of *England's Great Happiness, a Dialogue between Content
and Complaint* (1677) made his pro-enclosure speaker (*Content*) say:

'I confess I know no statute that gives full power to enclose all the
Common Fields in the Kingdom but in my weak judgement
there are several that do encourage it.'

He cited the Acts authorising the enclosure of fenland for improvement and the preamble to an Act of 1664 which he dubbed *Trade
Encouraged*.[4] This Act permitted export of corn when its price fell
below 48s. a quarter and in its preamble it praised tillage and commended the enclosure of wastes and their improvement

'if sufficient encouragement were given for the laying out of cost
and labour to the same'

—the 'Encouragement' being in fact not an Enclosure Act but an Act
to widen the market for corn. Despite *Content*, a vague commenda-
tion of improving wastes was some distance from an act encouraging
the enclosure of common fields. Bills to give encouragement had
recently failed. A Lords' bill of 1665 proposed to allow the owners
of unprofitable wastes to petition the Lord Chancellor or the Chancellor of the Duchy of Lancaster asking for a Commission to divide
the commons. It did not survive beyond a first reading.[5] In 1662
and 1663 the Commons rejected bills,[6] of which there survive no
details, entitled 'Common Fields' and 'For the Improvement of
Commons' and we may guess them to have been in the same vein as

[1] House of Lords Mss., 7 March 1621.
[2] W. Notestein *et al.*, eds., *Commons Debates of 1621* (1935), iii, p. 307.
[3] The 1563 Tillage Act was repealed in 1624; Coke also believed (correctly,
I think) that the Acts of 1597 also died in 1624 by non-continuance but the
Statute Law Revision Act of 1863 tidily repealed them.
[4] 16 Chas. II. c. 15; Acts such as 15 Chas. II c. 17 (Great Level of the Fens, 1663)
and 19 and 20 Chas. II c. 8 (Forest of Dean, 1668) extinguished common rights
in the cause of Improvement.
[5] Text of the Bill: House of Lords Mss. 20 Jan. 1665.
[6] *C.J.*, viii, pp. 423, 439, 466 and 486.

the Lords' bill of 1665. Another bill, which failed after its Committee stage in 1666, indicates the means whereby for nearly two generations local agreements had been finding legitimation independently of Parliament.

'Within these forty fifty and sixty years last past there have beene within this Kingdom multitudes of Enclosures of Commonable Grounds Wastes Heaths fermgrounds and Marishes by consent of partyes therein Interested made or ordered to be made, and the same uppon due Consideration thereuppon had been found to bee for the generall good and soe have been declared confirmed and established and decreed by decrees made in the Chancery or Exchequer Chamber or Duchy Court to generall satisfaction and contentment.[1]'

The bill proposed to give certainty to the legitimacy of these decrees by a retrospective blessing on all decrees for the previous sixty years. It did not propose any new machinery for future agreements but it did argue that the confirmation of past decrees would encourage other property owners who were considering an enclosure: yet the suggestion that a confirmatory Act was necessary was a tactless way of encouraging resort to decrees in the future.

In fact, confidence in the legitimacy of agreements registered in Chancery and Exchequer was strong in the 1660's and few decrees were brought in question. The early enclosures by Private Act were closely modelled on this well-established procedure of Decrees.[2] Many Acts simply ratified decrees, and even where there was no decree the early Acts were more akin to instruments for registering agreements among local proprietors rather than for overriding the obstinate opponents of Improvement.

[1] House of Lords Mss. 30 Oct. 1666.
[2] e.g. 4 Wm. & Mary (Private) no. 40 (1694) confirmed a Chancery decree for Hambleton (Rutland) of 1653 which had been brought into question: there may have been a genuine grievance of the villagers here (*Cal. S.P. Dom.* 1653, p. 330: petition against the purchaser of delinquent lands). 7 & 8 Wm. III (Private) no. 55 (1696) concerned Maidwell (Northants.) where there had been Chancery decrees of 10 May 1676 and 1 July 1692. A decree of 1716 for Huttons Ambo (Yorks), was confirmed by Act as late as 1805. As E.C.K. Gonner pointed out (*Common Land and Inclosure* (1912), pp. 187-8) there was an overlap in time between Acts and Decrees as a fashionable means of enclosing.

In general, enclosure by decree was enclosure by agreement, even where some pretence of disagreement was necessary before the court of Chancery could have jurisdiction.[1] Many enrolled decrees began by expressions of general local approval which were not cast in stereo-typed form and sound more spontaneous than the legal phrasebook.

'It would be convenient and pleasing to all men. . . and might be both good and profitable to all those who were desierous to live as paynefull men in theire callings,'[2]

declared the proprietors and commoners of Brandesburton (Yorks. E.R.) in their agreement of January 1630, one of the earliest to be registered in Chancery.

'It would raise and turne to a far greater benefitt to every of them then (*sc.* than) the enjoyinge of it in comon besides the generall good that would thereby accrewe to the commonWealth,'[3]

declared some Norfolk proprietors in 1627; while Endymion Porter, lord of the manor of Aston Subedge (Glos) claimed that his purchase of the manor at a stiff price had been encouraged by tenantry and freeholders assuring him that they wanted a general enclosure. They

'did much incourage and drawe him to proceed therein protestinge that if hee should have a hard bargaine thereof yett they would make him a good gainer thereby if he would agree to a generall incloasure to be made of the lordshipp'[4]

At another enclosure

'every man's part exceedingly improved in value;'

and at Thurcaston (Leics.)

'the said Inclosure tended soe much to the good of the common wealth and particular benefit of the said Parrishe. . . soe good a worke should not fayle.'[5]

When Charles I's Privy Council began to denounce and harry en-closure they had to meet the objection that agreed enclosures were

[1] In Leics. Dr. Thirsk identified 13 enclosures 1640-60 of which 'at least six' were by agreement. From these, three disputes arose. (*V.C.H. Leics.*, ii (1954), p. 218; C. 78/526 no. 8; C. 78/1214 no. 5.)

[2] C. 78/605; decree of March 1635.

[3] C. 78/273 no. 5.

[4] C. 78/273 no. 7: decree, Dec. 1629.

[5] C. 78/308 no. 21: decree, Dec. 1635.

harmless to the common weal. In March 1631 they described Leicestershire enclosures as

'very hurtfull to the commonwealth although they beare a fayre shewe of satisfaction to all Parties... but we well know what the consequences will be, and in conclusion all turne to Depopulation.'[1]

Where Chancery decrees speak of dissatisfaction over an enclosure the language must be construed carefully. It was a necessary fiction that a dispute existed, otherwise the jurisdiction of the Court might not run. The fictitious element appears near the surface in very many decrees, such as that of Bilton, (Warws), in 1661 which recited the agreement of 1657, alleging that the defendants were refusing to perform it; but no defence was entered—'they confess it'—and the agreement was duly registered.[2]

Where the defence is more fully and vehemently stated or the plaintiff more querulous it may be guessed that there was genuine disagreement. At Aston Subedge Endymion Porter's purchase had not been followed by the agreement which the villagers had promised him.

'some of them sometyme yeilded to a generall Incloasure yett some other of them at the same tyme yeilded only to a particuler Inclosuer and some others refused to yeild to any Incloasure, and some other of them were not present at any of the said meetings or propositions nor gave their consent.'[3]

This was just what Adam Moore had encountered in Somerset

'the vehement desires of the discreeter sort to proceed having been still crossed and cooled by the willful opposition of vulgar Spirits.'[4]

At Aston Subedge, the court of Chancery appointed a local commission of enquiry who admitted the difficulty of ever obtaining complete consent, and on the report of a majority consent the Court confirmed the agreement with small amendments—but nearly five years after the suit began.

'We finde most of the defendants contented... In a cause of this

---

[1] P.C. 2/40 f. 385: 7 March 1631.
[2] C 33/218 f. 263d: 3 July 1661.
[3] C. 78/273 no. 7
[4] Adam Moore, *Bread for the Poor* (1653).

nature concerninge a multitude we find it a matter difficult to please all.'[1]

It would need examination of a very large number of decrees and also examination of local estate records before any balanced judgement could be made on the proportions of fictitious and genuine disputes. In the cases so far encountered where there was disagreement the court was always told that there had been an initial agreement from which some parties had then retreated; it was on the equity of enforcing the agreement that the jurisdiction of the court rested.

The agreements which were brought to court for registration had very often been the result of long negotiation between the proprietors, the rector and sometimes the bishop. Endymion Porter had negotiated with all these at Aston Subedge. It became usual for the actual allocation of enclosed fields to be put in the hand of arbitrators appointed by the parties, and both in function and name these men anticipated the work of the enclosure commissioners appointed by eighteenth century Enclosure Acts. It was on the basis of commissioner-arbitrators that Shotbolt's proposal to James I had rested

> 'where men cannot agree betweene themselves Commissioners of worthe both for mindes and estates to be in all places selected to mediate all differences and questions in that kind... an unspeakable benefitt to the wholle Comonwealthe in generall.'[2]

At Aston Subedge the villagers appointed two commissioners, the parson one and Porter, as lord of the manor, the fourth. (The local commission of inquiry appointed by Chancery after the dispute was therefore a commission of appeal from commissioners.)

The numbers of commissioners to draw up the awards was sometimes large (again, like some of the early enclosures by Act), as at Brandesburton

> 'there beinge fifteene in number ympannelled;'[3]

and the awards could be voluminous. One decree recited 112 separate articles of the award by the six commissioners[4] but the majority of

---

[1] C. 78/273 no. 7.
[2] B.M., Royal Mss. 18A/XXV.
[3] C. 78/605 no. 3.
[4] C. 78/598 mm. 31 sqq.: Rillington, Yorks; decree, 9 July 1660.

decrees were shorter than this.

Surveyors also appear: at Aston Subedge Porter had met the full costs of a survey. At Claxton, (Yorks), the agreement of c. 1638 provided that

> 'a division should be made and the lands soe lyeing dispersed should be layed together to be inclosed in severalty and a proportionate part of the soyle of the waste should be sett forth in lieu of the right of common to be inclosed likewise in severalty. An expert surveyor shall be chosen to make the said division'.[1]

V

The exact date of the first Chancery decree concerned with an enclosure agreement is not yet known, there being 279 rolls for the period 1603-49 alone and their indexes inadequate for a search of this kind. The decrees and orders registered in books have to be sought in volumes of up to a thousand pages each, two volumes a year for most of the same period and just as inconveniently indexed for this purpose. (The note at the end of this essay offers some guide to the indexes.)

There is some evidence which suggests that the early 1630's saw the formal development of enrollment of agreements in Chancery. In 1631 the Privy Council threatened further action against Midland enclosers and demanded that promises not to decay houses nor lessen tillage upon enclosure should be embodied in a Chancery decree at the landowners' expense.[2] It was in 1633 that the wide approval of the court of the palatinate of Durham began to be extended to agreed enclosures. Miss Leonard traced 28 enclosure agreements registered there between 1633 and 1700, twenty of them relating to open fields, some 25,000 acres of the county.[3] The earliest date mentioned by Gonner is 1614 (Claypool, Lincs.) but he gave no reference[4] and this

---

[1] C. 78/598 no. 2: agreement, 1638; decree, 1659.

[2] P.C. 2/40 f. 540; also *Hist. Mss. Comm. Hastings* iv, (1947), p. 214.

[3] E. M. Leonard, 'The Inclosure of Common Fields in the Seventeenth Century', *Trans. Royal Hist. Soc.* new ser. xix (1905), pp. 111–14.

[4] E. C. K. Gonner, *op. cit.*

case cannot be traced in the index. Nor is it clear whether 1614 was the date of the agreement or of the enrollment.

The considerable lapse of time between an agreement and its enrollment at the end of a Chancery suit makes the date of the earliest enrollment of only minor interest. A decree made in May 1630 dealt with an agreement of about 15 years earlier;[1] another case on the same roll hinged on an enclosure 50 years earlier; a third agreement, known to have been made c. 1615 formed the basis of a suit begun in 1665 with its decree[2] in 1667. A fortunate minority was less afflicted with the law's delays: one agreement was made in 1662, the fields enclosed in 1663 and the decree confirmed the agreement[3] in 1664.

It will also be found that statements about enclosure by agreement also appear on the decree rolls in disputes of another kind which appear from their language to have been genuine and not fictitious suits. These concerned the quantity and quality of the glebe land which had been allocated by a local enclosure, the church's strips having lain promiscuously with the other open field lands. Just as the parochial surveys of glebe land in this period[4] often allude to the date of an enclosure (and sometimes to disputes) so the Chancery cases involving glebe may often give the date of an earlier general enclosure by agreement. One of 1580 is mentioned in a suit[5] concerning the glebe of Hardwick which was heard in 1630.

Being principally concerned in this essay with the provision of opportunities to legitimise enclosure agreements it would be wrong to see too much significance in the beginning of formal enrollment in Chancery. That court had been used as a means of establishing title long before 1630: how often cannot be said in view of the limited character of subject-indexes to the tens of thousands of cases. At Toddington, Beds. in 1589 a suit[6] was 'to establish an inclosure' and

---

[1] C. 78/360 no. 4.

[2] C. 78/669 no. 13.

[3] C. 78/669 no. 18.

[4] M. W. Beresford, 'Glebe Terriers and Open-field Leics.', *Tr. Leics. Arc. Soc* (1949), pp. 77-126; D. M. Barrett, ed., *Ecclesiastical Terriers of Warws. Parishes* (Dugdale Soc. xxii (1955).

[5] C. 78/360.

[6] C. 2/Cc12/34.

the great twenty-sheet plan of the manor drawn by Ralph Agas in 1581 may have been commissioned for this purpose.[1]

Even more utilised than Chancery was the jurisdiction of the court of Exchequer, the most prolific documentary source for the progress of sixteenth century enclosure, legal and illegal. There is no need to rehearse here the many occasions when illegal enclosures brought their perpetrators before the barons of Exchequer. But Exchequer was also the means whereby new titles to land after enclosure were established and the partial indexing of Exchequer judicial records in this period make them more accessible than those of Chancery

The first beneficiaries seem to have been the tenants of ancient demesne, the old Crown lands, and those brought under the Crown by the Reformation confiscations. (The separate jurisdiction of the courts of the Duchy of Lancaster gives analogous documentation for the Duchy estates all over England.) The logic seems to have been this: local commissions, rather like the medieval inquiries *ad quod damnum*, were ordered by the court to investigate whether the Crown's interests would gain or lose by projects of all kinds. High among these projects were revenue-raising steps like the enfranchise-ment of copyhold and the establishing of questionable tenancies. But villagers were also willing to pay for the enclosure of their estates and the Crown, as lord of the manor, had a private as well as a public interest. Many thousands of acres of common rights, parti-cularly in the northern uplands, were extinguished in this unob-trusive way.

Thus, the villages of Raskelf and Sessay (Yorks., N.R.) inter-commoned on what is still rough scrub at Pilmoor. Raskelf was a royal manor and the enclosure decree of May 1580 declared[2]

'it were as benyfyciall or more commodious for her Majesties tennants of her lordshipp and manner of Raskall that the defendants lordshipp and manner of Sessay should be devyded and kepte severall. . . then (*sc.* than) to lye in comen without soveraine.'

In Northamptonshire, on Duchy land, the tenants of Irchester, Rush-den and Raundes made an expensive composition with the Crown in

---

[1] B.M. Add. Mss. 38065.
[2] E. 123/7 f. 95; E. 159/379 m. 326.

June 1618 for the security of their copyholds; five months later the agreements recited that

> 'the said manor doth for the most parte consiste of Arable groundes which lye promiscuously dispersed and intermingled, with the freehold and customary lands'

and asked for a commission to reallocate the field lands at the same time that the common wastes were being enclosed. This was granted:

> 'that they should have liberty of inclosing and Exchaunging his or their customary esteates.'[1]

For this liberty the tenantry of Rushden paid £ 2,166, those of Raundes £ 1,640 and those of Irchester £ 723.

Parts of the waste of Easingwold (Yorks., N.R.) were enclosed by decree the next year[2] but the records both of Exchequer and the Duchy show that cases of this kind had been considered favourably in the previous reign; thus, part of Bradford (Yorks.) moor was enclosed[3] in 1590. The registration of agreed enclosures in Chancery was no more than an extension to other proprietors of a facility which tenants and freeholders under the Crown had long known in Exchequer.

Finally, there is a parallel in the court of Exchequer to the incidental revelation of the date of agreed enclosure by subsequent disputes over enclosed glebeland in Chancery. The court of Exchequer after the Reformation had jurisdiction over tithe disputes similar to that of the bishops in Consistory Courts.[4] An enclosure, particularly if a change in land use or an improvement in land values was expected, raised issues of great interest to the owners of tithes and to tithe-payers. The opportunity was sometimes taken to commute tithes for an annual sum or to give the Rector a piece of enclosed land in lieu of tithe. Consequential disputes in the courts frequently caused witnesses to describe the date and terms of the agreed enclosure.

---

[1] D.L. 5/27 ff. 1285, 1308-9; D.L. 5/28 ff. 50-6, 68-73, 73-78; E. 314, Northants. nos. 36, 44-5.

[2] D.L. 5/28 f. 151d.

[3] D.L. 5/18 f. 776 and 20 f. 354.

[4] for example see J. S. Purvis, ed., *Select XVI Century Causes in Tithe* (Yorks. Arch. Soc. Record Ser., cxiv (1949).

Thus, enclosure by agreement was facilitated by the death of some old prejudices; by the discrediting of regulation by unsavoury agents; by the registration of a good legal title to newly enclosed fields; by the acceptance of local variations in land-use as normal so that the countryside could be now 'a Barne' and now 'a Dayrie howse' in response to market forces. A century after the member for Shropshire had used this figure of speech in the debate of 1597 English agriculture was dancing to a recognisable tune:

'Men are not to be compelled by penalties, but allured by profit, to any good exercise,'[1]

and in place of Tillage Acts the legislature was considering Corn Laws and Corn Bounty Acts.[2]

There was one final change before freedom to enclose and freedom to choose crops could have their head. The fears and prejudices aroused by enclosure had not all derived from misgivings about depopulation and Habitation. The decaying houses of husbandmen betokened fewer yeomen of England and weakness in the face of the Queen's enemies without: but the decay of tillage betokened shortages of corn for all Englishmen. As Shotbolt[3] had put it, decay of tillage not only diminished the number of mouths in the countryside but also took bread out of everyone's mouth, whether in countryside or in towns. These sentiments resurged in years of bad harvest when even those districts with large grass acreages thought regretfully of the displaced ploughs and resurrected old grievances. The proclamation of July 1607 asserted that the rioters of that year were not justified by any dearth of corn but the evidence runs the other way.[4] Conversely, abundance of corn induced the experiment of repealing the tillage laws in 1593: and in 1618 the patent appointing a commission

[1] The dictum comes from Henry Jackman's speech of 1597 quoted in J. E. Neale, *op. cit.* p 343.

[2] The contribution of protection and bounties to enclosure and improvement was stressed in the *Dialogue* of 1677 quoted above, p. 55.

[3] B.M. Royal Mss. 18A/XXV, f. 3.

[4] E. F. Gay, 'The Midland Revolt of 1607', *Trans. Royal Hist. Soc.*, new ser. xviii (1904), p. 213.

to give exemption from the Tillage Acts justified itself by the same argument: regulation made superfluous by abundance.

'Tillage is become much more frequent and usual. . . . corn is at reasonable rates and prizes. . . woodland and plains have been converted to tillage whose nature serves them most aptly.

There is noe wante of corne lande att this tyme but want of pasture and cattle for much woodland and barren grounds are become fruitfull corne landes in steed of pasture.'[1]

But despite Bacon's belief in 1592 that

'high corn prices invited and enticed men to break up more corn ground and convert it to tillage than all the penal laws could ever by compulsion.'[2]

the market mechanism could not be trusted even after 1618. In 1630, a year of poor harvests and high corn prices, the Privy Council again attacked enclosure in familiar terms:

'of evill consequence and example as at all tymes especially at this tyme of dearth it being a greate occasion of feare in the common sorte of people that such conversion being suffered will occasion more scarcitie hereafter;'[3]

and with the noise of bread riots in their ears the Council succumbed to the temptation to blame everything on the engrossing middleman and the depopulating encloser. The Council moved away once more from faith in an unregulated market mechanism and, although the common informer was not revived, a Committee of the Council on Depopulation appeared and gave rise to the local Commissions. The liberal view was temporarily in eclipse again.

That it prevailed by the end of the seventeenth century was partly due to the bad taste left behind by the agents of a regulated economy in the 1630's. Yet bad harvests did not cease with the execution of Charles I: as late as 1709, a year of very bad harvests, the price of wheat reached a height surpassed only twice in the whole eighteenth century (1799 and 1800) and then during a war-time

---

[1] C. 66/2134 m. 1d; also C. 66/2150 no. 17.
[2] quoted, without reference given, in W. H. R. Curtler, *The Enclosure and Redistribution of Our Land* (1920), p. 123.
[3] P.C. 2/40 f. 199: 30 Nov. 1630.

inflation. But in 1709 14,000 more quarters of wheat were exported than imported and 77,000 the next year.[1] It was a far cry from the bill of 1598 which had proposed to ban all export of corn until twelve months after each harvest when it could be seen if anything could be spared for foreigners.[2]

It was not sufficient for the advocates of general enclosure by agreement to be able to promise Habitation; it was essential that Improvement should show itself in improved supplies of food which kept pace with the rise in population. We might have worse evidence of the effect of agricultural Improvement[3] than the fact that in two years (1710-12) which Professor Ashton[4] puts 'among the worst of the (eighteenth) century' no one wanted to hang the graziers or have the enclosers in the ditch. The issue of Habitation versus Improvement seemed dead and English farming seemed to be able to offer both.

---

[1] Data from T. S. Ashton, *Economic Fluctuations in the Eighteenth Century* (1959), pp. 181 and 183.

[2] House of Lords. Mss. *sub* 21 Jan. 1598.

[3] 'Improvement' must include distribution as well as production. Imperfections of transport, wholesaleing and retailing had to be smoothed before full advantage could be taken of local specialisation; a little is known of the transport history of the seventeenth century but studies of the mechanism of internal trade are badly needed.

[4] T. S. Ashton, *op. cit.*, p. 141; the two years ran from summer 1710 to summer 1712.

A NOTE ON THE SOURCES FOR ENCLOSURE AGREEMENTS IN THE PUBLIC RECORD OFFICE

This note is not an exhaustive guide: it says nothing of agreements among estate records[1] in private and public custody; nor of the evidence from tithe causes in the bishops' courts; nor of the references to enclosure in the successive terriers of the parish glebe. It is a commentary on the references to agreed enclosure among documents at the Public Record Office and on the indexes which are available there.

Chancery

Agreements can be found fully recited or summarily approved by Enrolled Decree[2] (class C78) or by a Decree registered in the Entry Books of Decrees and Orders (class C33). The *Enrolled Decrees* form a large class which are imperfectly indexed except by surname of the plaintiffs. If this name is known the manuscript indexes at Long Room Shelf L should be searched. There are ten volumes[3] of these in semi-chronological order, given to overlapping and thus mirroring the interior confusion of the decree rolls themselves. All that can be safely said is that C78/1 contains a decree from 26 Henry VIII; that the decrees of Elizabeth's reign seem to begin at C78/15, the end of the reign being reached near C78/111; C78/214 is unequivocally from Charles I and C78/389 from 1649. A volume also shelved at L in the Long Room is an alphabetical *index locorum* to the ten volumes of manuscript Calendars but it is far from exhaustive: Brandesburton (C78/605 no. 3 (1630)), Miss Leonard's main example, does not appear in it, for example.[4]

The *Entry Books of Decrees and Orders* comprise two series, 'A' and 'B'. Before 1629 there was no logic in the division of cases between the two series, but after 1629 the 'A' book of each year covered cases where the plaintiff's surname lay between A and K, and the 'B' book the remainder of the alphabet. The 'A' books make up the odd numbers of the class, C33/1 onwards, and the 'B' the even numbers from C33/2. A list of books identified by years will be found in the Chancery Class List shelved at 24/26B in the Round Room.[5] There are separate indexes to each year of each series but the index is solely by plaintiff's names.[1] No place-index has been found.

---

[1] e.g. the Brudenell documents cited by M. E. Finch, *op., cit.* p. 162

[2] One of these decrees is discussed by G. N. Clark *Eng. H.R.* xlii (1927) pp. 88 sqq. (C 78/586 no. 1: 12 Feb. 1662).

[3] These are numbered Index 16950-9. Index 16950 has additionally a Calendar for the reign of Elizabeth.

[4] Index 16951 (Eliz. to Chas. I) has a partial index of cases concerning manors at pp. 309-17 and 321-4.

[5] Thus Book B of 1661, Miss Leonard's reference *(art. cit.)* for the Bilton decree is now C. 33/218.

Maurice Beresford

Duchy of Lancaster

The *Decrees and Orders* form Class DL5 and are calendared by counties in a manuscript volume shelved at 27/82G in the Round Room. The adjoining manuscript calendars to *D. L. Special Commissions* and *Depositions* should also consulted.

Exchequer

Decrees in the court of Exchequer were not separately enrolled but some could be entered on the Queen's or Lord Treasurer's Remembrancer's Rolls (E159 and E368). Enclosure cases are more common on the former.[2] Most Exchequer decrees found their way not to the Memoranda Rolls but to the *Entry Books* (E123 to E131).[3] There are two Index volumes which attempt to cover the principal cases in the above classes involving land, and in addition a series of indexes and calendars to each class. The first of the two general indexes is Adam Martin, *Index to Various Records preserved in the Court of Exchequer*, published in London in 1819. Martin's index is alphabetical mainly of place-names with a few personal names. It is shelved at 7/136 in the Round Room. Hutton Wood's *Index* is a manuscript index covering very much the same ground but arranged county by county; the order within the counties is not alphabetical.

Other manuscript indexes follow individual Classes of Exchequer documents and, unlike Martin and Wood, aim to be complete. They overlap somewhat but can be listed as follows.

Round Room volumes 7/1 to 7/15 cover the *Entry Books of Decrees and Orders* (Classes E123-5) from Elizabeth to the Commonwealth. These index volumes are of plaintiffs' names.

Round Room volumes 7/16 to 7/19 cover the *Entry Books of Decrees* (Class E126) from 1604 to 1697 in the form of a detailed calendar.

Index volumes 16854-60 form a calendar to the *Entry Books* in chronological order but give the surnames of parties with no other data.

Index volume 16879 ('Vanderzee's Index') is a Calendar to the *Entry Books* from 1558 to 1675; the particulars are brief and where the same ground is covered by Round Room volumes 7/16 etc. the latter are to be preferred.

---

[1] Thus Index 1538 is to the 'A' book of 1630 (C. 33/159) and Index 1539 to the 'B' book of that year (C. 33/160). These indexes, term by term, do not more than place all the surnames of the same letter in one group.

[2] Thus, the Raskelf commons decree of 1580 is on membrane 326 of the K.R. M.R. for Mich. 22 Eliz. (E. 159/379).

[3] Thus, the decree for Ingleby and Barwick commons is in the Entry Book of Decrees and Orders for Mich. 26 Eliz. (E. 123/10 f. 215); those for the Forest of Galtres in 1632 and 1634 in E. 126/4 ff. 46-7 and 155.

In the course of Exchequer proceedings it was common to appoint local commissions to put specific questions to local juries and to return depositions. While a few sets of depositions were enrolled on the Memoranda Rolls (E159) each term the majority were simply filed away and form the class E134 to which there are Calendars on the shelves of the Round Room. Ancillary to these are the *Depositions Taken before the Barons* (Class E133) to which there are good manuscript calendars at Round Room 7/119C-E. Another manuscript calendar at Round Room 7/118R leads to the interesting class E134 Misc., a collection of 2,361 sets of depositions. The commissions sent to the provinces, often with the questionnaires attached, form class E178. As with the parallel classes, D.L. Special Commissions and Depositions, these Exchequer classes are extraordinarily informative in their verbose questions and answers.

Miscellaneous

Enclosure cases in *Star Chamber* and *Requests* may sometimes turn out to be over agreements or alleged agreements.

The varied classes which have been drawn on for the printed *Index of Rentals and Surveys and Other Analagous Documents* (P.R.O. Lists and Indexes no. xxv (1908)) are also rewarding in attempting to trace the progress from open to enclosed land. To these may be added the *Close Rolls* (C54) which aided Dr. Thirsk in her dating of some early Leicestershire enclosures (*V. C. H. Leics.*, ii (1954), pp. 254-9) e.g. Nether Broughton, 1651; C54/3668 no. 19.

INDUSTRIES IN THE COUNTRYSIDE

IN 1634 William White, William Steventon, and John Perkins, gentleman, were plaintiffs in a suit filed in the Court of Exchequer against William and Oliver Trotter, Richard Haygarth, Henry Mason and seven others. It concerned the customs of the lordship of Dent, a manor in the west Yorkshire dales which embraced Dentdale and Garsdale. In consequence, justices were appointed to make personal investigation, and at the free school in Dent on a wintry day in the middle of January questions were put to the oldest inhabitants with the longest memories. Edward Lande, an octogenarian of Dent, declared that if a customary tenant died seised of a tenement without having devised or disposed of it by will, then it descended 'to all his sons equally to be divided amongst them.' And, he added, 'by reason of such division of tenements, the tenants are much increased in number more than they were, and the tenements become so small in quantity that many of them are not above three or four acres apiece and generally not above eight or nine acres so that they could not maintain their families were it not by their industry in knitting coarse stockings.'[1]

Here is an illuminating contemporary explanation for the rise of a local handicraft industry. It does not attribute it to the energies of an entrepreneur, or to the ease with which supplies of wool could be procured locally, or to any compelling market demand, but to the special social and economic circumstances of the inhabitants of Garsdale and Dentdale, which compelled them to seek some employment in addition to their farming. It suggests that in other districts were rural industries are known to have played an important part in augmenting farm incomes, it would be rewarding to

---

[1] Public Record Office [= PRO] E 134, 10-11 Chas. I, Hil. 22.

consider the agricultural and social situation in which they began.

Such an analysis is, of course, beset with pitfalls. There is no certainty or finality in any explanation for the growth of a rural industry in one district rather than another. Its location may seem logical enough if it uses raw materials which are available in the district. But many rural industries have achieved national importance which do not fit into this category. It is usual, for example, to attribute the cloth industries of the West country, of Kent, and of Suffolk, to the availability of certain natural resources necessary for the making of cloth, namely, a local supply of wool, a plentiful supply of water, the existence of local seams of fuller's earth, and good communications with markets and ports. None of these reasons is completely satisfying. As Thomas Fuller observed in the mid-seventeenth century, local wool did not make a cloth industry. Counties like Leicestershire, Lincolnshire, Northamptonshire and Cambridgeshire, which had 'most of wool, have least of clothing therein'. The wool was usually available in a neighbouring farming region, but not in the region where the industry was situated. The clothiers of the Weald of Kent could procure wool from the fat sheep of the Romney marshes or from the sheep on the Downs, but in the Weald itself, in the words of a fourteenth-century commentator, 'there is not an abundant growth of wools.' The Wiltshire industry could obtain its wool from the Cotswold hills and from Salisbury plain, but much of the industry was concentrated in north-west Wiltshire where wool was among the least important products of the farm. The clothiers of central Suffolk could have bought some of their wool in east or west Suffolk but seem, in fact, to have relied on the wools of the Midland counties, particularly Leicestershire, Lincolnshire, Northamptonshire and Cambridgeshire. As wool was so easily transported, and since also it is doubtful whether there was any corner of England which did not have a wool-producing area in the vicinity, it can never have been the factor which made or marred a nascent industry.[1]

[1] Thos. Fuller, *The Church History of Britain* (1845), II, p. 287; Robert Furley; *A History of the Weald of Kent*, II, part 1, p. 336; *V.C.H. Wiltshire*, IV, p. 44, J. E. Pilgrim, *The Cloth Industry in Essex and Suffolk, 1558-1640*, unpublished M.A. thesis, London University, 1939, p. 2.

Local seams of fuller's earth were evidently no more vital to a cloth industry than wool, for the East Anglian cloth centres relied on supplies from Kent. Nor was a convenient local port essential since the West country cloth merchants in the Tudor period managed without undue inconvenience to carry their burdens by road to Blackwell Hall in London. Water was essential for the fulling process, but water alone did not make a cloth centre, or the embryonic industry of Hertfordshire in the early fifteenth century would not have died a mysterious death in the early sixteenth. It may be argued, of course, that the location of a handicraft industry can be an accident due to the enterprise of a single individual. It is not difficult to find both abortive and successful examples in the better-documented eighteenth and nineteenth centuries. But even in these instances it is impossible to dissociate their survival from their success in procuring and organizing an adequate labour force, and we are once more brought up against the question of the social and economic environment. Finally, since the geographers are permitted to enumerate the circumstances favouring the growth of a market town or port without claiming that these were the chief or only determinants, it seems reasonable (with encouragement from the inhabitants of Dentdale) to seek in an analysis of the farming economy and, more particularly, the social structure of the local community some of the circumstances which favoured the growth of rural industries in one region rather than another.[1]

It is impossible in a brief essay to consider all the country industries which flourished in England in the fifteenth to seventeenth centuries. Nor is there enough information about local economies to permit such a prodigious task to be undertaken here and now. Attention will therefore be given only to those industries which were carried on in conjunction with farming, and which catered for a national rather than a local market. But such a definition embraces the extractive industries, whose location was determined by the presence of minerals in the ground. In these mineral-yielding areas, industry and agriculture were ancient bedfellows, and in most places it is doubtful whether the beginnings of settled agriculture preceded or followed

[1] *Cal. S.P Dom*, *1623-5*, p. 216; *V.C.H. Hertfordshire*, IV, p. 210.

the mining for tin, lead, copper, iron, stone, and chalk. There is, therefore, no need to seek for pre-disposing social and economic circumstances to account for the rise of the industry. This is not to deny, however, that many interesting problems concerning these regions await investigation. The historian cannot fail to ponder how the resources of families were disposed in such communities to enable the two occupations to be dovetailed together. In general, mineral production was concentrated in the western half of England where much of the farming was pastoral, and since it required less labour than arable farming, it left the householder free to engage in mining while his family attended to the land and the animals. In this way, the mining-farming family made a success of the two occupations. But what of the social conflicts and economic problems that must have developed as populations grew and an increasing number of workers took to mining without farming? Over England as a whole there is no doubt that the mining-farming communities were large and frequently populous. A description of Derbyshire by the local justices of the peace in 1620 affords one example of a county where, already it seems, the farmers were in danger of being outnumbered by the industrial workers. 'Many thousands live in work at lead mines, coal mines, stone pits, and iron works.' 'The hardcorn gotten therein will not serve above the one half of the people that live in it, a great part of our county bearing nothing but oats.' Hence, the population was heavily dependent for its food on Danzig rye brought from Hull via the Trent.[1]

These and other problems of rural-industrial communities deserve proper study in any complete account of industries in the country-side. Here they are omitted in order that attention may be given to the handicraft industries which developed within communities already engaged in farming. Of these, the Wiltshire cloth industry was more ancient than any and grew to maturity earlier than any other. Its geographical and economic situation furnishes an apt illustration

[1] G. R. Lewis, *The Stannaries*, pp. 185-7; PRO SP 14/113, no. 17. For earlier examples of economic conflict, *see* H. P. R. Finberg, *Tavistock Abbey*, pp. 177-8 For a map of areas of mineral production in the fourteenth century, see H. C. Darby, *An Historical Geography of England before A.D. 1800*, p. 257.

of some general propositions which can be tested elsewhere.

The first signs of a cloth-making industry in the countryside, supplying a national market, date from the second half of the fourteenth century. Before that clothmaking had been an industry of the towns like Marlborough and Salisbury. But when once the fulling mill began to drive the industry to the banks of fast running streams and so into the countryside, the villages immediately in the vicinity of the old cloth towns, in the Kennet valley around Marlborough and in the Wylye and Nadder valleys around Salisbury, began to attract a population of weavers, dyers, and fullers. When the industry began to expand and to serve a national market, in the late fourteenth century, a larger labour force had to be found, and at this point new rural centres, not nurtured by the old cloth towns, began to emerge—in the north-western sector of the county, between Malmesbury and Westbury, a region given over to the small pasture farms of cheese-making dairymen, and in the south-western corner around Mere, in the country of small butter-making farms. Wiltshire had two main types of farming. The dairy farms lay in country that was early enclosed, while a sheep-corn husbandry sustained the chalk and limestone lands of Salisbury Plain and the Cotswolds, and kept many of the fields and commons open until the end of the eighteenth century. Owing to the paucity of documents in the Middle Ages, the sharp contrast between the two types of farming is not visible until the sixteenth century. But distinctions so fundamental are not made overnight. It is certain that they were of long standing, and later gave a very different character to the agricultural revolution in each region in the eighteenth and nineteenth centuries. The contrast has been summarized thus:—'the inclosed, non-manorial countries—the cheese and butter countries—were the lands of family farmers and self-employed persons, while the manorialized, champion, sheep-and-corn countries—the chalk, Cotswold, and Corallian countries—were the main field for the development of agrarian capitalism and for the agricultural revolution.'[1]

The identity of the clothing and dairying regions in the west coun-

[1] E. Carus-Wilson, 'The Woollen Industry before 1550,' *V.C.H. Wilts.*, IV, p. 115 *et seq.*; E. Kerridge, 'Agriculture, 1500–1793', *ibid.*, p. 43 *et seq.*

try did not escape the notice of Daniel Defoe. The logical sequence of his remarks, describing first the cloth industry and then the dairying in the same region, is somewhat obscured by his liking for digressions. But in fact his observation is precise. In the area enclosed between the towns of Bristol, Sherborne, Devizes, and Cirencester, in a district spreading through part of Wiltshire, Somerset, and Gloucestershire, Defoe found a flourishing cloth industry *and* 'large feeding farms which we call dairies' where cheese was made and pigs fattened on the waste products.[1]

In this Defoe saw no sociological significance. But it may be more than a coincidence that exactly the same type of farming should characterize the area of Suffolk in which its cloth industry lay. Here the speciality was coloured cloth for which demand was at its height in the late fifteenth and early sixteenth centuries. Apart from a few scattered centres further north and east where a different cloth, called kersey, was made, the industry was centred upon the southern portion of central Suffolk in and around Sudbury. The farming region of central Suffolk which covers some two-thirds of the county is traditionally known as the wood-pasture region—the region of dairy farms exporting cheese and butter to London in large quantity in the sixteenth century. It was old-enclosed country, possibly it had never been open, but had been cleared of woodland and the land henceforth held in severalty. The other farming regions of Suffolk consisted of a small area of fenland in the north-west corner of the county, and two strips of sand and breckland lying to east and west of the wood-pasture region, where sheep-folding and barley production kept the land fertile and yielded wool for the clothier. But the sand lands had no cloth industry. The economies of the wood pasture region and the eastern and western sands were succinctly described by the local justices of the peace in 1622. 'Our county consists of two several conditions of soil, the one champion, which yields for the most part sheep and some corn; the other enclosed pasture grounds employed most to grazing and dairy, so as the champion doth not only serve itself with corn but is forced continu-

[1] Daniel Defoe, *A Tour through the whole island of Great Britain*, ed. G. D. H Cole (1927), II, pp. 280, 284-5.

ally to supply the woodland especially in wet and cold years.'[1]

The situation of the Suffolk cloth industry was remarkably similar to that of Wiltshire except in one respect. It did not spread throughout Suffolk's wood-pasture region, but was concentrated at the southern end. This may be due entirely to the network of rivers in the southern half of the county emptying fast-flowing waters into the estuaries of the Stour, the Orwell, and the Deben, and so far superior to the slow-moving waters of the river Waveney on the northern border of the county. But consideration must be given to some of the social factors which may have affected central Suffolk unevenly. Unfortunately, Suffolk is a problem county where it is easier to pose questions than to answer them. Its settlement history, for example, is impossible to unravel without a study of its place names, and this is only the first difficulty in the way of understanding the social organization of central Suffolk. But if the inhabitants of Dentdale were correct in implying that large populations could sometimes attract industries to them, then we must consider the possibility that the clothing district of Suffolk, which was more thinly settled than north Suffolk in Domesday times, had grown more populous by the fourteenth century, and posed problems of unemployment and overpopulation which industries alone could solve. Had its land proved specially attractive to immigrants in the Middle Ages, or did its natives, for some reason inherent in their own social institutions, produce and support larger families than elsewhere? Neither of these questions can be satisfactorily answered at present, but since they concern a problem of general importance to the study of all rural industries— namely the causes of differential rates of population growth—it is worth pausing to discuss them. The manorial organization of central Suffolk was weak. Its manors were small, and frequently consisted of little more than a demesne farm with two or three small holdings. A weak manorial framework could and did permit an unusually rapid growth of population through immigration in regions where there was land to attract the landless.[2] Since by the sixteenth century parts

[1] J. E. Pilgrim, *op. cit., passim*; PRO SP 14/128, no. 65.
[2] *V C.H. Suffolk*, I, pp. 633, 640; cf. R. H. Hilton, *Social Structure of Rural Warwickshire in the Middle Ages*, Dugdale Soc. Occ. Paper, no. 9, pp. 10–15.

of central Suffolk were suffering a distinct shortage of commons and waste, earlier migration to the district for lack of any strong manorial control is a factor to be reckoned with. The second possibility is that local customs of inheritance had contributed to the large populations. In the fen villages of Lincolnshire, the custom of partible inheritance, by providing all the male children with a portion of the paternal land, is known to have played a decisive part in the growth of large village communities.[1] Partible inheritance was practised in Suffolk, though no one has yet defined exactly the districts in which it was most commonly found. The custom of Borough English was also well known in Suffolk and seems to have been widespread in the northern half of central Suffolk and in the south-east coastal area. It is usual to assume that this custom had the same effect as the rule of primogeniture in keeping one male member on the family holding and sending the others away. But, in fact, no assumptions concerning the effects of Borough English can yet safely be made, for there is reason to suspect that when the youngest son inherited the residue of his father's estate, his older brothers had often already received their share. If this were generally true, Borough English may have differed little from partible inheritance in its effect on the ownership of land, and the two customs, working their effects in certain districts while the rule of primogeniture governed others, may have had significant consequences for the uneven distribution of population in the county as a whole.[2]

We can do no more than speculate on the effects both of immi-

---

[1] H. E. Hallam, 'Some thirteenth century censuses'. *Econ. Hist. Rev.*, 2nd Ser., X, no. 3 (1958), p. 340 *et seq.* This article suggests not only that partible inheritance caused young people to stay in their native places because they had land to inherit, but also that they married younger and had more children. *See* pp. 354, 355.

[2] Some Suffolk examples of partible inheritance are listed in G. C. Homans, *English Villagers in the Thirteenth Century*, p. 428, note 16. On Borough English, *see* the inconclusive account in Thomas Robinson, *the Common Law of Kent with an appendix concerning Borough English* (1822), pp. 386, 389, and G. R. Corner, 'On the Custom of Borough English', *Proc. Suffolk Inst. of Archaeology*, II, pp. 227-41. I wish to thank Mr Norman Scarfe for a map of places in Suffolk where Borough English was the custom.

gration and of native inheritance customs. And local historians may well prove these factors to be irrelevant in Suffolk. But they may not be irrelevant in all industrial areas, and they require careful consideration before we accept a purely geographical explanation for the location of industries in the countryside. In some of the districts to be discussed below, in the moorland and fenland regions, with their ample common rights, and in woodland regions with their stores of timber, contemporaries deplored immigration. In at least four out of the six districts examined here, partible inheritance is known to have been practised, and in one of these it was declared to be the cause of overpopulation. Its influence cannot summarily be dismissed. In the first place, local studies show that partible inheritance was a far more widespread manorial custom than the nineteenth-century writers on gavelkind believed. Secondly, the extent to which it persisted among freeholders who could alienate their land, and among customary tenants who claimed a tenure almost as secure as a freeholder, is unknown. Despite the lawyers' insistence that the rule of primogeniture became almost universal after the thirteenth century, a small sample of early Tudor wills from Bedfordshire, a county where there is no reason to suspect the survival of partible inheritance as a strong manorial custom, shows how often men still shared their land among all, or some, of their sons.[1] Thirdly, the rule of primogeniture is a most unnatural law to inflict upon a parent. Was it perhaps not until the sixteenth century, when primogeniture became the law of Wales, when much Kent land was disgavelled piecemeal, and private agreements were reached within manors to discontinue the practice of gavelkind, that it became the almost universal rule on small estates? In our present state of ignorance, it is a reasonable hypothesis, and a reasonable argument for considering inheritance customs among the causes of the uneven rate of population growth in different districts.

For Kent there is somewhat more information about the social

---

[1] Ed. A. F. Cirket, *English Wills, 1498-1526*, Beds. Hist. Rec. Soc., XXXVII. Of 69 wills containing bequests of land, only 40% insist that, after the death of the wife, all land shall descend to the eldest son. The remainder divide the land between some or all the children.

composition of its population than for Suffolk, but rather less about the cloth industry. The lawyers accepted the view that all land in Kent was subject to gavelkind unless the contrary was proved. Since this custom tended to keep people in their native places, it gave rise to large and immobile populations. But in Kent they were not evenly distributed throughout the county. In the mid-sixteenth century the Wealden parishes had much larger populations, and by the end of the eighteenth century, its farms were noticeably smaller than in east Kent.[1] A second factor contributing to this uneven development must, therefore, be considered, namely the existence in the Weald of forest resources which yielded men a living from occupations other than farming, such as timber-felling and carpentry, wood-turning, charcoal-burning, and iron-smelting. In the fourteenth and fifteenth centuries, yet another industry was established in the Weald, that of clothmaking. It was important in towns such as Canterbury and Maidstone, but the rural industry was situated in the Wealden parishes of Cranbrook, Goudhurst, Tenterden, Hawkhurst, Headcorn and the neighbourhood. Supplies of fullers' earth were found locally, and the narrow valleys enabled the streams to be pent up by dams, and so to drive the fulling mills.[2]

---

[1] William Holdsworth, *History of English Law*, III, p. 262. For the sixteenth-century population of Kent, see British Museum [= BM] Harleian MS 594. This census of 1563 covers the diocese of Canterbury only (the return for the diocese of Rochester is missing), but it is enough to show how much larger were the populations of the Wealden parishes than those in the rest of Kent. The usual population of a Kent parish was something less than sixty families. For example, 22 out of 26 parishes in Sittingbourne deanery had less than sixty households, and 14 (53%) had less than 30. But in the Charing deanery, which includes most of the Wealden parishes associated with the cloth industry, only 6, out of 24 parishes had less than 60 families, and only 2 out of 24 (8%) had less than 30 families. The larger size of the Wealden parishes does not invalidate this comparison because they all contained great areas of woodland, parks, and commons. On the size of farms in the eighteenth century, see John Boys, *General View of the Agriculture of the county of Kent* (1813), p. 3, footnote.

[2] Robert Furley, *op. cit.*, II, part 1, pp. 325, 329-31; *V. C. H. Kent*, III, p. 403 *et seq.*; E. Straker, *Wealden Iron*, p. 264 *et seq.* For a valuable and suggestive comparative study of the forest areas of Northamptonshire, where populations were large, the commons attracted immigrants, the custom of inheritance was a

The Weald was ancient woodland where much settlement consisted of hamlets and scattered farms. Some of these did not come into existence until the twelfth and thirteenth centuries, and all were probably enclosed from the beginning. If we may again assume that the farming of the sixteenth century had a long tradition behind it, it consisted in the breeding and fattening of cattle with some dairying. This was in marked contrast to the mainly arable, corn-growing, and corn-exporting, region of east Kent.[1] Most probate inventories of Wealden farmers in the early seventeenth century mention a milkhouse and stores of cheese and butter, and the clothiers seem to have dealt in both wool and cheese. William Hugget of Pluckley, clothier, had 264 lbs of cheese in his house in 1614 as well as 568 quarters of wool together with cloth and dyestuffs. John Mills of Smarden, clothier, had thirteen cheeses weighing 100 lbs as well as eleven quarters of wool. Were these clothiers adapting their business to the needs of their clients and selling them wool in exchange for their cheese? It is a reasonable guess. But it would be inaccurate to describe the Weald as a mainly dairying region in the early seventeenth century. Much effort was being directed by that time towards the rearing and fattening of cattle and sheep. A single probate inventory will illustrate the point. Isaac Hunt of Woodchurch had four swine, six geese, three hens, two kine and two heifers, four 2-yearling steers, three twelve-monthings, 31 fatting sheep and 22 others, three mares and a colt, and 27 acres of grass. His storehouse contained three flitches of bacon, 24 lbs of hempyarn, three gallons of butter, and ten cheeses. He had a milkhouse, the usual farm accommodation of a modest yeoman, and a shop. He was evidently something of a dairyman but he fattened sheep and cattle as well. The Weald by this time was an important supplier of London's meat and its grazing interests were implied by Gervase Markham in the remark that the improved soils could produce 'a very good and sweet pasture...

form of Borough English, and a weaving industry developed in the later eighteenth century, *see* P. A. J. Pettit, *The Economy of the Northamptonshire Royal Forests, 1558-1714,* unpublished Ph. D. thesis, Oxford, 1959.
[1] PRO SP 14/112, no. 12; Kent County Archives [= KCA] Probate inventories, *passim.*

profitable both for sheep and bullocks.'[1] In short, it was again in a populous pastoral area where breeding and some dairying were combined with fattening, where farms were small and enclosed, that the Kent cloth industry lived and died.

The last centre of the cloth industry to be considered here is that of Westmorland. Its centre was Kendal, which was already famous for its cloth at the end of the fourteenth century. The industry did not spread into the countryside until the fifteenth century when it assumed great local importance. By the beginning of the Tudor period there were eighteen fulling mills in the parish of Grasmere alone. The industry died a mysterious death in Elizabeth's reign as did the Kent cloth industry in the seventeenth century. A full inquest has not yet been held though two causes of death have been put forward, that Kendal cloth fell out of favour with the London tradesman, and that plague decimated the population in the 1570's and 1590's.[2] The first explanations seems inadequate by itself while the second is demonstrably incorrect. Nevertheless, the plague in these two decades did reveal the precarious balance of the farming economy of the region which had caused the cloth industry to play such an important rôle in supplementing incomes.

Westmorland is a small county of which half comprises mountain and moorland. Its farming consisted in the breeding of cattle for sale to lowland farmers and in sheep-keeping for the sake of the wool. The cornland was meagre—the farmer was fortunate who had twelve acres to sow each spring, and on this he grew mostly oats, with a certain amount of bigg and March wheat and rye. Meadow, pasture, and moorland grazings were plentiful. In the early nineteenth century Westmorland butter had a high reputation for quality, but there is no sign that dairying served more than domestic needs in the sixteenth century.[3] In short, this was a county of pasture farms

---

[1] KCA PRC 28/5 & 8; Gervase Markham, *The Inrichment of the Weald of Kent* (1625), p. 13.

[2] M. L. Armitt, 'Fullers and freeholders of the parish of Grasmere' *Trans. Cumb. & Westm. Antiq. & Archaeolog. Soc.*, N.S. VIII (1908), pp. 195-8.

[3] Cumberland Record Office, Carlisle, and Lancs. Record Office, Preston, probate inventories, *passim*; F. W. Garnett, *Westmorland Agriculture, 1800-1900*,

which, though small, had appurtenant common rights on extensive moorlands. The most remarkable feature of Westmorland, however, was the very large populations which it supported in its narrow valleys. A number of rural parishes had between two and three hundred families apiece which may be compared with a normal average of thirty to sixty families for Kent parishes and between one and two hundred families for the more thickly settled Weald parishes. It is true that the fell parishes were vast but they consisted mostly of moorland and had a comparatively narrow strip of valley land. Yet the parish of Orton had 211 households in 1563, and a survey of the manor in 1589 describes many recent improvements of land and new-ly-built cottages suggesting a continuously growing population. Grasmere accomodated 186 families, Ravenstonedale next door had 116 families, Kirkby Stephen 300 and Wharton 284 families. Considering that Westmorland was so barren and rugged, it was extra-ordinarily populous, and we may well accept the substantial truth of the statement of the Westmorland justices in 1622 that 'the smallness, barrenness, and the multitude of inhabitants in the habitable places of this country is such and so far incomparable to the other counties of this kingdom.'[1]

The paradox has to be explained. The valleys in the fells were thickly populated and yet their farming economy was ever tilted on the verge of a crisis. It was not properly self-sufficient in corn. The climate made every harvest more than ordinarily hazardous, and the cornland was in any case limited. A crisis of famine and consequent plague could easily be precipitated by a harvest failure. The justices of the peace who remarked upon the large populations of Westmorland in 1622 were explaining the gravity of a crisis caused by the scarcity of bread. The harvest failure of 1597 had brought just such another disaster affecting all four northern counties. In vivid language the bishop of Durham described to Lord Burghley how 'in the bishopric of Durham five hundred ploughs have decayed in a few

---

p. 137. Twelve acres represents statute measure. The local measure, as it appears in the probate inventories, was eight acres.

[1] BM Harleian Mss. 594; Cumberland Record Office, 1589 Survey of the Lands of Leonard Dacre, attainted; PRO SP 14/131, no. 25.

years and corn has to be fetched from Newcastle, whereby the plague is spread in the northern counties. . . Of eight thousand acres lately in tillage, now not eight score are tilled; those who sold corn have to buy. . . tenants cannot pay their rents.'[1]

Farming was precarious, but it was not precarious enough to drive people from the narrow congested valleys of the fells. Two reasons suggest themselves. Meadow and pasture were plentiful for the keeping of cattle and sheep. A man who looked naturally to the land for his living could count himself a king of infinite space if he had no more than a small piece of arable and unstinted common rights. In the seventeenth and eighteenth centuries, writers viewing the agrarian problem of the Midlands bewailed the attractions of open commons to migrant paupers seeking a corner of land on which to settle.[2] By that date, people were perambulating the Midlands in search of a somewhat rare commodity. But in the pastoral regions of England, open commons were not scarce. They might now attract migrants from elsewhere, but for centuries before this they had held out an encouraging hand to the young, and had kept the children in their native places to marry, earn a living, rear their children, and die. The wide moorlands bred contentment because they offered a satisfactory living, and this in turn kept people at home and fostered what outsiders regarded as clannishness. If it is legitimate to see in some more isolated modern communities a pale reflection of the traditions and attitudes of the past, then we may suspect that the strong ties of family unity, which even now keep young men and young women in the fells on the farms of their fathers till long after others of their generation have married and moved away, were bonds of iron three or four hundred years ago. The family was and is the working unit, all joining in the running of the farm, all accepting without question the fact that the family holding would provide for them all or else that

---

[1] Quoted in Henry Barnes, 'Visitations of the plague in Cumberland and Westmorland', *Trans. Cumb. & Westm. Antiq. & Archaeolog. Soc.*, XI, 1891, pp. 178-9. Similar shortages in the 19th century were mentioned by F. W. Garnett, *op. cit.*, p. 19.

[2] See, for example, Samuel Hartlib's remark—'There are fewest poor where there are fewest commons.'—*Samuel Hartlib, his Legacie*, 1652, p. 42.

the family's savings would go to buy a lease or an interest in land nearby. The custom of partible inheritance fosters this attitude, and its survival among a small number of families in Gosforth in Cumberland to this day suggests that it was once more common in the northern fells.[1] Hence, a society which does not drive its children away to earn their living elsewhere, which pursues a pastoral economy that is not greedy of land, that does not compel men to enclose every rod in the quest for survival and profit, such a society may well breed large populations and create for itself an increasing problem of feeding them. For these people did not live in paradise. Some of their herds and the flocks which they grazed on the fells in summer had to be found fodder and shelter in winter, and this the narrow valleys could not always fully provide. Many fell communities supplemented their farming incomes by iron-mining, lead-mining, stone, and slate quarrying. Others were not so advantageously placed but they had the labour force to engage in rural handicrafts if the opportunity occurred. Nowadays they cater for the holidaymaker.[2]

Another society of small peasant farmers possessing some of the features common to fell communities existed in the Lincolnshire fens. Farmers were engaged in rearing cattle and some sheep, fattening beef and mutton, breeding horses and keeping geese. It was another area where the commons were large and unstinted and where common rights included not only grazing rights but generous allotments of peat, sedge, willows, and the right to catch fish and fowl. The community had enough resources to support a custom of partible inheritance, and in the Middle Ages, when this custom was practised in some villages, there is persuasive evidence to show that populations grew faster than in villages where primogeniture was the rule. It is not certain how long this custom survived, but, even in the seventeenth century, the population of Elloe wapentake, which had the largest amount of open commons in the Lincolnshire fenland, whether

---

[1] W. M. Williams, *The Sociology of an English Village: Gosforth*, pp. 37-55.
[2] When the cloth industry ceased, it seems to have been replaced by stocking-knitting. The first evidence which I have found in Westmorland dates from the 1690's. It persisted longest in the Orton, Ravenstonedale, Kirkby Stephen district.—F. W. Garnett, *op. cit.*, p. 4.

through immigration or by its own efforts, grew at a far greater rate than that of the rest of Lincolnshire.[1]

In such circumstances, we can understand why the weaving of hemp, flax, and wool was a by-employment in many fen households. It is unlikely that this industry met a national demand, and since it did not compete in the export market, it does not receive attention in public records. But if one compares the personal property of Suffolk farmers, who grew hemp in quantity but wove none of it, with the fen farmers who grew it, processed it, wove it, and had many yards of cloth in store, it is reasonable to rank this industry as a handicraft serving more than merely domestic needs, and supplementing the resources of yet another populous pasture-farming community.[2]

Finally, we may return again to the hand-knitting industry of Dentdale and Garsdale, and summarize briefly certain known facts about its farming and its industry. Gavelkind inheritance, aggravated no doubt by the general rise of population in the sixteenth century, caused its population to outgrow the resources of the land. This seems credible in view of the fact that the parish of Sedbergh had a population of 663 families in 1563: 346 in the town of Sedbergh, 251 in Dentdale and 66 families in Garsdale. The husbandry of Dentdale and Garsdale was devoted to rearing and dairying. Wensleydale cheese achieved its greatest reputation in a later age, but it was already marketed in the sixteenth century. Hand-knitting became an important local industry in the Tudor period, and from then until the nineteenth century, Dentdale was considered to be the principal home of the knitters. Now, in the mid-twentieth century, the small dairy farmers of the dales still pose economic problems to the agri-

[1] Joan Thirsk, *English Peasant Farming*, pp. 28-31, 140-41; H. E. Hallam, *op. cit.*, p. 361.

[2] More domestic weaving of flax, hemp, and wool seems to have been carried on in the whole county of Lincolnshire than in many other counties. Therefore, it is difficult to gauge the relative importance of the industry in the different regions. But insofar as it is possible to measure it by reference to the probate inventories, I believe that it was economically more important in the fens of Holland than elsewhere, though the fens also had other by-employments such as rush-plaiting. In the Isle of Axholme the by-employment was undoubtedly sack-cloth weaving.

cultural economists who wish to see the land yield something more than subsistence to its occupiers.[1]

It is not the intention of this essay to propound a theory for the situation of rural handicraft industries which can be applied mechanically to them all, but to enumerate some of the common factors which seem to be present in a number of semi-farming, semi-industrial communities, and to suggest that attention be paid to them in any future study of rural industries such as lace-making, hat-making, glove-making, and basket-making, which are not mentioned here. The common factors seem to be these: a populous community of small farmers, often mainly freeholders (as in Suffolk) or customary tenants with a tenure almost as good as a freehold (as in the Yorkshire dales), pursuing a pastoral economy. This may rest upon dairying in which case the farms are usually early enclosed, and manorial organisation and cooperative farming, in consequence, is weak or non-existent. Or it may rest upon breeding and rearing on generous pasture commons, where there is no practical incentive to enclose, where the arable land is meagre, and where again there is no strong framework of open fields and cooperative husbandry. In the rearing districts the resources of the land (particularly the generous commons) are sufficient to support, and do support, a custom of gavelkind. In the dairying regions the same custom cannot certainly be held responsible for the large populations. Underlying all this, we may see a certain logic sometimes in the way these common factors are linked together. Some of the land best suited to pasture was not cleared of woodland until a comparatively late stage in local settlement history. It was likely to be immediately enclosed. It was likely to give rise to a community of independent farmers who recognized not the hamlet or the village, but the family, as the cooperative working unit. If the land was suitable for dairying, it had enough water to support a cloth industry too. In a less hospitable countryside, where there were wide moorlands or large fenland commons, and little suitable

---

[1] BM Harleian Mss. 594; Leeds Central Library, Archives Dept., and Lancs. Record Office, probate inventories, *passim*; Marie Hartley and Joan Ingilby, *The Old Hand-knitting of the Dales* (1951), p. 7 *et seq.*; W. Patterson, 'The New Pennine Dairy Farming', *Agriculture*, LXVI, no. 8, pp. 340-42.

cornland, the husbandry was bound to consist in rearing and sheep-keeping. The commons attracted landless youths. The farming required less labour than a corn-growing farm and left men time to engage in a subsidiary occupation.

Perhaps, indeed, the intelligent globe-trotters of Tudor and Stuart England took for granted some of the propositions which we, who are far removed from them in time and experience, have painfully to prove. The phrase 'scratch a weaver and find a parcener' sums up that part of this argument which is concerned with the effects of gavelkind, and says as much as the handknitters of Dentdale. The Somerset J.P's who summarized in a sentence the economy of four hundreds of Somerset seem to be describing just the landscape in which handicraft industries could flourish: 'The country, a great part of it being forest and woodlands and the rest very barren for corn... the people of the country (for the most part) being occupied about the trade of clothmaking, spinning, weaving, and tucking.' The inhabitants of Hertfordshire, resisting an attempt by the Crown in James I's reign to establish the New Draperies in their county, described, on the other hand, the kind of landscape which could not support a handicraft industry—a corn-growing region which gave full employment to all. 'The county of Hertford doth consist for the most part of tillage... it has better means to set the poor children on work without this new invention than some other counties, viz. by employing the female children in picking of their wheat a great part of the year and the male children by straining before their ploughs in seedtime and other necessary occasions of husbandry.' Does this, indeed, help to explain the strange death of clothmaking in Hertfordshire? It appeared in the fifteenth century in just the area where one would want to place it, east of Royston, Buntingford and Ware in a district much of which was not cleared of woodland before the twelfth century, where the land was immediately enclosed, and a landscape of hamlets and isolated farms took shape. The rivers would have yielded more than enough water for the cloth industry, but instead other influences were at work, and it became a corn county. And the cloth industry disappeared[1] in the early sixteenth

[1] PRO SP 14/144, no. 24; SP 14/96, no. 39; *V.C.H. Herts.*, IV, pp. 210, 249.

century when in other places it was at the height of its prosperity.

There seems to be enough positive evidence to support the proposition that the location of handicraft industries is not altogether haphazard, but is associated with certain types of farming community and certain kinds of social organization. One could go further and suggest that the period in which these industries arose in different districts deserves scrutiny. Professor Malowist has recently remarked upon the simultaneous rise of the cloth industry in the fourteenth and fifteenth centuries and the crisis in agriculture.[1] This phenomen is not peculiar to England but is found in the Low Countries, southern Germany, and Italy. One could reasonably postulate some association between the rise of population and pressure on the land in the sixteenth century, and the rise of the handknitting industry in the Yorkshire dales. One might then consider why the framework-knitting industry did not spread into Leicestershire until the later seventeenth century, while cotton and wool manufacture did not take root in the Peak district of Derbyshire until the eighteenth century.[2] But here we must end one discussion, not begin another.[3]

[1] 'It seems to me that this fact proves that agriculture did not suffice to give them a living, and this, in turn, may have been the result of the low level of their agricultural efficiency.'—M. Malowist, 'The economic and social development of the Baltic countries from the fifteenth to the seventeenth centuries', *Econ. Hist. Rev*, 2nd Ser., XII, no. 2, p. 178.

[2] W. G. Hoskins, *The Midland Peasant*, pp. 227-8; Owen Ashmore, 'The early textile industry in North-west Derbyshire', *Derbyshire Miscellany*, no. 9, June 1953, p. 129.

[3] I wish to thank Drs. A. Everitt, H. P. R. Finberg, R. Hilton, W. G. Hoskins and Mr Norman Scarfe for their helpful criticism of this paper.

THE FRUITS OF OFFICE: THE CASE OF ROBERT CECIL, FIRST EARL OF SALISBURY, 1596-1612[1]

A T all periods of English history most of the really large landed fortunes have been acquired not through the law, trade, marriage or successful estate management, but through royal favour and high political office. Though countless families have risen to the squirearchy by the former methods, it has usually taken the latter to hoist them up a further stage into the more exalted atmosphere of the great territorial aristocracy. The subtle alchemy by which favour and office have been transformed into money and land has varied from age to age in its techniques and in its success, and a study of these changes would throw more light on the workings of the English political system than constitutional and administrative historians are usually willing to admit. All too often, however, the chemical formula has been lost, and the surviving records reveal no more than the resultant accumulation of property. The case of Robert Cecil, 1st Earl of Salisbury, is of unusual interest for four reasons. He was the founder of a landed family which is still one of the largest and most distinguished in the country. He acquired his wealth under two sovereigns, and thus spanned a transitional period during which the nature and extent of the profits of office were widely believed to have undergone considerable change. His is a story of great complexity which throws light into many corners of Jacobean politics

[1] Most of the documents used in this study are preserved at Hatfield House and I am deeply indebted to the Marquis of Salisbury for permission to examine them. The following abbreviations are used for them: A—Accounts; B—Bills; D—Deeds; L—Legal; G—General; S—Salisbury MSS (bound volumes of official correspondence); Box G, Q, U, V, S—Box G. Q. U. V. S.

and finance. Lastly, of all the great political figures of the Elizabethan and Early Stuart period, only Cecil has left behind him sufficient papers to enable the historian to reconstruct a good deal of the acquisitive process.

Robert Cecil was the younger son, by a second wife, of William, 1st Lord Burghley. In a long life spent in public office his father had acquired a huge estate scattered over the home counties and the east midlands, and running up into Lincolnshire and Yorkshire. The custom of primogeniture made it inevitable that the lion's share of these lands should go to Robert's elder brother, Thomas. But it was not uncommon for a man whose wealth was the result of his own exertions rather than ancient inheritance to feel free to deal more generously than was usual with his younger children. Moreover Burghley's political hopes centred upon Robert, to whom in 1587 he left the reversion of the gigantic palace at Theobalds and most of his lands in Hertfordshire and the Home Counties. There is enough evidence for it to be fairly safe to assume that the average annual income of this property in the first years of the seventeenth century was between £1,600 and £1,800, of which under £700 came from the Theobalds group, and out of which the huge palace of Theobalds had to be maintained.[1]

This substantial inheritance was in prospect, not in possession, and Robert Cecil probably drew an annuity from his father as long as he lived. Apart from this he had to depend for his income upon the profits of office. After acting in a semi-official capacity for some years, he was finally made Secretary of State in 1596, which gave him a secret service allowance of £800 a year besides the official fees, he became Chancellor of the Duchy of Lancaster in the next year, and in 1598 he succeeded his father as Master of the Court of Wards. This last office offered great possibilities of gain by the sale of wards for personal profit and it is not surprising to find Cecil beginning to buy land soon after his accession to the Mastership. Between 1608 and 1612, when he was both Lord Treasurer and Master of the Court of Wards, it is possible to build up a picture of how and by how

[1] Box Q/2. A. 6/16, 20, 36; 7/2. N.E. McClure, *Letters of John Chamberlain*, Philadelphia, 1939, I, p. 42.

much Cecil increased his income from these official sources. Before this enough has survived to allow us to add circumstantial detail to the jocular comment of Sir Fulke Greville that 'In the point of profit I perceive you resolve now to multiply yourself.'[1]

The last years of Elizabeth were ones of acute financial stringency and all politicians complained of the drying up of the flow of official gifts and rewards. They tended to lose money heavily by their attendance at Court and as a result were driven more and more to the perversion of their powers and influence to corrupt uses, and to exploring every lucrative side-line that offered itself. Two possible ways of adding to official income were by speculative investment in new industrial undertakings and in privateering on the high seas. It is very doubtful whether Cecil got anything out of his shares in the Mines Royal and Mineral and Battery Companies, his purchase of a monopoly patent to manufacture iron, steel and lead using peat or coal, or his investment with Buckhurst and Shrewsbury in Bevis Bulmer's prospecting for minerals along the Scottish border.[2] More profitable, perhaps, was the acquisition with Lord Buckhurst of Sir John Packington's eight-year monopoly patent for the manufacture of starch, an exceedingly complicated transaction of which the details are obscure. Not surprisingly the full weight of the Privy Council was put behind the enforcement of the monopoly, the official production figures rose sharply in 1599-1601 and there is reason to suppose that the monopoly showed a profit, possibly a large one.[3]

But these tentative and mostly unhappy ventures into industry are over-shadowed both in scale and in success by Cecil's investment in privateering during the interminable Anglo-Spanish war of 1585 to 1604. This time-honoured method of naval warfare cost the Crown nothing, inflicted damage on the economic life of the enemy, and brought a fortune to the Lord Admiral, who took 10% of all prizes. One of the hazards of the business, however, was the uncertain legal position over neutral goods and neutral shipping en route for enemy

[1] *H. M. C. Salis. Mss*, XVI, p. 196.
[2] D. 45/2, 73/9, 94/8. College of Arms, Talbot MSS, I, f. 266.
[3] *H. M. C. Salis. Mss*, VIII, pp. 172, 233, 565; XIII, p. 559; XIV, pp. 59, 87, 102, 169. S. 204 f. 123.

ports, and in practice the distinction between legitimate privateering and indiscriminate piracy was hard to draw, despite efforts by the Crown and the Court of Admiralty.

It seems to have been the Lord Admiral, Lord Howard of Effingham, who first drew Cecil into this speculative business. It offered special attractions to both of them, since they could—and did—use their official positions to off-set some of the costs. Cecil could use some of the secret service money to fit out ships, on the grounds that one of their purposes was to hang about off the coast of Spain to pick up information about Spanish naval preparations; Effingham and Cecil between them could get ships put on the royal pay-roll and then use then for their private advantage.

Cecil's first venture was in the winter of 1595-6, when he joined Effingham in building the *Truelove*. The bare hull was said to have cost £800, but if the contractors were treated like the supplier of cordage, who had still not been paid his bill of £95 in 1603 and was by then in the Fleet for debt, the actual cost to the adventurers must have been much reduced.[1] After joining the Cadiz expedition in 1596, the *Truelove* set out on a half-commercial, half-privateering venture to Barbary in 1597, an expedition which cost Cecil and Nottingham little since the ship was added to the pay-roll of the royal fleet for this spring. Since the fleet was only commissioned for three months it looked a little awkward to put the *Truelove* down for six. This difficulty was overcome, however, by inflating the nominal muster of the crew, so that they were double victualled for three months, thus making the equivalent of the full six months. The voyage was a moderate success. Although there was trouble over one prize, whose contents turned out to be Dutch-owned, the capture of another with £1,800 worth of cargo, coupled with the fact that the Queen was bearing the costs of the voyage, must have brought substantial gains to Cecil and Effingham.[2]

---

[1] *H. M. C. Salis. Mss*, XV, p. 206. A Collins, *Sydney Papers*, I, p. 377.
M. Oppenheim, *The Naval Tracts of Sir William Monson* (Navy Record Soc.), 1902, I, p. 358. E. Edwards, *The Life of Sir Walter Ralegh*, 1868, I, p. 199.
[2] *H.M.C. Salis. Mss*, VII, pp. 79, 82, 148, 277, 522, 538.

In 1598 it became urgent to obtain information about Spanish
naval preparations. So Cecil and a London merchant hired a Dutch
ship, filled her with banned goods, mostly naval stores, put an English spy on board disguised as a Dutch factor, and sent her off on a
smuggling voyage to Coruña. It was a disaster, and Cecil lost his 500
ducats investment in the cargo, paid for out of the secret service fund.
Spanish suspicions were aroused, the spy confessed under torture
and was then strangled, the ship and its goods were confiscated, and
the unfortunate Dutch master, who was entirely innocent of any
knowledge of espionage, was condemned to eight years in the
galleys.[1]

This experience seems to have deterred Cecil for a while, and he
abandoned the sea during 1599. In 1600, however, he took the major
share with Nottingham and two other peers in setting out a large
London ship, the *Lioness*, on a privateering cruise in the Mediterranean. The voyage was a brilliant success, thanks to the capture in the
straits on 1st February 1601 of a large ship laden with sugar, and on an
investment of about £1,150 Cecil must have made a clear net profit of
about £6,000.[2] Between 1600 and 1602 Cecil's privateering activities
reached their peak. Three more expeditions financed jointly with
Nottingham or Lord Thomas Howard proved to be failures, but the
purchase of a share in a voyage launched by Sir John Gilbert brought
in a net profit of about £1,000.[3]

The fifth and most ambitious of the ventures of these years was
a large expedition to the eastern Mediterranean mounted jointly by
Cecil and Nottingham. For it they prepared a 100-ton pinnace belonging to the latter, and hired a 300-ton London ship, the *Marigold*,
with 100 men aboard her. Though there is reference to the 'excessive
charges' to which the adventurers had been put, unless there were two
London ships called the *Marigold*, she was certainly on the list of

---

[1] S.P. 12/268/95. L. Stone, *An Elizabethan: Sir Horatio Palavicino*, Oxford, 1956
p. 326. *H. M. C. Salis. Mss*, XI, p. 576.

[2] *H.M.C. Salis. Mss*. X, pp. 392, 400, 454; XI, p. 177; XVI, p. 168.
S. 87, f. 164; 142, f. 175. A. 6/9, 119/12. Essex R.O., D/DP. L. 38.

[3] *H.M.C. Salis. Mss*, X-XII *passim*; XIV, pp. 50, 135; XV, p. 127. Box S/7 f. 13.

merchantmen hired by the Crown for operations at Kinsale in Ireland from October 1601 until January 1602. Since the pinnace was certainly fitted out at the royal expense, nominally as part of the Channel Guard, it looks as if Cecil and Nottingham had managed to shift most of the cost of the expedition on to the Exchequer. How successful the voyage proved we do not know, the last report being of the capture off Sicily of a Hamburg fly-boat, claimed as prize largely because it had the temerity to offer resistance, and of the intention to pursue an English pirate who had just taken 4,500 pieces of eight off a Genoese ship. One would hesitate to decide whether it was righteous indignation at the piracy or an eye for the pieces of eight that inspired this latter project.[1]

By now peace with Spain was imminent, and Cecil finally withdrew from the privateering business. There can be no doubt at all that over a period of eight years he had gained handsomely on his investments. He had been prudent enough to spread his capital over a number of ventures instead of staking all on a single voyage, and he had avoided those over-ambitious projects that were the undoing of Cumberland and Lord Thomas Howard. He had also contrived to shift part of the expenses on to the Navy or his own secret service allowance. As a result his gains had far outweighed his losses, and in 1601-2 his share of captures must have brought him a net profit of about £7,000.

The only way in which Elizabeth knowingly allowed Cecil to increase his income from official sources—and even in this case it appeared to bring profit to the Crown—was by granting him the farm of the customs on imported silks. Under pressure of an insatiable demand for luxury clothing by the upper classes, imports of silks, satins and velvets were rising rapidly. Hitherto most of them came overland from Venice and were imported to England from the Low Countries. Although it was evident that the use of these rich textiles was growing in England, and thus that imports must be rising, the Customs figures actually showed a sharp fall in the late 1590s. There

---

[1] *H.M.C. Salis. Mss*, XI, pp. 408, 453-4, 457; XII, pp. 25, 549-51. Oppenheim, *op. cit.*, I, pp. 281, 358; II, pp. 126, 169, 170.

was good reason to believe that the cause of this was extensive smuggling in the Port of London, and the Exchequer officials finally decided that the only way to put a stop to it was to enlist the aid of the profit motive by leasing the silk customs to a contractor at a fixed rent. There was a precedent for this method both of producing a stable revenue and of rewarding deserving courtiers, for the Sweet Wine Farm had for years been one of the financial supports first of the Earl of Leicester, and then of the Earl of Essex. This was the precedent upon which was based Cecil's successful request for a ten-year lease from January 1601 of the silk customs at a rent of £8,882. This was £1,200 a year higher than the average for the previous seven years, and the lease therefore involved the Crown in no financial loss. But in view of the fact that the average receipts for 1589-93 had been £9,675, it was clear that Cecil had only to reduce smuggling to its previous proportions to be able to make a handsome profit.[1]

With the advent of the new reign the long years of Crown parsimony were at last over. The pork barrel was broached again on a scale that had not been seen since the days of Edward VI, and James at once hastened to show his gratitude to Cecil for the brilliant engineering of a peaceful accession. First the latter obtained a pardon for almost a whole half-year arrears of rent of the Silk Farm, which put £4,441 into his pocket, and in 1604 he got a new lease for 15 years at the same rent. He promptly sub-let the farm to a merchant syndicate for six years for a sum that guaranteed him a clear net profit of £1,333 a year. Moreover in the same year the introduction of a new Rate Book enhanced the value of the farm, and this improvement Cecil sold to the sub-contractors for £3,286 in cash. Finally in 1610 Salisbury obtained from James a fresh grant at the old rent for no less than nineteen years. By now the value of the farm had greatly increased, so much so that by 1612 the sub-contractors had agreed to pay Salisbury the gigantic sum of £7,000 a year clear.[2] If it had

[1] *H.M.C. Salis. Mss*, XI, p. 1. B.M. Harl. Mss 1878/59. *Cal. S.P. Dom.*, *1598-1601*, p. 499. L. 85/3.
[2] D. 209/2, 164/1. *H.M.C. Sackville Mss*, I, p. 122. S. 129, ff. 129, 133. Leeds City Library, Temple Newsam Mss, English Customs IV/1. D. 114/4, 8; 216/8.

run its course, this single grant to the Earl of Salisbury would have been worth a sum not far short of a million pounds in money of today.

Nor were these Salisbury's only pickings from farms of the customs. In 1604 the Privy Council decided to lease the general body of the customs in a single 'Great Farm', and tenders were invited. One of the competing syndicates of merchants rallied behind Cecil, who acted as their spokesman, though as Secretary he was also a leading member of the selection committee. After a struggle his syndicate (of which his silk farmer, Francis Jones, was a member) was awarded the contract—and he promptly sold his interest to the Farmers for £6,000 down.[1] As so often happens, it is difficult here to be dogmatic about Salisbury's motives. He was probably genuinely anxious to provoke competition for the contract in order to get the best possible offer for the Exchequer. On the other hand his public spirit was rewarded by a dubiously acquired £6,000.

Between Michaelmas 1608 and Michaelmas 1612, six months after Salisbury's death, the chance survival of his receiver-general's accounts makes it possible to give some statistical precision to allegations of official corruption, and to examine the workings of the system in some detail.[2] As they stand, however, they do not tell the whole story. In the first place there is evidence that fairly large sums of money were passing to and fro without being recorded in the accounts. In some years the receiver, Roger Houghton, paid nothing at all into the Earl's privy purse, which was evidently fed from elsewhere. From time to time Houghton records the receipt from the Earl, usually in gold, of large sums with which to make certain payments, while at other times he notes that money he has paid out is in addition to other payments made directly by Salisbury from his private reserves. Moreover there must have been further sums paid out of this private account of which the receiver-general had no knowledge or which he

[1] F. C. Dietz, *English Public Finance, 1558-1640*, New York, 1932, p. 332.
A. P. Newton, 'The Establishment of the Great Farm of the English Customs', *T.R.H.S.*, 4th Ser. I, 1918, p. 150.
[2] A. 160/1. Box G/13.

had no reason to record. For example Houghton received all the official payments from the Exchequer for secret service, totalling over £5,500 during these four years, but he only made the most obvious and open payments, amounting altogether to a mere £732. It would be quite false to assume, however, that Salisbury was making a profit by pocketing large balances on the secret service account, for a memorandum, drawn up for purely internal purposes, observes that the money was 'nearly all spent'.[1] Consequently most of the payments on the secret service account must have been made from the Earl's private cash reserves. In view of other sources of gratuities and other secret expenses which do not appear, one may reasonably guess that at least £1,500 a year was passing through Salisbury's hands without being entered in the accounts.

Although these accounts are, as far as I am aware, unique in the degree to which they record illegal and quasi-legal sources of income, their value to the historian is diminished by some rather half-hearted efforts at concealment. Although no politician had yet been prosecuted for peculation on the basis of impounded private papers, there was always a risk that this might happen, and Houghton was evidently instructed to be as discreet as he could without falsifying his accounts. He did his best. When he referred to the 'w. of one Ponies in Essex, £400', 'of Lady Derby to your use for a certain w. £500', or 'the wardshippe of one L, £200', there is no doubt that he is talking about the unofficial sale of wardships for his private profit by the Master of the Court. But many very large payments are merely recorded with the name of the payee, and one can only guess at their true significance. It may be assumed that all payments by Exchequer officials are for the sale of offices and other perquisites of the Lord Treasurer, and that all payments by Court of Wards officials are for the sale of wards. One of two other items can be identified with some confidence. 'Mr Wright for a certain quarter's pay, £115', which recurs up to 1609 and then ceases, is presumably the pension from the King of Spain, which Salisbury is known to have been receiving since 1604. In 1609 he asked that it should stop, and that he should be given instead occasional special gratuities,

[1] Box Q/2.

which no doubt went to swell his private treasure-chest outside Houghton's cognisance. It was certainly a safer method.[1] But when all these more or less identifiable items have been eliminated there still remains a residue of unexplained receipts, while on the payment side there are one or two mysterious items, such as 'to one at your Lordships order £400', 'to the same partie £200', and so on. Even allowing for these deficiencies, however, we are still left with a set of figures which throw a good deal of light upon the gigantic but precarious finances of a great Jacobean courtier.

During these years Salisbury was engaged in two large-scale land transactions, which will be described later. They involved him in very heavy purchases and sales, and as a result his landed revenue fluctuated considerably. On an average, however, after deducting fixed charges like fee-farm rents and rents for leasehold land, and after including fines and casualties and the rent of the New Exchange, Salisbury's receipts from land came to about £7,000 a year. Far more important sources of income were those derived directly or indirectly from the tenure of political office. From the Silk Farm he drew his regular annuity of £1,333 till 1610, soon after which he engineered the new lease from the Crown and then sublet at the huge figure of £7,000 a year. This new rent hardly appears in the accounts, however, as it was almost immediately diverted directly to debt repayment. A further, but relatively minor source of income was the average of £340 a year received for the sale of surplus plate which poured in at the New Year in gifts from Exchequer officials, suitors, courtiers, and other seekers after favour.

Salisbury's most important office was the Lord Treasurership, which carried with it an official fee of £366, together with about £30 a year in casual fees. The real income came from other sources. The £1,000 a year average paid in by Sir Walter Cope, Chamberlain to the Exchequer, may well be the profits from the sale of numerous lesser offices in the Treasurer's gift. But other sums have a more sinister flavour. What are we to make of the £2,400 paid into the Earl's account in 1608-9 by various Tellers of the Exchequer? They were certainly not private loans, for they are not listed under that

[1] S. R. Gardiner, *History of England, 1603-16*, 1863, II, App. III.

heading. They may be further receipts for the sale of offices, though there is no reason at all why they should pass through the hands of the Tellers. A possible explanation is that they are raids on the royal Exchequer made by Salisbury to assist his own financial position. That this was a practice among Jacobean Lords Treasurer is known from the confession a few years later of the Earl of Suffolk, who admitted 'borrowing' money from the Tellers for his own purposes, and retaining it, interest free, for over four years. Indeed he only repaid the money in a hurry after investigation into his peculations had already been opened.[1] It is certainly not unlikely that in this practice Suffolk was merely copying the habits of his predecessor. Other items are equally suspect. The Royal jeweller paid Cecil £1,581 and the Royal goldsmith £762—and very shortly afterwards they obtained warrants from the Lord Treasurer for the repayment of debts owed them by the Crown. Since Suffolk later admitted that his wife took bribes to get warrants signed for the repayment of Crown debts, and since one such episode actually involved the same individual, the close correlation of these payments with the issue of warrants is certainly very suggestive. Finally there is a further £1,000 paid into Salisbury's account between 1608 and 1610 by Henry Spiller, an Exchequer official in charge of recusant fines.[2] If these are all accepted as probable fruits of office as Lord Treasurer, they come to about £2,800 a year. Twenty years later the office was estimated to be worth at least £7,000 a year.[3] If this is at all accurate, it is evident that Salisbury was relatively honest by subsequent standards, for the unidentified and unaccounted items cannot possibly fill the gap. At the very most Salisbury's profits as Lord Treasurer cannot have exceeded £4,500 a year, and it is clear that we are still at a period when some vestiges of the tolerable mid-Elizabethan standards survived in official circles to exercise a restraining influence. And yet, as the Earl of Newcastle

---

[1] Wilts R.O., Suffolk and Berkshire Mss, Moore's Boxes, 5/21.
[2] *Cal. S.P. Dom.*, *1603-10*, pp. 574, 625, 377. Chancery Proc., Ser. I, Jas. I, S 32/27.
[3] *Cal. S.P. Dom.*, *1635*, p. 120. P. Heylin, *Cyprianus Anglicus*, 1668, p. 285. *Clarendon State Papers*, I, pp. 158-9. cf. S. Pepys, *Diary*, 9 Sept. 1665.

observed some 40 years later, 'that profitable place is a greate temtation to honestye, & as the Earle off Strafforde tolde mee, thatt iff the Lord Tresorer woulde streatch his Contience, thatt hee mighte gett the Divell & all—& I never harde off anye Lorde Tresorer's Contience butt was off Streatchinge Leather'.[1]

The full profits of the Mastership of the Court of Wards are as difficult to estimate accurately as those of the Lord Treasurership. Official fees for diet and casual fees for the seal of the Court and for the passing of Liveries came to about £480 a year. Clearly identifiable private sales of wards by the Master came to about £1,400 a year, while at least another £700 may reasonably be guessed as coming from the same source. It is likely, therefore, that the total recorded income of the Master in these accounts is about £2,600 a year. To this may probably be added some of the payments that otherwise cannot be explained, and certainly about £2,000 of the debts noted as due to the Earl by others in 1612.[2] We should not be far wrong in estimating Salisbury's total income as Master at about £3,000 a year, the bulk of it derived from the private sale of wards on his own account.

Even before his father's death and his appointment as Master in 1598, suitors were approaching Robert Cecil with offers of bribes to obtain wardships,[3] and thereafter there is plenty of evidence that he was carrying on his father's practice of selling wards for personal profit. For example in 1602 his secretary Michael Hicks asked him for a ward but was refused. Cecil explained that 'the Court is absolutely full of Importunity for it', and that he intended to profit by this competition 'to draw some benefite to myself.'[4] With the help of the accounts, the way the system worked can be traced in detail in a number of cases. To give but one example, John Gobert paid £370 to the Court and £1,400 to Salisbury for the wardship of John Jennings. This is the sort of transaction that goes far to explain the popular hatred for the Court and its corrupt beneficiaries, and it may

[1] S. A. Strong, *A Catalogue... of Documents at Welbeck*, 1903, p. 194.
[2] A. 6/7.
[3] *H.M.C. Salis. Mss*, IV, p. 554; VI, pp. 363, 425; VII, p. 115.
[4] B.M. Lansd. Mss. 88/45.

be significant that thirty years later the former ward, John Jennings, was one of the leading opposition Members in the Long Parliament.[1] On the other hand these private sales are neither more numerous nor more extortionate than those negotiated by Lord Burghley in the 1590s.[2] There is no sign of any growth of corruption during the rule of Salisbury, while there was certainly an increase in official receipts due to Salisbury's success in cutting down the middlemen's profits that had flourished so luxuriantly in the days of Burghley, a policy which included measures to protect the interests of the ward and of his family. Moreover attention should be drawn to the astonishing altruism shown by Salisbury when he promoted the Great Contract in 1610, by which the Crown was to surrender its rights of wardship in exchange for a fixed grant by Parliament.[3] Had it been accepted, it would have resulted in the abolition of the Court of Wards and the suppression of the office of Master. Salisbury could certainly have relied on receiving compensation for the loss of office, but he could hardly have anticipated that it would equal the full amount of his official *and* unofficial profits.

Of the hard core of the unexplained payments, some are recorded as being received from or on behalf of the Countess of Derby, a fair number of which were undoubtedly gratuities passed to Salisbury *via* his favourite niece. Others are flotsam from transactions the nature and propriety of which we now have no means of discovering, and lastly there is the £4,755 paid over in gold from the Earl's private treasure chest. Since all other possibilities have been explored, one is forced to conclude this store of gold was built up partly from accumulated reserves from pre-1608 transactions, and partly from further undisclosed irregular sources. There were the large casual presents which were said to have replaced the regular Spanish pension in 1609. The lessees of the Wine Licence monopoly had paid an annuity of £400 to Lord Treasurer Dorset for his goodwill, and in 1608 they

---

[1] A. 6/7. P.R.O., Wards, Misc. Books 408. M. F. Keeler, *The Long Parliament*, Philadelphia, 1954, pp. 233-4.
[2] J. H. Hurstfield, 'Lord Burghley as Master of the Court of Wards, 1561-98, *T.R.H.S.*, 4th Ser., XXXI, 1949, p. 108.
[3] J. H. Hurstfield, *The Queen's Wards*, 1958, ch. 15.

transferred it to Salisbury. Since there is no sign of this annuity in the accounts, it must have passed directly into the Earl's treasure chest.[1] Another likely source was bribes from the Spanish and French trading Companies which were set up in the first decade of the seventeenth century and which probably enlisted Salisbury's support.[2]

Thanks to land speculation and an extravagant building programme these huge sums were inadequate to cover expenditure, and in these four years Salisbury borrowed £61,000, took responsibility for £14,000 worth of debts in return for the surrender of land, and repaid a mere £36,000. The net increase in the Earl's indebtedness in the last four years of his life was therefore £39,000. Since he was already heavily in debt before 1608 it is not surprising to find that in July 1611 the Earl's debts by bond and bill came to no less than £53,000.[3]

The lenders of this £61,000 over these four years were the usual restricted list of Jacobean creditors, but it is disturbing to find that no less than £23,400 came from merchants engaged in one or other of the customs Farms, the money presumably coming at least in part from customs revenue balances held by the farmers. Since it was Salisbury's duty as Lord Treasurer to keep a strict eye on the Customs administration and to negotiate new leases on terms favourable to the Crown, these huge advances to bolster up the Earl's private finances were, to say the least of it, unfortunate. They open up disquieting vistas of private pressure upon the Lord Treasurer. The uneasiness is strengthened by the discovery that in 1611, while negotiations were proceeding for a new grant of the Great Farm of the Customs, the farmers formally took over £20,000 of the Earl's debts, including £9,450 already due to them. The interest on the £9,450 was apparently secured by their taking over the management of the New Exchange at a rent of £1,000 a year, while the capital sum was to be paid off out of part of the profits of the silk farm, which Salisbury later sublet to the same syndicate. It is this sort of transaction which 20 years later led Sir John Harrison to the conclusion that the

[1] *H.M.C. Sackville Mss*, I, p. 90.
[2] G. 28/1.
[3] Box U/39.

vested interest of the current Lord Treasurer in the customs farms was one of the main causes of their retention.[1]

Although, as has been pointed out, the accounts do not record the full receipts of the Earl of Salisbury between 1608 and 1612, they at least serve to give some idea of the order of magnitude. As they stand, after certain corrections, the accounts show average receipts of about £49,800 a year. Of this £15,300 came from loans and £14,300 from the sale of land. Of the remaining £20,200, £6,900 were certain or probable legal and illegal profits of the three offices of Lord Treasurer, Master of the Court of Wards, and Secretary of State. Other sources of income that derived ultimately from political office, the pension from the King of Spain, the sale of plate, the annuity out of the Silk Farm, payments by the customs farmers, cash paid into the account by the Earl himself, and other large unexplained payments together amount to about £5,300. Compared with these huge sums from official or semi-official sources, the recorded receipts from land (excluding the £1,000 from the New Exchange) were relatively modest, amounting to just on £6,000. The remainder was made up of £700 from or on behalf of the Countess of Derby, which might be loans, purchases of wards, bribes, or receipts concerned with her estates, £700 a year from the repayment of money lent, and £600 from arrears and other miscellaneous payments.

To appreciate the astonishing scale of these figures, it is necessary to compare them with others. If we exclude 'extraordinary' sources like borrowing and sale of land, but add the full rents of the Silk Farm and of the New Exchange and the estimated £1,500 a year of unrecorded gratuities, we find that Salisbury in the last two years of his life was in receipt from recurring sources of at least £25,000 a year. This was a time when the unskilled manual labourer could not expect to earn more than £10 to £15 a year, when the greatest landed income in the country did not exceed £8,000 ,and when the 'ordinary' revenue of the State itself was only about £300,000. Several of the overmighty subjects of the Middle Ages could boast of an income

---

[1] S. 141, f. 352. B.M., Stowe Mss 326, ff. 89-89v. I owe this reference to the kindness of Dr. Robert Ashton.

equal to a twelfth of that of the King. But the difference, in which lies one of the most significant transformations of English society, was that this huge income now depended very largely on the personal whim of the monarch. Withdraw that favour, remove the profits of office, and the whole edifice would come tumbling down.

There were three main pressures which obliged Salisbury to accept these large and irregular sums from clients and suitors, and to run up such a terrifying load of debt. The first was the need to maintain a lavish household establishment with which to entertain royalty, maintain his circle of clients and supporters, and impress the public at large. In a situation where power depended in no small measure on prestige, and prestige in turn upon a high level of expenditure, conspicuous consumption was both a public duty and a political necessity. Salisbury's personal and household expenditure was running at about £8,500 a year during the last four years of his life. At the same period his son was sent on the grand tour, married, and given a handsome allowance, and a daughter was expensively married into the older aristocracy. As a result his children were costing him another £6,000 a year.

The second and heaviest burden during these years was on building. Lord Burghley had been a passionate builder, with Theobalds, Burghley House, and Exeter House in the Strand to show for it. At the first opportunity Robert Cecil had also begun to build, first at Chelsea House, then at Salisbury House in the Strand. But it was the surrender of Theobalds to the King in 1607 that spurred him into the most astonishing building programme of the age, a programme so grandiose in its scope as to strain even Salisbury's gigantic financial resources. At one time he was building simultaneously at Hatfield, Cranborne, the New Exchange, and Salisbury House.[1] The total expenditure on building in the last five years of the Earl's life came to over £63,000, the average between 1608 and 1612 being £13,500

[1] See L. Stone, 'The Building of Hatfield House', *Arch. J.*, CXII, 1956, and 'Inigo Jones and the New Exchange', *Arch. J.*, CXV, 1959; H. A. Tipping, 'Cranborne House', in *English Homes*, Period III, vol. II, 1927, pp. 353-71; 'Salisbury House', in *L.C.C.*, *Survey of London*, XVIII, 1937, ch. 18.

a year. It was this that caused the soaring debt which so alarmed the Earl's agents before he inaugurated the great land-sale campaign of 1611-13.

The third main item of expenditure was the massive programme of land purchase which between 1597 and Cecil's death in 1612 turned the modest inheritance from his father into one of the greatest estates in the kingdom. In 1597 his father gave him Beaufort House in Chelsea, where he had no sooner put on a new front than he lost interest and sold out for £6,000 to the Earl of Lincoln.[1] The cause of this hasty sale was the decision to buy a more central site on which to build a town house that would be worthy of his position as one of the leading courtiers of the day. Beginning in 1599 he gradually acquired a substantial frontage on the south side of the Strand where he erected two opulent mansions.[2] Though a late-comer on the scene, his skilful and persistent efforts had secured him a large site for a town house in this highly coveted area, at the expense of the Bishop of Durham, the Bishop's former lessee Sir Walter Ralegh, and Lord Herbert. Later still, he acquired from the Bishop the whole Strand frontage of Durham House, where he built the New Exchange, which was intended to rival Gresham's famous building in the City and act as a sort of bazaar or multiple store in this fashionable quarter. Lastly in 1609-10 he made what was eventually to prove the most successful investment of his life, the purchase for less than £500 from a variety of owners of some nine acres of undeveloped land running part of the way up the west side of Saint Martin's Lane.[3]

Meanwhile substantial acquisitions were being made in the coun-

---

[1] C.R. 42 Eliz. pt. 20; 41 Eliz. pt. 23. D. 117/5, 104/1, 102/13. A. W. Clapham and W. H. Godfrey, *Some Famous Buildings and their Story*, pp. 79-91. *H.M.C. Salis. Mss*, VIII, p. 387.

[2] *L.C.C., Survey of London*, XVIII ch. 18. C.R. 44 Eliz. pt. 8. *H.M.C. Salis. Mss*, XI, pp. 343, 349, 358, 367, 397; XV, pp. 37, 111. E. Edwards, *Life of Sir Walter Ralegh*, 1868, II, pp. 262-65. L. 67/24; D. 183/14. House of Lords Mss, 3 Jas. I, Private Acts, cap. 1.

[3] A. 112/6; D. 111/18, 226/14 and 16; L. 233/14, 67/24. Box S/7, f. 87. House of Lords Mss, I Jas. I, Private Acts, cap. 6. *L.C.C., Survey of London*, XVIII, pp. 87-96, 120 note.

try. In 1559 Cecil paid the Crown £4,661 for a group of estates in the west country that included Cranborne manor in Dorset.[1] This Cranborne purchase was of great importance for the future history of the family, as it first directed Cecil's attention to this part of the world, where in his methodical way he began to build up a large and compact estate. Between 1601-1612 he spent £14,450 on buying land in the area, mostly from the Crown and the Earl of Pembroke.[2]

The tracing up to 1612 of the growth of these London and west country estates should not be allowed to conceal the extraordinary scale of Cecil's land purchases all over the country in the last two years of the Queen's life. After spending £5,600 in 1599-1600, there can be little doubt that in 1601-2 Cecil spent at least another £25,000 on buying land, besides completing the building of Salisbury House. Although some of the purchases of these months were designed to consolidate or extend existing properties, most of them were scattered lots purchased in bulk from the Crown, which was throwing large areas of its land on to the market in order to pay for the Irish war.[3]

The money for this gigantic operation came from a variety of sources. There was the £6,000 he had extorted from the Earl of Lincoln for Chelsea House. Between his father's death and 1601 he raised £4,400 from fines and the sale of woods on his Hertfordshire and Middlesex estates. As we have seen, there were unknown but possibly substantial profits from the starch patent, the private sale of wardships must have been bringing in several thousand pounds a year, privateering realised about £7,000 in 1601-2, and the silk farm showed a profit of £434 in 1601 and £4,441 in unpaid rent in 1602. Yet all this was not sufficient for Cecil's needs, and his agents were soon busy borrowing large sums from London aldermen.[4] Moreover to add to his worries a large purchase of Cornish lands turned out to

[1] G. 44/16. Box S/7, ff. 43v, 45, 67; Box S/8 A. 135/4. Land Revenue Office, Misc. Books 72, 73. *Cal. S.P. Dom. Eliz., 1601-3*, p. 260.
[2] G. 71/27, 56/1; D. 201/18; L. 233/14; A. 112/6, 9/5. Box S/7, ff. 66, 105. C.R. 42 Eliz. pt. 10. *H.M.C. Salis. Mss*, VII, pp. 405, 434; X, p. 282; XI, p. 17.
[3] G. 44/16; Box S/7, ff. 95, 103, 105. D. 151/3, 238/1-6; A. 112/6. C.R. 43 Eliz. pt. 5; 44 Eliz. pt. 22. S. 204 f. 139. Land Revenue Office, Misc. Books 73. *H.M.C. Salis. Mss*, XV, p. 361.
[4] *ibid.*, XI, p. 397; XII, p. 408.

have been a bad investment. The details of the intrigue elude us, but the fact remains that Cecil succeeded in selling these unwanted estates back to the Crown early in 1603 for £ 5,200.[1]

There are several possible explanations of this outburst of land purchasing. We have seen that in various ways Cecil had acquired about £20,000 of free capital. He may have regarded the massive Crown sales as an opportunity for profitable investment that with the approaching death of the Queen and the inevitable peace and consequent recovery of Crown finances was unlikely to recur. No doubt his political influence and contacts gave him access to information from Exchequer officials that enabled him to make particularly successful purchases, while if things went wrong it seems he could even get the Crown to take the property back again. But the fact remains that Cecil was actually running into debt in order to increase his holdings in land. Can it be that he was uncertain of his political future on the death of the Queen and was desperately trying to salt away the profits of office while there was still time? Unlike money, land safely conveyed to trustees was fairly immune from confiscation, even after a conviction for treason.

Early in 1603 Cecil bought from the Queen at an unknown price the Great and Little Parks of Brigstock, Northants., and followed this up two years later by the purchase of the manor and rectory.[2] His attention had first been drawn to this prize in 1601, when Sir Francis Carew told him that he was proposing to ask the Queen for a reversion of the parks after the death of the existing lessee, Lord Hunsdon, for which he was willing to pay £666. With an unscrupulousness that goes far to explain the popular hatred that surrounded him, Cecil promptly seized the opportunity to obtain the parks for himself, behind the back of Lord Hunsdon and without regard for the prior claims of Carew.[3] Under the ownership of Lord Hunsdon

[1] *ibid.*, XII, pp. 289, 348. A. 6/16; D. 5/20.
[2] Box S/7, f. 99; D. 81/4, 181/10. C.R. 2 Jas I, pt. 19. *H.M.C. Salis. Mss*, XV, p. 361; XVI, p. 99.
[3] *ibid.*, XI, p. 190; XV, p. 361. *H.M.C. Buccleuch (Whitehall)*, I, p. 236.A. 160/9; S. 98 f. 177. B.M. Add. Mss, 38444, f. 8.

the local inhabitants had exercised extensive rights of common over the parks, which were stocked with deer. But Sir Robert Cecil had other ideas, and all this old-fashioned administration at once gave way to brisk commercial exploitation by means of a group of heavily defended private sheep pastures. Despite bloody rioting by the local inhabitants, the revolution was forced through at a ruthless pace, and by the end of 1603 it was complete. There can be no doubt that enclosure and conversion resulted in an enormous increase of income, for by 1612 this great ranch was on lease to a large-scale grazier at a rent of over £1,200 a year.[1]

Though various purchases and sales continued during the next few years the only really important alteration to the emerging pattern of the Cecil estates was the Theobalds exchange of 1607. When Lord Burghley had finished improving and extending Theobalds, it had become a gigantic palace more suitable for a monarch than a subject. Indeed apart from Westminster Palace and Hampton Court, it was probably the largest building in England. It had been inherited by Robert Cecil, who lost no time in putting it to its intended use as a residence in which to entertain the sovereign. Unfortunately, however. James began to take far too keen a liking to the place, and in 1607 Cecil thought it only prudent and tactful to offer it to the King. By the terms of the exchange Cecil handed over nearly all his property in Cheshunt, the rental of which was probably under £500 a year, and was granted extensive manors and lands in ten counties, including the Early Tudor palace of Hatfield. As a result he was left with a moderate-sized, rather old-fashioned house instead of the huge and up-to-date showpiece of Theobalds. It is doubtful whether in the long run the Cecils lost very much by the exchange, for they received about £25,000 in cash from the subsequent sale of part of the exchange lands, and a 1640 rental of the remainder of £1,500 a year, whereas the Theobalds rental is very unlikely to have increased to this extent. They had also got rid of a house that was far too large for comfortable and economic occupation by a private individual.

---

[1] *H.M.C. Salis. Mss*, XV, pp. 60, 71, 361; XVI, pp. 38, 266, 318, 451. A. 112/6, 133/1, 160/1; G. 11/22.

In the short run, however, the £40,000 needed for building the new house meant a terrifying load of debt, nearly all of it at 10% interest. The real gain was in imponderables—in the goodwill of King James from whom yet greater rewards might be expected. If the renewal of the lease of the silk farm is regarded as a part of the deal, there can be little doubt that it paid off handsomely.

One might have supposed that the huge transaction of the Theobalds-Hatfield exchange, involving rapidly rising debt and the endless difficulties of finding buyers for the land, would have deterred Cecil from anything more than limited purchases to consolidate the existing estate. In fact, however, he simultaneously involved himself in a series of very complicated transactions by which he acquired the bulk of the property of his brother-in-law, the attainted Lord Cobham. Loss of royal favour had tempted Cobham into treasonable speeches, and led to his arrest and condemnation in 1603. Cecil certainly laboured to save his life, though the dramatic last minute reprieve at the scaffold may have been the personal whim of James himself. Subsequently, Cecil's attitude was ambiguous. Though Cobham apparently regarded him as his leading advocate at Court, he continued to languish in the Tower, and the remorseless carve-up of his property made it clear that influential persons were acquiring an interest in the irrevocable ruin of the house of Brooke. And of those with a stake in the Brooke estates Salisbury very soon became by far the most important. But the steps by which this hold was acquired were so involved, and took place over so extensive a period, that it is doubtful whether they can be seen as predetermined stages in a Macchiavellian plot by Salisbury to dispossess his brother-in-law. It is more reasonable to suppose that Salisbury at first was torn between calculated self-interest and a genuine desire to come to the help of his afflicted relatives, and that only at a later stage did he succumb to the temptation to take over the Brooke estates altogether.

In 1602-3 Lord Cobham's net landed income was about £3,700, a figure that put him in the front ranks of the Elizabethan peerage. About £650 of this came from leases from the Crown and from ecclesiastical authorities, to whom rents of about £150 were due.[1]

[1] S. 145 ff 90-99. Exchequer, Declared Accts., Pipe Office, 412.

The title to all this property was very varied. By the conviction of Lord Cobham there came into the hands of the Crown all his personal estate, including the leases, and such land as was not entailed. Most of the property was tied up by an entail of George, 1st Lord Cobham, and the Crown's interest was limited to the lifetime of the Lord Henry, after which it should descend to William, son of his executed brother George, on whose death without heirs it should revert to Lord Cobham's cousin, Duke Brooke of Templecombe. There were therefore three persons with interests to be considered: William, the infant son of George Brooke, Duke Brooke, and Lord Cobham's wife, the dowager Countess of Kildare, who had claims for maintenance so long as her husband lived, and for a jointure after his death.

Lady Kildare had long been on bad terms with her husband, and had no compunction in salvaging what she could for herself out of the wreck of the Brooke fortunes. It was in thanks for assistance in this and other endeavours that in 1607 she sold to Salisbury for a mere £1,000 her life interest in the very valuable estate of Canterbury Park. As she put it—somewhat crudely—to Cecil, 'I know you have been better to me than any commodity I should ever make out of Canterbury Park.'[1] And indeed she had been well provided for in a private act of Parliament of 1604 which assured her a present jointure of land valued at £481 a year, and the reversion after Lord Cobham's death of a further £501 a year.

The main problem was the disposal of the remainder, valued at over £962 a year. Despite the Crown's doubtful title in view of the entail, a good deal of it had already been given away by James to various prominent courtiers, both the leases and Canterbury Park having gone to Cecil himself.[2] And so another act was pushed through Parliament, which declared the forfeiture of all these estates by Lord Cobham and George Brooke and their heirs, and which confirmed the royal grants. The purpose of clearing the Crown's title was to

---

[1] *H.M.C. Salis. Mss*, XVII, p. 176. C.R., 4 Jas. I, pt. 32.

[2] J. Hutchins, *History of Dorset*, 1861-70, II, pp. 82, 84, 111, 115. J. Collinson, *History of Somerset*, 1791, III, pp. 303-4. T. D. Fosbrooke, *A History of Gloucestershire*, I, 1807, p. 265. *Cal. S. P. Dom., 1603-10*, pp. 227, 169, 106, 206. Pat. Rolls, 2 Jas. I, pts. 13, 27. *H.M.C. Salis. Mss*, XVI, p. 352; XVII, p. 628.

allow it to sell to Duke Brooke all the remaining estates for £8,000, together with its reversionary interest in the Countess of Kildare's jointure for a further £3,500. By this transaction, the property was transferred to a loyal branch of the Brooke family, the Crown gained a handsome windfall, and the children of George Brooke were ruined for ever. When in 1610 the children got themselves restored in blood by an act of Parliament, the Lords, presumably under the watchful prompting of Salisbury, put in a proviso expressly excluding them from all rights and claims to any property of the late Lord Cobham.[1]

The only difficulty was that Duke Brooke simply did not possess the £11,500 needed to pay the Crown and he was obliged to borrow it from great London financiers.[2] But since the Act had cleared the estate of encumbrances, he was therefore free to sell parts of it to pay the purchase price. He had already raised some £8,000 to £9,000 by sales, when he died and was succeeded by his brother Charles.[3] Charles was evidently a wild and extravagant young man, and within a year his position had become desperate. No doubt through the mediation of his friend and creditor, John Daccombe, who was also Lord Salisbury's solicitor and chief financial adviser, he began borrowing heavily from the Earl on the security of his estate, while at the same time plunging more deeply into the toils of the leading London money-lenders.[4] Gradually he found himself more and more dependent on Salisbury to support his credit and keep him out of the Fleet prison, and gradually the Earl came to assume control of more and more of his estate in return for taking on the burden of his debts. By April 1610, when Charles made his will, his position was hopeless. Ignoring the claims of his wife and child, he left his whole personal and real estate to the Earl in return for the payment of his debts,

---

[1] *ibid.*, XVI, p. 224. House of Lords Mss, 1 Jas. I, Private Acts, cap. 18; 3 Jas. I, Private Acts, cap. 6; 7 Jas. I, Private Acts, cap. 18.
[2] L.C. 4/195 ff. 343, 385, 403.
[3] P. Morant, *History of Essex*, 1768, II, p. 535, 537. H.M.C. *Salis. Mss*, XVII, pp. 119, 539.
[4] A. 7/13, 9/12, 128/1. S. 141, f. 352. L.C. 4/186 ff. 138, 151, 220, 242, 287, 332, 338, 362, 421; 197, ff. 13, 15. Charterhouse, Founder's Papers, 1/14, 97, 123; 2/29; 11/11.

those to others being scheduled at £14,000. And so for a total investment of £36,700 the Earl of Salisbury had acquired nearly all the Brooke estates, both in Kent and in the West, together with a personal estate in goods worth about £4,000.[1]

Whatever his original motive there is little doubt that Salisbury acquired the land at well below the market price. On the other hand the wisdom of floating this great venture concurrently with the Hatfield building programme at the time seemed open to question. The consequence of running these two operations together was the rise of the Earl's debts to £53,000 which made imperative the massive and rapid sale of both the Theobalds exchange lands and the Brooke estate.

This undertaking was tackled with energy and success by the Earl's agents. Coming at the end of nearly a decade of post-war prosperity and during a period of rapidly rising rents, the time could hardly have been more favourable for such an operation. In all the Cecils realised about £74,000 from the sale of land and goods in return for an investment of at most £36,700.[2] But this apparent profit of 100% takes no account of the interest money that had to be paid between 1607 and 1613 or of a £200 a year life annuity to Charles Brooke's widow, who lived on until 1626.[3] No exact calculation of the interest charges is possible, for the debt burden rose to a peak in 1611 and then fell sharply as the money from land sales poured in. But even if £10,000 is added to the investment to allow for the interest charges, the net profit is still over 55%. In this case, as with the Theobalds exchange, most of the property was sold within six or seven years of the purchase, during which time land values had certainly not risen under the general inflationary pressure by more than 10 or 15% at the very most. Was it this happy speculation in Brooke lands to which John Daccombe—Charles Brooke's 'friend'—

---

[1] A. 9/4, 13/54, 112/6; L. 64/16; G. 56/16; S. 145, ff. 118, 128. P.C.C., 38 Wingfield. C.R. 4 Jas. I, pts. 5, 29.

[2] A. 12/7; 13/53, 112/6, 154/1, 157/3, 160/1, 5; B. 109; D. 40/10, 102/13, 19-23, 27, 28, 40, 125/31, 160/27; L. 44/1; Box G/13, box N/3.

[3] Box G/13; A. 133/1; 160/5, 6.

was referring when he claimed in May 1612 to have gained for the late Earl £1,000 a year in rents and £35,000 in cash?[1]

Such were the methods by which in a mere fourteen years Salisbury built up a great landed estate which has remained the support of one of England's leading families from that day to this. It is evident that a crucial part was played by political influence. It was not merely that most of the money used for land purchases came from the profits of office. Other sources such as the windfalls from privateering or the annual income derived from the silk farm were ultimately derived from royal favour or political power. Part of the land was granted by the Crown as a reward for services, part of it was given in exchange for the surrender of Theobalds. Most of what was bought came from the Crown, and much of the rest from fellow peers: successful fellow-courtiers like Nottingham and Pembroke, hard-pressed countrymen like the Earl of Derby and Lord Windsor selling up family estates to pay off debts and settlements, and the family of Brooke, Lords Cobham, broken by political folly and then ruined by personal extravagance. In all cases it was his political position that gave Salisbury the necessary contacts and capital.

It is not the business of the historian to strike moral attitudes. And indeed, owing to his happy lack of personal experience, an Englishman living in the twentieth century is singularly unfitted to form a balanced judgment about corruption in public life. As Lord Keynes once remarked, in some societies corruption is the simplest and most convenient method of taxation. Under certain circumstances, and practised with moderation, it is not incompatible with a devotion to the public interest. 'I hope I may get nobly and honestly with profit to the King', confided Pepys to his diary as he negotiated to receive £300 a year for the award of the victualling contract for Tangier.[2] Nevertheless contemporary observers of the Early Stuart scene were

---

[1] G. 16/17. Daccombe ended up as owner of some of the Devon property, so that his relationship to Charles Brooke as friend, executor, financial adviser of the principal creditor, and personal beneficiary from the dissolution of the estate, was, to say the least of it, equivocal (S.P. 14/95/53; P.C.C., 19 Meade).
[2] S. Pepys, *Diary*, 2 July, 1664.

intensely—almost pathologically—preoccupied with the theme of the spread of corruption throughout the central organs of government. As he lay dying a lingering death in 1612 Salisbury himself clearly felt that his career had left much to be desired. In a somewhat tactless attempt to comfort him, his Chaplain observed that whereas King Herod had been cut off in full career, Salisbury should be thankful that God had given him leisure for repentance by afflicting him with a slow, wasting disease.[1] So oppressed was he by a sense of his sins— among which that of peculation must surely have been one—that the dying man made no objection to the invidious comparison. Less interested contemporaries were also worried by this canker eating into the body politic. Letter writers like John Chamberlain filled their pages with rumours of financial scandals; in the 1620s two great public figures, Bacon and Cranfield, saw their careers blasted by well-founded charges of peculation, and a third, the Duke of Buckingham, was only saved by the hasty dissolution of Parliament. Time and time again, the House of Commons came back to this theme of corruption at Court, as a principal cause of the wastage of the revenues of the State and of the inability of the King to live of his own. There is reason to believe that it was a powerful factor in turning the country gentry against the administration, and in the development of what came to be called 'the Country party', or 'the Patriots', a new phenomenon of open political opposition to the Court and all it stood for. This suspicion of corruption goes far to explain the obstinate refusal of Parliament to contribute to the burdens of government, a refusal which in turn made even more outrageous resort to corruption almost inevitable.

Sir John Neale has suggested that there was a substantial deterioration of financial probity among politicians in the 1590s, and much of his evidence for this deterioration comes from the correspondence of Robert Cecil and his secretary. A careful examination of Cecil's private papers amply supports the contention that he used his official position for personal financial gain on a very large scale. If the profits of office were less than those that were being made by his successors a few years later, there can be little doubt that they were

[1] F. Peck, *Desiderata Curiosa*, 1732, I, lib. VI, p. 10.

a good deal larger than those of Lord Burghley before him. Whereas the latter took half a century of almost uninterrupted public office to acquire his estate and build three great houses, Robert Cecil had to cram his territorial acquisitions and his five building operations into no more than sixteen years, from 1596 to 1612. The conclusion seems inescapable that Cecil must bear some responsibility for the decline of official morality that was in the end to have such serious political consequences. For if in his handling of the wards he was no more corrupt—and a great deal more efficient—than his father, his conduct as Lord Treasurer is more open to question. A number of transactions carried out by him in this capacity are clearly very unsavoury. Moreover one of the most sinister features of the early seventeenth century is the stranglehold obtained upon government finances by the customs farmers, and here Salisbury's personal financial dependence upon these predatory creatures is both new and alarming. When the Lord Treasurer is as deeply in their debt as Salisbury found himself by the end of 1611, it is vain to expect the cancellation of the system, the grant of the contract to a rival syndicate, or even the negotiating of a new lease of the farm on the most advantageous terms for the Crown. Here, at any rate, things had clearly gone downhill sharply during Salisbury's tenure of office.

On the other hand it is quite wrong to suppose that Salisbury was merely the unscrupulous careerist described by his enemies. Unlike so many of his contemporaries in Early Stuart politics, he was a shrewd and clear-headed statesman who worked actively to further what he conceived to be the best interests of his country. He greatly improved Crown revenues, both as Master of the Court of Wards and as Lord Treasurer. As Master he took novel—even revolutionary—steps to protect the interests of his charges. There is not the slightest evidence that he allowed his Spanish pension to affect his judgment on foreign policy, and on at any rate one occasion, when he proposed the Great Contract, he was deliberately putting the public interest before his personal advantage. Moreover in his position, scrupulous honesty would have been not merely eccentric, but impossible. The stagnation of official salaries during a price revolution coupled with Elizabeth's parsimony in the 1590s made corruption a necessity for a younger son living at Court with his way to make in the world. And when his position should have improved thanks to the generosity of King James, he found himself caught up in a fiercely competitive struggle for conspicuous consumption, and in particular in a race for ostentatious building. It was in order to raise money for his buildings that during the last four years of his life Salisbury was obliged to use his official powers for corrupt personal ends. When we seek the causes of the decline of financial probity at the Jacobean Court, we must not forget Audley End and Hatfield, Bramshill and Cranborne, Northumberland House and Holland House.

ENGLAND AND THE MEDITERRANEAN,
1570-1670

THE growing strength of the English economy in the half-century or so before the Civil War is nowhere more clearly expressed than in its relations with the Mediterranean. In this period English industry solved technical problems which had hitherto held it back, and flooded the markets of the eastern and western Mediterranean with woollen goods, incidentally reducing Turkey and Italy to the role of suppliers of industrial raw materials. English shipping solved the problems of combining self-defence with commerce, plied a large traffic through the Straits of Gibraltar and captured a leading place in the carrying trade within the Mediterranean itself; English merchants established themselves all over the Mediterranean and the Near and Far East, passing directly to England a trade which had largely been channelled through the cities of Italy, and making superfluous the presence of Venetian or Florentine merchant houses in London. There are well-known reasons why these developments took place at this particular time. The collapse of the Antwerp entrepot and the intense if short-lived disturbance of economic life elsewhere in the Netherlands, during the Dutch War of Independence, not only made it necessary to open new channels of trade, but also made it easier to establish direct connections with the old customers of the overland routes; the engrossment of Venice in war with Turkey in 1570-73 turned attention to opportunities in the carrying trade between western Europe and the Mediterranean; finally, the fusion of Portugal with a hostile Spain in 1580 strengthened the determination to trade independently with the Portuguese-dominated Far East.

These successive political events on the continent in the decade of the seventies, were the occasions which directed English efforts towards new avenues of profit; but the occasions would have come and gone unnoticed had not the English economy already grown strong enough to provide the capital and organisation for opening new and distant trades, re-creating a merchant fleet and developing industrial responses to the new demands. Escaping from economic tutelage at the hands of Germans, Flemings, Italians and Spaniards, the English had in the course of the sixteenth century grown in capacity and confidence and begun to push beyond their old markets on the western coasts of Europe when these ceased to provide scope for expansion. In the new century opportunities were widening and the Mediterranean footholds which had been secured were extended, as England took over more and more of the functions of the weakening mercantile and industrial cities of Italy.

The influence upon industry of the new developments is seen specially clearly through the trade with the Iberian peninsula and the Levant. The former, associated with the development of the 'new draperies' has been closely examined by Professor Fisher, and will not be discussed here.[1] But changes in the older cloth industries, though rather longer delayed, were hardly less important, and the progress of the English Levant trade is closely connected with them.[2] This trade was opened just after 1580, following some years of cautious negotiation, when war was making overland connections with Italy, and through Italy with Turkey, very difficult; but it continued to expand rapidly even after these troubles were past and the land routes were operating freely again. It may reasonably be asked, therefore, why it was that English traders and their products were able to maintain themselves permanently in these new markets, which had for so long been dominated by the Italians and the French.

The staples of the early English trade to the Levant were goods which had long been exported from England—kerseys, lead, tin.

[1] F. J. Fisher, 'London's Export Trade in the Early Seventeenth Century', *Econ. Hist. Rev.*, 2nd ser. III (1950-51), pp. 151-161.

[2] Dr. T. S. Willan's useful account of the trade in *Eng. Hist. Rev.*, LXX (1955) pp. 399-410, stops at 1600 when vital changes in the character of the trade were about to take place.

These are the goods which John Sanderson, in his letters from Aleppo and Constantinople in the nineties, constantly refers to;[1] the lead and tin supplied much of Turkish needs, but the kerseys touched only the surface of the great market for woollen cloth which existed in the Near East. Fynes Morison wrote in 1596 'The English bring to the Turks kersies wrought and dyed, of divers kinds and colours, but they bring little broadcloth, wherewith they are aboundantlie furnished from Venice.'[2] Kersies, wrought and dyed, were old-established products of English industry; but in the principal centres of the much larger broadcloth manufacture, in Wiltshire and Gloucestershire, attention had long been directed on supplying to London merchants, for export to Antwerp, a semi-finished material for dyeing and dressing on the continent. In the face of increasing difficulties in their old markets, merchants continued to attempt the export of these white cloths, through Hamburg or Middelberg or Dort; these vested interests prevented a rapid development of English dyeing and finishing industries, though the immigration of skilled artisans in the sixties and the direct import of eastern dyestuffs by the Levant Company from the eighties onward must have provided opportunities for it.[3] A much smaller producing region, however, along the Essex-Suffolk border, had long been making dyed broadcloths, though of a different quality. Its chief markets were in the Baltic, and in the last quarter of the sixteenth century (again, principally because of the struggle in the Low Countries) Baltic trade was booming and making rapidly increasing demands on the Suffolk industry. This trade, after reaching a peak when the famines of 1594-97 drew vast corn imports from the Baltic, began to fall away;[4] and from this time dyed Suffolk broadcloths were shipped among the kerseys in English ships bound for the Levant. In 1598, alongside an

---

[1] *The Travels of John Sanderson, 1584-1611* (Hakluyt Society, 1930).

[2] *Itinerary Containing Ten Years Travels* (1907) IV, p. 124.

[3] The development of dyeing of these cloths may have been held back by the attempts of the London dyers to secure control of it, culminating in the Cockayne project of 1613. London water was unsuitable for high quality dyeing with the techniques then available.

[4] R. W. K. Hinton, *The Eastland Trade and the Common Weal* (Cambridge, 1959), p. 24.

export of 18,031 kerseys, 750 broadcloths went to the territories of the Levant Company.[1] The introduction of these broadcloths quickly revealed to the English traders a large potential demand in Smyrna, Constantinople and Aleppo. Exports were rapidly expanded, partly at the expense of kerseys, partly to the detriment of Venetian manufactures of heavy cloth which had previously held the field. During the next two decades kerseys were first driven from the main Turkish trading centres to find outlets in the minor ports of Ragusa and Spalato which served the north Balkans and Hungary, and then swept completely into oblivion. In 1606 2,776 Suffolk broadcloths went into Italy and the Levant[2] alongside 10,349 kersies;[3] in 1621, to the Levant Company's territory, about 7,500 broadcloths and 2,300 kerseys; and 1629 was the last year when kersies appeared in the Mediterranean in any quantity.[4] By 1621, when the Levant Company records first become regularly available, an average of over 6,000 broadcloths a year was being exported. It is true that shipments were intermittent, and as they grew larger became less frequent. The 1621 fleet took 7,500 broadcloths; that of 1629 12,000—but the following year none went at all; and the largest shipment before the Civil War, of 17,000 cloths in 1634, was followed by two years without exports.[5] The yearly average, however, was at least maintained. There was a growing re-export of English cloths from Leghorn to the Levant, which if it was handled by foreigners did not pay the Levant Company's dues when it arrived in Turkey; it was always quite small in relation to the direct export from England, but its growth implies a

---

[1] T. S. Willan, *op. cit.*, p. 409.

[2] A. Friis, *Alderman Cockayne's Project and the Cloth Trade* (Copenhagen, 1927), p. 62. Some kersies, and a very few broadcloths, also went overland to Venice and on to Turkey at this time. The share of Italy in the seaborne export shown in these figures was almost certainly negligible.

[3] A broadcloth was officially reckoned to be worth at least four times as much as a kersey.

[4] From the Levant Company's ledgers in the Public Record Office: SP 105-57/159.

[5] This partly accounts for the wildly excessive estimates of the total export made by contemporaries, English and Venetian; estimates which have been repeated in modern works on the subject.

gradual increase in the total amounts of English broadcloth going to the Levant. During the Civil War and its aftermath there were few very large shipments to the Levant, but the average export was virtually maintained, and after the Restoration there was a very rapid expansion of the trade; average annual export was from 1666-72 13,762, and from 1673-77 20,075 cloths.[1] Even the chief mourner of English decay, the author of *Brittania Languens* (1680) was driven to the reluctant conclusion that 'It must be confessed, that we have supported our Turkey-trade better than any other'[2]—an unfortunate lapse, for at this very date the trade was turning towards slow decline in the face of French competition, a decline in which it was not accompanied by any of the trades for which the writer had promised a disastrous future.

Broadcloth export to the Levant had been pioneered by the relatively small Suffolk industry. From the twenties onward, the developed and stabilised export came to be based increasingly upon a new source of supply in the west country, which during the second quarter of the seventeenth century was quickly turning, amid the collapse of its old markets for unfinished cloth, to the creation of dyeing and finishing branches to deal with its products.

The history of cloth dyeing in England is still obscure. One thing is absolutely clear, however; that in the first decade of the seventeenth century very much more than half the cloth exported from England was undyed, whereas before 1670 undyed cloth had become an unimportant part of England's export trade.[3] The decisive changes had taken place before mid-century, when dyeing had become securely established in the great strongholds of the white cloth industry, Gloucestershire and Wiltshire. Dyeing at Stroudwater had its origin about 1605, according to the tradition of the next generation;[4] the 2,545 cloth workers listed in Gloucestershire in 1608 included 47

---

[1] *Historical Manuscripts Comm., House of Lords Mss., 1706-08*, p. 251.
[2] J. R. McCulloch, ed., *Early Tracts on Commerce* (1856), p. 401.
[3] This is not due to the development of new types of cloth; even at the end of the seventeenth century over a quarter of cloth exports were broadcloths of one kind or another, and in the 'sixties the proportion was probably well over a third.
[4] SPD Charles I, 287-97.

dyers—a number which suggests an already considerable output of dyed cloth.[1] Fuller, writing in 1661, took dyeing for granted as something long settled in Gloucestershire, based on 'the benefit of an excellent water for colouring their cloth, being the sweet rivulet of Stroud.'[2] In Wiltshire and Worcestershire dyed cloths, at first of Spanish wool but soon using English material, were appearing after 1620 and their production was spreading fast in the thirties.[3] The counterpart of such developments was the decline of the Suffolk broadcloth industry, turning to baymaking in the face of this competition from a section of the cloth manufacture which had greater resources than its own.

These changes within the industry are plainly reflected in the Levant trade. The Port Books of 1618 show a few 'long westerns' and 'long Glosters' appearing among the Suffolk cloths; by 1632 these western cloths have far advanced in numbers; a decade later they dominate the trade. In February 1642 the House of Commons spared a moment from more desperate concerns to set up a committee which should consider 'how the Suffolk cloths may be vented in Turkey, as they formerly have been'.[4]

Dyed and finished broadcloths, first from Suffolk but later from the west of England, replaced Italian heavy cloths in Turkish markets, gaining a foothold in the last years of the sixteenth century and rapidly making their grip more secure. The new light cloths of East Anglia and Devonshire never found a sale in the eastern Mediterranean, where cottons and silks were so readily available for summer wear; but when the cold gales of autumn blew from the uplands of Asia

---

[1] R. H. Tawney, 'An Occupational Census of the Seventeenth Century', *Econ. Hist. Rev.* VIII (1934), p. 55.

[2] *The History of the Worthies of England* (1811), I, p. 374.

[3] *Victoria County History of England, Wiltshire*, IV, p. 153; *Worcestershire*, II, pp. 301-2. See also the petitions on dyeing from Wiltshire, Gloucestershire, Somersetshire, and Worcestershire, in *Calendar of State Papers Domestic, 1640*, pp. 188-89. Dr. G. D. Ramsay in *The Wiltshire Woollen Industry* (Oxford, 1943) has closely examined the growing manufacture of dyed 'Spanish cloth'; but this is far from being the whole story of west country dyeing, and the Levant Company's exports never included many Spanish cloths.

[4] *Journals of the House of Commons*, II, 429.

Minor and the Balkans the prosperous Turk or Persian counted himself lucky to be wrapped in the thickest and heaviest of English woollens. Though the sale of these in eastern markets could not be promoted until adequate quantities of dyed and finished cloth were produced in England, the fulfilment of this condition does not by itself explain their success in capturing Turkish markets; and in particular why they were able, from the twenties onward, to replace Venetian cloth to an extent which English broadcloths dyed and finished at Antwerp had never done. 'The Londons do the greatest harm to Venetian cloth' wrote the Venetian bailo at Constantinople in 1630 'as they not only imitate its colours, but can sell it at a lower price, thus tempting the lower and middle classes to buy... cloth like it cannot be made at Venice except at a much higher cost, because wool is so plentiful in England.'[1] And again, five years later 'The English devote their attention to depriving our people of the little trade that remains to them in the mart of Constantinople, as they imitate Venetian cloth and make borders after the Venetian manner.'[2]

Though it is true that the English used native wool, while the Venetians relied in the main on imports from Spain, this was clearly an English advantage of long standing; indeed, it was precisely at this point of time that England herself was beginning to import Spanish wool for the making of certain kinds of cloth. It may be true that Spanish wool prices were rising faster than English, but the data to establish this do not exist. As to labour costs, the position is much clearer. The sharp fall in real wages in England during this period is well known;[3] among the Wiltshire cloth workers 'in spite of the upward movement of prices, wages rose little, if at all, between the middle of the sixteenth and the first ten years of the seventeenth century.'[4] In Italy, on the other hand, municipal and gild controls

---

[1] *Calendar of State Papers, Venetian*, 20th April 1630.
[2] *ibid.*, 14th March 1635.
[3] See, for example, E. H. Phelps Brown and S. V. Hopkins, 'Wage Rates and Prices; Evidence for Population Pressure in the Sixteenth Century', *Economica*, n.s. XXIV, 1957.
[4] *Victoria County History, Wiltshire*, IV, p. 149.

appear to have kept industrial wages much more closely in line with the rising price level.[1]

The stability of the English cloth industry's costs in this period had many repercussions. Mr. Supple has pointed out how rigid costs kept prices too high to retain markets in central and eastern Europe where currency adjustments were making local products relatively cheaper.[2] Professor Fisher cites the inability to lower the prices of existing types of cloth as a reason why expansion had to take the form of new materials for new markets.[3] But in the eastern Mediterranean the effect was different again. For, with the costs and prices of Italian competitors here actually rising, this same stability of English costs enabled traditional broadcloths to capture the Turkish market.[4]

The great export of broadcloths secured for England, during most of the seventeenth century, an exceptionally healthy balancing of imports and exports in the trade with Turkey.[5] 'Of all Europe' wrote Thomas Mun in 1621 'this nation drove the most profitable trade to Turkey by reason of the vast quantities of broadcloth, tin, etc. which we exported thither, enough to purchase all the wares we wanted in Turkey, whereas a balance in money is paid by the other nations trading thither.'[6] Indeed, the Levant Company at times expressed alarm at the difficulty its members had in securing enough goods in Turkey to balance the supply of English cloth sent there.[7] The view

[1] C. M. Cipolla 'The Decline of Italy', *Econ. Hist. Rev*, 2nd ser., V (1952–53), pp 183–185.

[2] B. E. Supple, 'Currency and Commerce in the Early Seventeenth Century', *Econ. Hist. Rev.*, 2nd ser., X, (1957) pp. 246–254.

[3] *op. cit.*, pp. 156–159.

[4] The same reason may go far to account for the success of English cloth in Spain, Portugal and Italy in this period; the new draperies which went to these countries were to some extent, at least, competing with Italian cloth.

[5] This was probably not true in the sixteenth century, before broadcloths appeared in quantity; Dr. Willan considers that there was then an excess of imports. *op. cit.*, p. 410.

[6] 'A Discourse of Trade from England to the East Indies', in J. R. McCulloch, ed., *Early Tracts on Commerce* (1856), pp. 32–33.

[7] Levant Company Register Book, SP 105–143, 11th October 1633. *Historical Manuscripts Commission, Finch Mss.*, II, p. 165.

that the English, alone among traders to the Levant, exchanged goods for goods rather than taking large quantities of cash to meet an excess of imports, was widely repeated by foreign observers as well as by interested English parties, and such trade statistics as are available do not contradict it.

Moreover, the exchange was of English manufactures[1] for foreign raw materials. The trade can almost be reduced, in fact, to the exchange of broadcloth for raw silk; in ordinary years the greater part of export and import values was in these two commodities. Not only did the opening up of the connection with Turkey lead to new opportunities for the English woollen industry; it also stimulated entirely new industries in England, because of the character of the goods which were offered in return. Raw silk, which was imported in negligible quantities in the mid-sixteenth century, came in substantial and rapidly rising volume from the time of the opening of the Levant trade, and became the largest of English raw material imports; from 11,904 lbs. in 1560 its volume rose to 117,740 lbs. in 1621 and 357,434 lbs. in 1669.[2] By James I's time a silk industry of some size existed in England, and it continued to grow rapidly for nearly two hundred years. Similarly the cotton industry established itself, though on a much smaller scale, as the raw material began to flow into England from Smyrna and Cyprus.[3]

The Levant trade, then, fulfilled all the dreams of the mercantilist; balanced, offering raw materials in exchange for English manufactures, employing large ships on a distant voyage, handled throughout by English merchants. The mercantilist and his dreams may be abstractions of the modern historian; the merchant was real, and for him, it appears, the Levant trade had great bounty to offer. It was a trade handling valuable goods in great quantities, for which large capital or very extensive credit was necessary; this restricted indis-

[1] The value of lead and tin exports was very small.
[2] Figures for 1560 and 1621 from A. E. Millard, 'The Import Trade of London, 1600-1640' (unpublished London Ph. D. thesis, 1956), Vol. III, table 3; for 1669 from BM Add. Mss. 36785. There was a small import of silk by the Russia Company in the 1560's and later, and by the East India Company after 1620.
[3] It is not suggested that the import of raw materials was the sole basis of these industries; but it contributed very much to their establishment.

criminate entry to the trade, which was further reduced by high apprenticeship premiums, and by the practice of sending the young men under training to learn a part of their business in Aleppo or Smyrna, where death rates were extraordinarily high. For those who could survive the obstacles to become Levant merchants in London, it was an immensely profitable trade; the roll of the wealthiest merchants of the early seventeenth century includes many whose chief trading interests lay in the Levant—Sir Paul Pindar, Sir Henry Garway, Sir Morris Abbott, Sir Thomas Soame, Sir Andrew Riccard. The title of 'Turkey merchant' was later a general synonym for vast riches, and in the eighteenth century the apprenticeship premiums taken by these merchants—500, 1000, 1200 guineas—were never exceeded by those of any other trade or profession, or even equalled except by a rare entrant to the dignified and lucrative craft of banking.

Hardly less important were the opportunities which appeared in the Mediterranean for the expansion of English shipping interests. It may be doubted whether English ships ever entirely ceased, during the sixteenth century, from passing into the Mediterranean;[1] but it is certain that their appearances during the middle decades of the century were very rare. The European shipping industry was dominated during these decades by a recently developed class of large cargo carriers—vessels which were short, beamy and slow, but operated very cheaply in relation to the tonnage they could carry. The great hulks used by the Hanseatics in northern Europe, the Portuguese carracks which brought the wealth of the Indies to Europe, the Mediterranean argosies of Venice and Ragusa—these held the carrying trade of Europe, to the detriment of trading nations such as England which were backward in adopting them, possibly because their trade was not large enough to warrant the use of vessels of such size. The Dutch flyboat which emerged late in the century was a modified type of this slow and almost defenceless cargo carrier; it transported most of the cargoes of north European waters throughout the seventeenth century.

English building of large ships emerged in a different school. The

[1] T. S. Willan, op. cit., pp. 399-404.

opening of English long-distance enterprises, in which some large vessels were used, dated only from the fifteen-seventies; trading to a Mediterranean whose gateway was commanded by an already hostile Spain, illegal trade and privateering in the Caribbean and on the coast of Brazil, operations on the coast of Africa in the face of armed Portuguese and Dutch opposition. For more than a quarter of a century of open or disguised war, English ships of any size were built with an eye to speed, manoeuvrability and defence, sacrificing cheapness of operation so that in ordinary commercial conditions it was impossible to compete (except in the carriage of high-value goods) with Dutch flyboats or Hanseatic hulks.

English ships were successful in their re-entry to the Mediterranean, and in maintaining and extending the place they won there, because for a long stretch of time 'ordinary commercial conditions' did not exist in that sea, and relative costs of operation could no longer be absolutely decisive in determining the kind or nationality of ships to be employed. The Anglo-Spanish-French-Dutch war which occupied the last decades of the sixteenth century created in England, Holland and France a vast privateering industry, partly large-scale and organised on business-like lines by rich merchants, but also to some extent a freelance affair of ships' captains who were more interested in the value than in the nationality of potential prizes. The signing of the Franco-Spanish peace in 1599 and of the Anglo-Spanish peace in 1604 left many of these seamen without legitimate occupation in the highly specialised profession which they had been practising for a decade or more. Many of them were suspect in their own countries owing to their lack of discrimination in taking prizes. Those who continued to operate after their countries made peace found themselves outlaws and pirates, enemies of Christendom, and they turned naturally to the older-established anti-Christians, the Moorish corsair communities of the south Mediterranean coast and Morocco. To these technically backward warriors they brought the example of the use of the latest fighting ships of north-west Europe. From the first years of the new century records are full of reports of the deeds of English, French, Dutch, Scots and Germans, operating from Algiers, Tunis or their own base at Mamora.[1] The respectable merchants of London and Nantes, erstwhile financiers of privateering, learned to shudder at the names of Ward and Danziger, Bishop and Sansom. Their European crews were gradually replaced, as time passed, by Moors; one after another they died, retired or took service under the Moorish rulers; Moorish captains adopted their ships and their tactics. In twenty years the European renegades had served their purpose and most of them had disappeared from the Mediterranean scene. They had taught the Moors to abandon their galleys and create sailing ship fleets; and the sailing ships were modelled upon English and French fighting ships. To one of the many protests at corsair activities directed to the Turkish Sultan who was nominally their suzerain, he replied that 'the fault lay with those who introduced the pirate *bertons*[2] at Tunis and Algiers, who were English, French and Flemings. They taught the people of Barbary, who before that time had not known what *bertons* were.'[3] In making this transformation so quickly, the Moors were alone among the European states;[4] the Italian maritime cities remained faithful to their unwieldy argosies until far past the middle of the century, the Spanish Mediterranean marine was still largely composed of galleys; the French operated a multitude of fast, but tiny, craft from Marseilles. First the west Mediterranean basin, then after about 1612-13 the eastern Mediterranean and even the Atlantic coast of Europe up to the mouth of the English Channel, came to be terrorised by the corsairs.[5]

[1] Near Sallee. It was destroyed by a Spanish expedition in 1611, and those pirates who still used it were driven into the Moorish cities or, a few of them, to bases in southern Ireland.
[2] A Turkish name, subsequently adopted into Italian, for these handy and strongly armed sailing ships; there is no equivalent English word.
[3] *Calendar of State Papers, Venetian*, 27 May 1624.
[4] An estimate of *naval* strength in the Mediterranean in 1618 suggested that the strength of the corsair fleets in African ports was larger than that of all the other Mediterranean powers together. (*Calendar of State Papers, Venetian*, 21 July 1618).
[5] The history of the corsairs is dealt with in S. Lane-Poole, *The Barbary Corsairs* (1890) and L. Playfair, *The Scourge of Christendom* (1884). Sir Godfrey Fisher's *Barbary Legend* (1957) presents a different view of them.

The English ships which were by this time passing in and out of the Mediterranean had in this situation great advantages. The corsairs were not anxious to attack ships which could defend themselves, since there was so much easier prey. The great ships employed by the Levant Company, of 400, 500, 600 tons—ships regularly incorporated in the line-of-battle fleet in every English war before 1689—were powerfully gunned and adequately manned; they were usually too strong to be successfully attacked.[1] They, and similar Dutch vessels, were for some decades the safest ships in the Mediterranean; Turks, Venetians and even the Spanish Viceroy of Naples sought to hire them to augment their fighting fleets in wartime. Even the smaller English ships, of 150-250 tons, which came only into the western and central Mediterranean to trade with Malaga, Alicante, Genoa, Leghorn, Naples and Messina were strongly armed for their size and could defend themselves against single corsairs.[2] The Dutch, too, normally used defensible ships in the Mediterranean trades, and therefore failed, in those trades, to secure the great competitive advantages over English shipping which they had everywhere else.

These English (and Dutch) ships therefore came to be demanded, not only for the carriage of goods from western Europe, but also for the maintenance of much of the inter-Mediterranean traffic. From the end of the Anglo-Spanish war in 1604 they are to be found carrying Spanish wool to Italy, Sicilian corn to northern Italy and Spain, as well as sugar, hides and bullion from the Portuguese and Spanish ports just outside the Mediterranean to Italy. By the twenties English carriers were acquiring a strong position in the eastern Mediterranean as well, and even Venetian merchants, whose ships had formerly met their own needs adequately, were seeking to hire

[1] The artillery of the time could not, without great luck, do much harm to an ocean sailing vessel; to capture her she must be boarded. A manoeuvrable ship, well handled and with a reasonable broadside of guns, could do immense havoc among the men clustered to board her, and had a good chance of defeating their intentions completely.

[2] A large part of the heavy loss of English merchant ships to the corsairs in the twenties and thirties took place around the south and west coasts of England, to which the corsairs were then giving much attention, and where they found a multitude of small and lightly armed coasters and short sea traders.

English vessels.[1] It is quite clear that the defensibility, not the cheapness, of English ships was securing them these cargoes. As early as 1609, it had been noted that the Levant Company 'fit out their vessels excellently, and never let themselves be tempted to take such cargo as would hamper the navigation of the vessel or hinder them from fighting if occasion offered.'[2] In 1627, when Venetians at Constantinople wanted to hire English ships, they admitted that freight rates were 10% higher than their own; but they expected to save much of the excess by paying lower insurance premiums.[3] The following year the Venetian ambassador at Constantinople reported that the freight of English ships was higher 'as they carry more sailors and gunners and less cargo, leaving plenty of room for fighting.'[4] English ships became heavily engaged in the great traffic in corn from the Greek Archipelago to Italy,[5] and the Levant Company itself was eventually driven to complain that its members were suffering from 'the great trade driven by strangers in English shipping' between Turkish ports and Leghorn, Genoa and Marseilles.[6]

The second half of the century saw the growth, in rivalry, of English and Dutch (and later French) naval power. Rapidly eclipsing all others at sea in the creation of large fleets of specialised warships it was natural that when not engaged in mutual destruction they should turn their forces to the suppression of the piratical war which incessantly threatened their merchant ships in the Mediterranean. Under Charles I an effort had been made to exert pressure; but Mansell's expedition of 1621 was a failure which enraged while it emboldened the corsairs. In the thirties a serious effort was made to clear the Irish coast which they were by this time infesting, but in the

[1] See, for example, *Calendar of State Papers, Venetian*, 20 September 1625, 13th February 1626, 2nd October 1627, 16th September 1628, 1st March 1629.
[2] *ibid.* 6th May 1609.
[3] *ibid.* 2nd October 1627.
[4] *ibid.* 3rd March 1629.
[5] *ibid.* 14th October 1627, 11th September 1629, 24th November 1629, 27th December 1631. See also the Levant Company letter to Constantinople, 3rd June 1626 (S.P. 105-111) and Court Minutes of 30 March 1636 and 5 February 1638 (SP 105-149).
[6] Court Minutes, 15 February 1636 (SP 105-149).

Mediterranean they were left to themselves. Blake's Commonwealth
fleet which drove the Dutch from the Mediterranean, however, was
turned to the corsair problem in 1655; it destroyed the port and
fortifications of Tunis and its menace drove all the corsair communities to treat with him and agree to grant immunity to English ships.
With the decline of English prestige after 1658 there were new attacks
on them, but under naval pressure the authorities at Tunis, Tripoli and
Algiers signed treaties from 1662 onward guaranteeing immunity
to English ships; the system of Mediterranean passes, to be issued by
the English Admiralty to establish identity, was brought into being.
Difficulties did not cease at once, for the Moorish seamen were not
conspicuously obedient or loyal to their rulers. In particular, the practice of taking foreign goods and passengers from English ships was not
entirely abandoned, though specifically forbidden by treaty; it was
indeed to some extent encouraged by the treaties, for English seamen
who could feel that surrender no longer meant slavery for them became less anxious to risk life and limb by fighting to defend the
ships they sailed in and the property they carried. There were serious
scandals which damaged the English reputation, and the government
endeavoured to meet them by passing the *Act Against the Yielding up
of Merchants Ships*[1] in 1665, which laid down penalties on masters
of ships 'who shall yield up the said Goods to any Turkish Ships or
Vessels or to any Pirate or Sea Rover.' A further naval expedition
under Allin and Spragge in 1669-71 blockaded Algiers and destroyed
a corsair fleet at Bougie; thereafter the English flag seems to have given
complete protection to merchant ships. Until far into the eighteenth
century this capacity to force the Moors to respect treaties was considered to give English shipping great advantages over vessels of the
weaker Mediterranean states and the smaller maritime powers such
as Hamburg and Denmark.[2]

The exercise of naval power changed the conditions under which
English ships held their large share of Mediterranean carrying trade.
Formerly based on the merchant ship's own defensive capacity, it

[1] 16 Charles II, c. 6. It was renewed in 1671 by 22/23 Charles II, c. 11.
[2] M. S. Anderson 'Great Britain and the Barbary States in the Eighteenth Century', *Bulletin of the Institute of Historical Research*, 1956, p. 89.

was after 1655 increasingly dependent on the corsair's fear of the later consequences of attacking English ships. The need to carry many guns and strong crews therefore declined, and English ships in the Mediterranean were more cheaply operated. At the beginning of the century, for example, the crews of ships going into the Mediterranean commonly numbered one man to every 4.5 to 5 tons. In the early sixties, when the pass system was instituted but was too new to be completely relied on, the figure was one man to 5.9 tons; at the end of the eighties, when this system had been shown to offer a high degree of safety, it had gone up to one man to 7.5 tons. At this latter figure manning for the Mediterranean was comparable with the levels which had long been adopted for similar English ships in many other trades.[1]

The Mediterranean was the first, and for a long time the only, region where English ships took a large part in the carrying trade between foreign countries. This situation was created and for long maintained by the special dangers of Mediterranean navigation; its basis was strengthened by the growth in the volume of English cargoes going to and coming from the Mediterranean, by the creation of an English commercial base at Leghorn, and by the appearance of English naval power in the Mediterranean after 1655. Though Dutch competition was met at the beginning, it faded during the Thirty Years' War, and apart from a brief period between 1649 and 1653 English shipping always held—despite the wails of the propagandists —a rather stronger position than Dutch in these waters.

The expansion of England's Levant trade and of her Mediterranean shipping interests are both manifestations not only of the growth of English economic strength, and of the effects of particular political circumstances, but also of Italian economic decline. The mercantile interests shouldered out of Constantinople and Aleppo were Italian interests;[2] the vessels which rotted at their moorings while English

---

[1] Figures from many cases in the High Court of Admiralty, and (after 1662) from the registers of Mediterranean passes in the P.R.O. Adm. 7-75 *et seq.*
[2] The other Levant power, France, concentrated its interests on the more southerly Turkish territories in southern Syria and Egypt, and successfully fought against English influence there.

ships were sought after to take cargoes were Italian vessels. Italy, as Professor Cipolla has shown, was suffering the pains of economic decline between 1600 and 1670, and England, France and the Netherlands profited from its troubles to take over many of the Italian commercial functions in the Mediterranean.

'The economic prosperity of Italy, at the end of the sixteenth century, was mainly dependent on two things; the export on a large scale of manufactured produce (especially woollen and silk textiles) and large invisible exports in the form of world-wide banking operations and maritime transport... By the end of the seventeenth century Italy had become an economically backward and depressed area, its population was too high for its resources, its economy had become primarily agricultural. The great change had come mainly between 1600 and 1670.'[1]

This study of the English in the Mediterranean may therefore be concluded by examining the changes in the character of English relations with Italy itself. Though of less importance to English economic development in the seventeenth century than the Turkish trade or the expansion of shipping operations in the Mediterranean, Anglo-Italian trade showed changes which were even more striking, involving in important respects a complete reversal of the economic roles of England and Italy.

First in point of time was the capture of the trade between Europe and the Indian Ocean, formerly channelled through the Italian cities and the Middle East. Here the decisive event was the entry of England and Holland into direct relations by sea with the lands bordering the Indian Ocean. Though the opening of this route by the Portuguese in 1497 had damaged Mediterranean trade with the east, this trade was by no means destroyed; and during the wars in which Portugal was engaged from 1580 onward the old routes and their trade flourished. When the English and Dutch penetrated the Indian Ocean in 1598-1601, and particularly after the immense expansion in the scale of their enterprises from about 1615-17, the situation quickly changed. A glance at the supply of pepper to Europe makes this clear. The division of power in the east gave England a large part

[1] C. M. Cipolla, *op. cit.*, pp. 178, 180.

of the pepper trade, and pepper constituted, for a long time, a high proportion of the imports of the East India Company. Like other states which had to export bullion to carry on eastern trade, England secured much of that bullion by the re-export of many of the goods brought in. Though the principal markets for pepper were found in north-western Europe, records of the cargoes of English ships going into the Mediterranean begin after 1612 to include pepper and other eastern goods, and within a few years pepper was found in quantity in most of these ships. In 1623 a London merchant wrote of the distribution of eastern goods to 'Germany, Poland, many parts of Ita'y and even Venice.'[1] In 1640 the East India Company settled its own agents at Leghorn (and temporarily at Venice and Messina) to sell pepper;[2] in 1654, it estimated that four-fifths of the annual pepper imports were re-exported to 'Turks, Italians, French, Germans and Poles.'[3] Occasionally, as in 1626, 1643 and 1644, pepper was even carried to Turkey to compete with supplies coming overland or through Alexandria;[4] but Italy, so lately the entrepot for eastern goods on their way to western Europe, was now the chief Mediterranean market for these same goods entering that sea through the Straits of Gibraltar.

Secondly, though Italy was still the centre of a great woollen industry, it began towards the end of the sixteenth century to expand its small imports of English woollen cloth. Its old imports had been kerseys, possibly for shipment further east; the new imports were the 'new draperies' of Norfolk and Suffolk. The growth of these imports to Italy was slow, but by 1640 the trade was firmly established, and many Italians were becoming accustomed to being clothed in English woollens, while their own woollen industry was falling into decay around them.

Pepper and other eastern products, and cheap English woollens, needed a port of entry into Italy. They found such a place in Leghorn, declared a free port in 1593 and rapidly developing its resources

[1] *Calendar of State Papers, Venetian*, 2nd June 1623.
[2] *Calendar of Court Minutes of the East India Company, 1640-09, passim.*
[3] *ibid., 1650-54*, p. 349.
[4] Levant Company Ledgers, SP 105-157/159.

under enlightened rulers, with the financial support of Genoese merchants whose activities were restricted by their city's close association with Spain.[1] From Leghorn the Plain of Lombardy, where much of the Italian population was concentrated, could be reached by a short journey by waterway and land to Bologna. Once ships began to call at Leghorn with cargoes for disposal, the port began to attract from the overland route Italian exports bound for England, and the outbreak of the Thirty Years' War accentuated this tendency. As late as 1621 England's direct imports from Italy were negligible, while quantities of silk goods, obviously in the main Italian, came in via the Netherlands and Germany. A few years later this overland trade had been replaced by direct import from Italy, and nine-tenths of this import was shipped from Leghorn.[2] The overland route never completely recovered. Leghorn, therefore, quickly became a depot for English goods, and a port of call for nearly all English ships going to southern Italy, the Levant or the Venetian islands. Moreover, by 1630 English ships were lading Florentine textiles at Leghorn not merely for England but also to carry on to Turkey,[3] and a few years later the Levant Company was imposing special dues on English ships which went from Leghorn to lade goods in Turkey without its license.[4] Before the Civil War Leghorn had become the chief port of Italy, and, unlike the other Italian cities, one in which the foreigner could live and trade on the same terms as the native. Its streets were thronged with merchants of all nations of east and west—Armenians and Indians as well as Germans and French—and among these the English held an important place. Meanwhile in London, where once there had been whole colonies of Venetian and Florentine merchants, hardly one remained.

More slowly, but even more decisively, the structure of the English import trade from Italy was changing. Little had come from Italy to England, before 1570, except silk goods, and these had travelled by the overland route. With the growth of wealth in England, and

---

[1] See *Calendar of State Papers, Venetian*, 16 April 1628, 18 March 1645.
[2] A. Millard, *op. cit.*, Vol. I, Appendix, Table 14; Vol. III, Table C.
[3] *Calendar of State Papers, Venetian*, 15 April 1628.
[4] Court Minutes, 11 October 1633 (SP 105-149).

especially with the spreading habit of proclaiming wealth by ostent-
ation in dress, the import of these silk goods was fully maintained;
they were hardly affected by the appearance of the English silk
industry, which made stuffs of poorer quality competing with French
imports. Silks began to be supplemented, however, by other imports
from Italy, and these were all of agrarian products.[1] First were cur-
rants, coming from the Venetian islands of Zante and Cephalonia,
imported after 1570 in quantities which expanded continuously and
rapidly right up to the Civil War, and stabilised at the high level then
reached. Growing demand over-stimulated production in the islands,
and prices fell heavily, so that the value of the import possibly showed
little change between 1600 and 1640, though its volume increased
fourfold. English merchants settled in the islands early in the seventeenth century and were soon handling all the crop, buying it from
the peasants and holding it to sell when the English ships arrived;
Venetian merchant houses were completely driven from the trade.
Rather later an import of Italian olive oil was undertaken, which
gradually replaced the Spanish supply; by the 1630's Italy supplied
the greater part of England's rapidly growing needs. In 1635 it was
complained that so many ships from England were lading oil in
Apulia that a shortage was created at Venice.[2] Again, the trade was
handled, even before 1640, by English merchants settled in the south
Italian ports.

Still later in time, but ultimately to be of the greatest importance,
came the import of Italian raw silk or silk yarn. The date of its beginning is uncertain, for silk imports from Leghorn included Turkish
silk; but Italian silk was the subject of argument as to its quality in
London in 1656, and appears not to have been very well known at
that date.[3] In 1672, when Venice was considering whether direct
export of silk to England should be allowed, a substantial export was
already being carried on from Venetian territory through Bologna

---

[1] There were other imports of course, of goods for which Venice was famous—
glass, gold thread, paper—but their value was small in relation to that of imports dealt with here.

[2] *Calendar of State Paper, Venetian*, 24 March, 1635.

[3] *Calendar of State Papers, Domestic*, 3 June 1656.

and Leghorn.[1] In 1669, nearly one-third (by weight) of the silk imported to England came from Italy; most of this was yarn, not raw silk.[2] From the 1680's the English silk industry began to grow very rapidly, and Italy steadily overtook Turkey as the supplier of material for it, perhaps because of the efficiency of the Italian silk-throwing machinery whose secrets John Lombe brought to England in 1717. The obverse of this expansion was the collapse, in the early eighteenth century, of the trade in Italian silk manufactures to England; but English imports of Italian silk were in 1750 three times as great in value as the manufactures had ever been.

The character of English imports from Italy was, then, rapidly altering during the seventeenth century; the total was increasingly made up of the products not of industry but of agriculture, and the completion of this development soon after 1700 turned Italy into yet another country which exchanged its agricultural products for English manufactures. The whole enormous expansion of English Mediterranean interests between 1570 and 1670 was in a Mediterranean becoming complementary to the English economy, a contributor towards English industrial and commercial expansion; the old focus of European wealth and mercantile influence was sinking back into the role of another Baltic, subservient to the requirements of the powers bordering the Atlantic Ocean.

---

[1] *Calendar of State Papers, Venetian*, 18 November 1672.
[2] BM. Add. Mss. 36785.

CHARLES I AND THE CITY[1]

I

AMONG the most familiar and acceptable commonplaces of textbooks on seventeenth century political history is the notion that the hostility which the economic and financial policies of Charles I created among the business interests of London was one of the most important reasons for the defeat of the Crown in the Civil War. But the reasons why the great majority of businessmen opposed the Crown in 1642 are not always so straightforward as is sometimes assumed. In particular, the normal orthodoxy which sees capitalists in general becoming increasingly exasperated by a monarchy which was determined to keep the economy in a strait-jacket is one of the dangerous half-truths of historiography. In recent years one school of thought has tended to see the opposition of business interests to the Crown as the natural result of the divergence of interest between a rapidly maturing business class and a monarchy which had still not emerged from the 'feudal' stage. Conversely, the fact that certain important business men, who were undoubtedly capitalists by any rational criteria, are to be found on the royalist side in the Civil War, has led some non-Marxist historians to assume that, because these facts are difficult to fit into that economic interpretation of the choice of allegiance in 1642 which sees the conflict as a straight struggle between the 'bourgeois' and the 'feudal' elements in English society, *all* economic causation must therefore be ruled out of court. The long-derided Whig interpretations are once again in fashion. In the clash of conflicting theories a middle view which sees in econo-

---

[1] The term 'City' is here used to denote the business community not the city corporation. For a detailed account of Charles I's relations with the latter we await the publication of Mrs. Valerie Pearl's book.

mic factors a vitally important, but by no means exclusive, determinant of the allegiance of contemporaries is all too rarely considered, though Mr. Christopher Hill's recent study of the economic problems of the Church suggests one line of approach which scorns the over-simplifications of exclusively economic, political or religious causation.[1] The purpose of the present essay in historical interpretation is to spotlight the economic attitudes of some important sectors of the London business world *vis-à-vis* the economic and financial policies of the Crown. It suggests that these attitudes cannot be neglected by any serious student of the rôle of the city in the events leading up to the Civil War, a problem which has been unduly overshadowed in recent years by the fierce debate on the respective economic fortunes of the gentry and the nobility. It does not suggest, however, that the factors with which it is concerned are the only, or even in many cases the most important, determinants of business men's choice of allegiance.

II

The notion of a straightforward divergence between the interests of the Crown and those of businessmen in general will hardly survive even the most cursory examination of the economic history of the period. The interests of different types of businessmen—of, for example, the members of privileged exporting agencies, and of the interlopers who defied them, of manufacturers and of exporters, of Eastland merchants and of Merchant Adventurers—crossed at every point, and their attitude to a government which attempted, however unsuccessfully, to lay down a basic framework of policy within which their operations were to be conducted was likely to be as divergent as these operations themselves. The Court and Country alignment, which has—correctly, I think—been given so much prominence in recent writings on the period, extended into the city itself. For example, policies of financial retrenchment at Court were likely to bring

---

[1] C. Hill, *Economic Problems of the Church From Archbishop Whitgift to the Long Parliament.* (Oxford, 1956). See also his admirable essay 'Recent Interpretations of the Civil War', reprinted in *Puritanism and Revolution*, (1958), pp. 3-31.

protests from merchants no less than from the courtiers whose perquisites were threatened, as Cranfield had learnt to his cost.

In our own times a government which attempts in peacetime to
impose drastic controls or limits upon the freedom of private economic enterprise is *ipso facto* anathema to all but an eccentric minority of
businessmen. The standard description of the reaction of the city to
the policies of the early Stuarts is in many ways more appropriate to
the conditions faced by a twentieth century Labour administration
than to those which confronted the advisers of Charles I. At the beginning of the reign, the opposition among business circles was a
good deal less than solid for the reason that the economic fortunes of a
not inconsiderable number of capitalists were closely tied up with
those of the Crown. More than one historian of Elizabethan and early
Stuart England has been at pains to stress the opportunities which
were offered to the aspiring businessman by a combination of economic and administrative circumstances, the essence of which is to be
found in the familiar fact that the firm official conviction that economic control was necessary was not backed up by the administrative
resources which alone could render that control effective.[1] It is true,
of course, that our own contemporary experience suggests that, even
in the twentieth century, not a few business nests have been feathered
by the exploitation of the administrative weaknesses in a system of
state economic control. But this fact serves to strengthen rather than
to confute our argument, when it is considered how much greater—
relative, that is, to the total volume of business transactions—such
opportunities must have been in early Stuart England, when the
government, lacking the professional bureaucracy of the modern
state, had to fall back upon business interests to put into effect large
and vital sectors of its policy decisions. In these circumstances the
effect of royal policies of economic control and restraint cannot be
summed up in the simple assertion that they gave rise to antagonism
to the Crown among businessmen. They split the city, though admittedly by no means down the middle. Moreover, the acquisition

---

[1] See, for example, L. Stone, *An Elizabethan: Sir Horatio Palavicino*, (Oxford,
1956), pp. xiv–xvi and *passim*; R. H. Tawney, *Business and Politics under James I*
(Cambridge, 1958), pp. 80–120.

of those economic privileges which stemmed, to some extent at least, from the vesting of functions of public control in the hands of private individuals offered, as Professor Fisher has pointed out,[1] a peculiarly attractive field for the investor and entrepreneur in an age when the opportunities for increasing profits through technological innovation were relatively slight, and those of economic rationalization by making improvements in the pattern of the division os labour necessarily limited. Unless the early seventeenth century is considered as an exception to the rule that capital must always seek its most profitable outlet, it was surely natural that much business capital would flow into the acquisition of such privileges, investment which, by their very nature, helped to create a close tie of economic interest between the Crown and the investor. In these circumstances, that form of investment which adds to the community's stock of wealth and which is one of the conditions of economic progress might have to give way to the purchase of patents of monopoly, shares in a customs farm, licences, or the right to sell titles, to quote four obvious examples. Thus in a small way Professor Hauser's celebrated 'haemorrhage of capital' might well have been an English hardly less than a French phenomenon. To courtiers and other notabilities who stood to gain by acting as middlemen between the royal fountainhead of privilege and the business world this was a situation which offered golden opportunities. The divergence of interest between economic *ins* and *outs* cannot be confined to the familiar division between Court and Country, for its roots went no less deep in the city itself. Here the distinction in terms of economic interest is not that of Court *versus* City, but of Court and a section of the City *versus* the rest. This is the essential starting point of any discussion of the problems with which this essay is concerned.

III

It is, of course, incontestable that the situation described above created a much wider focus of economic opposition to, than support

[1] F. J. Fisher, 'Some Experiments in Company Organisation in the Early Seventeenth Century', *Econ. Hist. Rev.* IV (1933), 178-9.

for, the Crown. Among the familiar and irreconcilable sources of such opposition were those merchants who were excluded from participation in large and important sectors of the nation's foreign trade, those manufacturers who were excluded from earning a living as a result of the royal patent policy, or, at best, bled white by the patentees in return for permission to do what they had formerly done as of right, the consumers of monopolized commodities, and the dealers such as Grocers and Salters[1] who sold them. In addition there was a multitude of special interests, often themselves concessionaires of the Crown, whose operations were affected in no small way by the grant of such privileges. The successive soap monopolies of the Westminster and London soapboiling companies in the 1630's were bound to be unpopular with the Greenland and Eastland Companies. The Westminster Company was probably the more objectionable of the two, because of its avowed intention of dispensing with the use of whale oil and potash, the former being the staple commodity traded by the Greenland Company, and the latter an essential return cargo in the Baltic trade.[2] But the ability of its successor to exploit its monopolistic position to beat down the price of these materials was hardly less a source of disquiet.[3] Similarly, the bitter opposition of the planters of Bermuda and Virginia, and, far more important, the merchants of the Somers Islands Company, to the royal tobacco monopoly precipitated an appeal to and a favourable response from

---

[1] *Cal. S.P.D. 1634-5*, pp. 393-4; W. Notestein (ed.), *The Journal of Sir Simonds D'Ewes from the Beginning of the Long Parliament to the Opening of the Trial of the Earl of Strafford*, (New Haven, 1923), pp. 54, 540.

[2] W. R. Scott, *The Constitution and Finance of English, Scottish and Irish Joint-Stock Companies to 1720*, (Cambridge, 1912), II, 71-2; R. W. K. Hinton, *The Eastland Trade and the Common Weal in the Seventeenth Century*, (Cambridge, 1959), p. 45. The Westminster Company was ultimately allowed to make soap using the old materials. But the fact that the government did its utmost to prevent such materials from getting into the hands of unlicensed manufacturers must certainly have restricted effective demand. See *Cal. S.P.D. 1637*, pp. 53-4, 100.

[3] Hinton, *op. cit.*, p. 81; Privy Council Register, P.C. 2/48/299-300, 337-8; *Cal. S.P.D. 1637*, pp. 480, 513. *(1639)*, p. 45.

parliament in 1628-9.[1] Another example of a collision of interest between a chartered company and a patentee relates to a profitable sideline of the East India Company. In 1626 the company received the right to make gunpowder for its own use out of the saltpetre which it imported, a concession which in subsequent years was construed by the company to include production for the market also. The subsequent suspension in 1632 of its right to manufacture gunpowder at all is attributable to the complaints of the gunpowder monopolist, John Evelyn, and was a source of great annoyance to the company.[2] Finally, the greatest royal financial concessions, the customs farms, were extremely unpopular with all merchants who were not themselves financially interested in the farms either as directors or investors. There can be no doubt that customs duties were far more efficiently collected when they were in farm than when directly administered. Indeed, one critic of farming roundly condemned 'the extreame course taken with the Subject to paie to the uttermost exaction, with which severitie it Cannot be denyed that they were not formerly vsed.'[3] To this general grievance might be added the more particular objections of the chartered companies in foreign trade, the efficient enforcement of whose monopolistic privileges depended to no small extent upon the obedience of farmers and customs officials to conciliar orders not to allow the goods of interlopers to be landed or shipped. The Levant Company, with men like the Garways and Salter as directors of the great farm under James I, and Pindar under Charles I, had long been aware of the importance of maintaining a sphere of influence at the receipt of custom. The

---

[1] Scott, *op. cit. II*, 291-2; W. Lefroy, *Memorials of the Discovery and Early Settlement of the Bermudas or Somers Islands, 1615-1685*, (1877), I, 339-40, 347-8.

[2] P.C. 2/39/533, P.C. 2/42/87, 294; *Cal. S.P.D. 1625-6*, pp. 93, 99, 109, 111, 376; 407, *1629-31*, p. 496; *Calendar of State Papers Colonial. East Indies and Persia* (hereafter cited as *Cal. S.P.E.I.*) *1630-4*, pp. 116, 266, 273, 289, 315, 317-9. The prohibition was removed in 1635, when the company was allowed to manufacture powder for itself and for the King, but this arrangement lapsed in 1637. *Cal. S.P.D. 1635*, p. 513: E. B. Sainsbury (ed), *A Calendar of the Court Minutes etc. of the East India Company* (hereafter *C.M.E.I.C.*) *1635-1639*, pp. 49-50, 76, 101-2, 131-2.

[3] B. M. Harleian Mss. 1878, fos. 79-80.

Eastland Company was less fortunate, and appears on more than one occasion to have suffered from the fact that, so long as the most important branches of the customs revenue were administered by private concessionaires for their own profit, the dictates of self-interest would inevitably impel them to ignore the activities of the interloper so long as he paid duty.[1]

These examples are not least significant in that they demonstrate how the value of privileges granted in one sector of the economy might substantially detract from the value of privileges granted in another, a fact of some importance to which we shall have occasion to refer later. But divergence of economic interest is not simply to be found as between different sectors of the economy, nor, within a single sector, in the simple distinction between *ins* and *outs*. In the sphere of foreign trade, for example, there was no great measure of homogeneity of economic interest as between different privileged groups or even within a single group. Thus the Merchant Adventurers had no reason to love either the Eastland or the Levant Company, while their attitude to the government must have been unfavourably coloured by its discrimination against them on the behalf of these companies.[2] And even within a single privileged group there was ample room for divergence of economic interest. Professor Friis has shewn how the controversies over the location of the Merchant Adventurers' staple in the reign of James I, reflected the contradictory interests of larger and smaller adventurers,[3] while on at least one occasion the Privy Council was forced to act upon the complaints of the Eastland Company, not against interlopers, but against merchants free of the company, whose regular use of foreign ships ran counter to the terms of the proclamation of 1630.[4] Similarly, within the East India Company there were clashes between the larger stockholders, who were vitally interested because they were deeply in-

[1] P.C. 2/39/652-4, P.C. 2/41/272-4, P.C. 2/42/324-5.
[2] A. Friis, *Alderman Cockayne's Project and the Cloth Trade* (1927), pp. 387-8, 399; Hinton, *op. cit.* p. 31. For a specific example of the working of these discriminatory practices, see P.C. 2/43/482-4.
[3] Friis, *op. cit.*, pp. 390-1.
[4] P.C. 2/51/262-3, 419-20; Hinton, *op. cit.*, p. 78.

volved in the trade, and the smaller investors, whose interest was more marginal, and who were prepared to move out of East India stock when times became difficult for the company.[1] In the 1630's the Courteen project, backed as it was by Crown and Court, provided an additional element of fissure by attracting away some of the members of the company.

Similar differences can be discerned within the sphere of internal trade and manufacture. A government which was anxious to strengthen the hands of the traditional instruments of industrial control, the gilds, was bound to view sympathetically the proposals of companies such as the Weavers and the Goldsmiths that all persons practising these crafts should be members of the appropriate company.[2] But if this vague sympathy should at any time be translated into positive action, the Crown was likely to incur a hostility which was far more widespread than the support which such action elicited. This was made plain in 1630, when, in response to long-standing complaints of the Brewers Company, the government attempted to insist that all brewers in London and its environs should become members of the Brewers Company. These proposals were doubtless very popular with that body, but they elicited outraged howls of protest from a number of other companies, many of whose members had long been engaged in this lucrative business.[3] The gilds were indeed the traditional instruments of government control, but no less traditional was the so-called custom of London, whereby any freeman might practise any trade, a custom which was clearly inimical to the establishment of any really efficient degree of government control

---

[1] This difference was accentuated by the democratic system of voting in the company's General Courts, by which voting power bore no relationship to size of holding, an anomaly which the directorate bitterly regretted, but seems to have been powerless to abrogate. [See W. Foster, Introduction to *C.M.E.I.C. 1635-9*, pp. viii-x].

[2] On this subject, see J. L. Archer, 'The Industrial History of London, 1603-1640'. (M.A. thesis. London Univ. 1934), pp. 165-70.

[3] *Cal. S.P.D. 1629-31*, pp. 420, 440-1, 488; P.C. 2/40/43-5, 316, 421, London Guildhall, Repertory (of Court of Aldermen) *XLIV*, fos 322(b)-3 Remembrancia *VII*, 61.

through the medium of the gilds.[1] Moreover, attempts to translate members of major livery companies, like the Grocers, Haberdashers, Fishmongers and Clothworkers, to a minor company might be construed as an act derogatory to the social prestige of the persons concerned, as well as a prelude to the introduction of an unwelcome degree of royal control, which their coalition in a single company would undoubtedly facilitate.

IV

The foregoing pages have served to demonstrate, *inter alia*, that the economic attitudes of merchants *vis-à-vis* the Crown present far more complex historical problems than is sometimes assumed. The fashionable game of discovering royalist merchants is a harmless enough pastime, provided that it is not assumed that each discovery is a fresh nail in the coffin of economic interest as a determinant of individual allegiance in 1642. A commercial magnate, such as Sir Nicholas Crispe, who combined in himself the rôles of customs farmer, office-holder, commercial concessionaire—as founder of the Guinea Company—and holder of several patents of monopoly[2], had every *economic* reason to be a royalist, as his subsequent treatment at the hands of the Long Parliament clearly indicates. Indeed a large proportion of those merchants, who, like Crispe, inhabited the topmost regions of the business world, where commerce and high finance were inextricably intertwined, must have been to a greater or lesser degree dependent for their economic—to say nothing of their social—well-being upon remaining *personae gratae* with Crown and Court. Withdrawal of favour, such as resulted from Sir Paul Pindar's refusal to join in customs farming with Lord Goring in 1638, might spell, if not economic ruin, at least a sensible deterioration in economic

---

[1] The solution finally reached was a *pis aller* for the Crown and the company. This was that brewing members of non-brewing companies should not be translated to the Brewers Company, but that this company would have the right of search etc. over all brewers. [See P.C. 2/43/397, 655].

[2] For copperas, dyewoods and vending beads. [Notestein, *op. cit.*, pp. 312, 497, 540; Bodleian, Bankes Mss. 11/68].

fortune, and call forth prodigious efforts to regain royal support, even when, as in the case of Pindar, who regained the farm in 1640, that support was rapidly ceasing to be worth having. On a somewhat lower economic plane, the members of the powerful sugar lobby, which under both James I and Charles I succeeded in persuading the government to prohibit the establishment of new refineries in and around London, had equally good reason to support the government; just as the excluded innovators—mostly aliens it would seem—the consumers of sugar and the grocers had to be dissatisfied with it.[1]

Similar arguments can be applied to the more notorious internal monopolies of the Caroline period. A familiar characteristic which distinguishes many of these monopolies from their predecessors of the two previous reigns is their corporate nature, for it is a well-known fact that incorporation provided one of the most obvious means of getting round the provisions of the statute of 1624. This fact has a further significance for us in the context of this essay. Since the 1590's agitation against monopolies had been if not a constant, at least a regularly recurring, feature of the English political and economic scene. During that decade the pressure of war had forced the government to strain every nerve to expand existing and create new sources of revenue, and, among the latter expedients, monopolies were prominent. The end of the war in 1604 had brought little relief, for domestic extravagance had replaced external strife, and the drain upon the Exchequer had continued. In the Elizabethan and Jacobean periods the interests which had profited from monopolies, and, consequently, those interests upon whom public disapprobation was concentrated, were a relatively small number of individuals—a Wilkes, a Raleigh, a Mansell or a Mompessen. By contrast, the corporate character of many of the Caroline monopolies created by its very nature a more widely diffused source of vested business interest, linked by the closest of economic ties with the Crown. Of few, if

---

[1] *Cal. S.P.D. 1611-8*, pp. 376-7, 396; *1619-23*, p. 407; S.P. Charles I, 279/79; P.C. 2/42/547-9, 556-7, P.C. 2/43/108-9; London Guildhall, Repertory *XLVII*, fos. 278-9; Remembrancia *IV*, 2, 3, *VIII*, 113; J.U.Nef, *Industry and Government in France and England, 1540-1640*, (Philadelphia, 1940), pp. 34, 55.

any, of these interests is it possible to agree with Professor Nef's assertion[1] that royal recognition merely confirmed the concessionaires in a position which they had previously attained without royal assistance.

V

However, perhaps the most interesting, and certainly the most neglected, aspect of the relations of the London business world with the Crown is the degree to which the government antagonized many of the vested interests which its own policies had been largely responsible for creating. As Unwin has shewn,[2] in that part of royal industrial policy which related to the gilds, a fatal ambivalence between paternalistic and fiscal motives was to ensure that the Crown got the worst of both worlds. On the one hand, there was the hostility of the business grandees of the city to the royal policy of incorporation of groups of small masters, which reached a new height in 1638-9 with the open defiance by the Lord Mayor and Aldermen of the royal order to enrol the newly incorporated Distillers Company as a free company of the city.[3] On the other, there was the opposition of these groups whose interests this policy was originally designed to serve. For a short time, indeed, the king may have appeared as a new messiah to scores of master craftsmen. But when he turned out to be a false prophet, their attention shifted from the Crown to a parliament whose anti-monopolistic proclivities soon made it clear that they had little hope of redress from this source either.[4] Disappointed of their hopes from both of the contending parties, they would remain a potential source of unrest and disruption, whose memories of the negative response of parliament to their appeals were hardly less bitter than those of their betrayal at the hands of Charles I.

[1] Nef, *op. cit.* pp. 116-7.
[2] G. Unwin, *Industrial Organization in the Sixteenth and Seventeenth Centuries* (1957 edn), pp. 142-71.
[3] *Cal. S.P.D. 1637-8*, pp. 318, 585; London Guildhall, Remembrancia *VIII*, 208, 217, 219, 223-4: Bodleian, Bankes Mss. 6/2, 12/20, 23.
[4] On this episode, see G. Unwin, *The Gilds and Companies of London* (1925 edn.), pp. 333-6.

Many of the Caroline monopolists experienced similar disillusionment. The Westminster soapmakers were superseded in 1637 by a company which could hardly feel any great debt of gratitude to the Crown, since it consisted of producers who had formerly been excluded by the earlier monopoly.[1] The reconstitution of the Starchmakers Company in 1638 and the subsequent internal discords within that body were the result of an injudicious and unpopular mixture of royal fiscalism and interference.[2] The same familiar combination had been the motivating force behind the formation of the Westminster Company of Brickmakers and Tilers in 1636. But although this company could easily afford to pay the royal excise of sixpence on every thousand bricks produced out of the swollen profits resulting from tight combination,[3] by the opening of the Long Parliament Charles had as irrevocably lost the good will of its members as he had that of the excluded producers of bricks and tiles, for the company's privileges had been swept away in that holocaust of patents and other grants which was one of the panic measures heralding the end of the period of Personal Government.[4]

VI

But there were far more powerful, if less numerous, city interests, whose affections were partially or wholly alienated from the Crown as a result of royal policy. The opposition of those who were excluded from privileged spheres of foreign trade requires no explanation, especially in the light of Professor Friis' thesis that such concessions as

[1] W. H. Price, *The English Patents of Monopoly* (Cambridge, Mass, 1913). pp. 122-3. And, of course, it had to pay heavily for its privileges, both in terms of excise to the Crown and compensation to the old company.
[2] P.C. 2/47/288-9, 327, P.C. 2/48/59, 303, P.C. 2/50/157-8, 262, 378-9, P.C. 2/51/87-9, 168, 198-200, S.P. Charles I, 279/77, 77(i); *Cal. S.P.D. 1637*, p. 240; *1637-8*, pp. 109, 552; *1638-9* pp. 165, 242-3; *1639-40*, pp. 93-4, 230.
[3] One member of the company claimed that the consumer would have to pay an additional 18d. per thousand bricks. [*Cal. S.P.D. 1639* p. 66].
[4] P.C. 2/47/70-1, P.C. 2/49/350-1, P.C. 2/50/209-10, 439, 692, P.C. 2/52/721-2; S.P. Charles I, 362/81, 386/71; *Cal.S.P.D. 1639*, pp. 30, 116, 374, 470; *1640-1*, pp. 31-2: Bodleian, Bankes Mss. 12/32-5.

were made to these interests during the early 1620's were due to parliamentary pressures rather than to spontaneous government action. But the hostility of the great chartered companies to the Crown is a far more puzzling phenomenon. While it is true that there were undoubtedly divided political loyalties among the members of these companies in 1642, there can be little doubt that the bulk of them supported the pretensions of parliament against a royal government to whose support they had once owed their very existence. It is true that organizations such as Crispe's Africa company and Courteen's East India association[1] were so closely bound up with the Court as to provide exceptions to this rule, but there is also a great abundance of evidence relating to continued government support for the older companies. Indeed, in the case of the Merchant Adventurers, the company's hold over the export trade in woollen cloth to Germany and the Low Countries was in some respects tightened as a result of government action. Since the depression of the early 1620's the trade in coloured cloths to these regions had been thrown open, but in 1634 the Merchant Adventurers received the sole right to export not simply unfinished but every type of cloth.[2] Even though a corollary of this new arrangement was a widening of the membership of the company to include the Staplers and other exporters of coloured cloth,[3] this decision was likely to be far more unpopular with these two groups than with the Merchant Adventurers, for the former would obviously have preferred the maintenance of the *status-quo ante* 1634 than to be offered the stark alternatives of seeking admission to the Merchant Adventurers—on payment of stiff entry fines—or of abandoning the trade altogether. The same year saw a clear rebuttal by the government of the Staplers' claim to participate in the cloth export trade *qua* Staplers, a decision which was meat and

---

[1] Courteen's association had however been dissolved long before 1642.
[2] P.C. 2/44/89-90, 224: S. P. Charles I, 277/124(i); *Cal. S. P. D. 1634-5*, p. 346.
[3] P.C. 2/44/131-2, 174-5, 224; *Cal. S. P. D. 1634-5*, p. 346. In response to a complaint of March 1639 that interlopers continued to trade without becoming free of the Merchant Adventurers, the Privy Council showed itself willing to adopt the remedy suggested by the company—viz the appointment by the company of officials to sit in the customs house and take bonds of suspects. [P.C. 2/50/170-1].

drink to the Merchant Adventurers.[1] What then was the nature of the economic complaints of this and other companies, or must an explanation of their hostility be couched in exclusively non-economic terms?

Any attempt to tackle this difficult problem in a comprehensive way in this essay is precluded not only by lack of space but also by inadequate knowledge, for the topic of commercial policy under Charles I has still to find its historian. Nevertheless, it is difficult to avoid the conclusion that many of the companies had reached a stage in their development, when they were inclined to take a large measure of government support for granted, and to be more conscious of those of their aims which remained unfulfilled than of the substantial gains which were actually achieved.[2] Given such an attitude of mind, apparent breaches of privilege were all the more likely to be resented and to assume a disproportionate importance in the eyes of the concessionaires. Such were the Council's permission to Newcastle to import timber for use in the coal mines, and to Plymouth to import naval stores in foreign bottoms, its decision of 1626 that the men of Yarmouth who wished to import Eastland goods might become free of the Eastland company at reduced entry fines, and its throwing open of the import trade in flax in 1630.[3] All of these actions were bitterly resented by the London members of the Eastland Company. *Mutatis mutandis*, the same is true of the Merchant Adventurers with regard to the permission given by the council in 1636 to the baymakers of Colchester to export new draperies to Germany and the Low Countries, and its refusal to prohibit the trade in the so-called 'Spanish' cloths direct from the West country ports.[4] Similarly, conciliar support for the exclusive whaling rights of the Greenland Company[5]

---

[1] S. P. Charles I, 274/51; *Cal. S.P.D. 1634-5*, p. 257.
[2] This is the view of Dr. Hinton (*op. cit.* pp. 81-2) with regard to the relations of the Eastland Company with the Crown. And some of the companies had greater cause for dissatisfaction than the Eastland Company.
[3] *ibid.* pp. 72-3, 77-9; P.C. 2/40/29-30, 56-7.
[4] P.C. 2/45/15, P.C. 2/48/476, 516, 535-6: *Cal. S.P.D. 1635*, pp. 91, 103-4; *(1637-8)*, pp. 164, 176, 185, 218.
[5] See, for example, *Acts of the Privy Council* (hereafter *A.P.C.*) *1628-9*, pp. 384-5; P.C. 2/39/697, 765, P.C. 2/41/202-3, 366.

was no more than that company expected from the government, in which circumstances the permission given to one Nathaniel Edwards to operate in Greenland waters under the specious excuse that his patent had been granted in Scotland was all the more resented by the Company.[1]

Among the more general reasons for the growing dissatisfaction of members of privileged chartered companies was the growing multiplicity of economic privileges which marked the years of Personal Government, thus greatly widening the scope for collision of interest between different groups of concessionaires. It has already been remarked that the monopolistic soapboiling schemes trod heavily on the toes of more than one company. Similarly, the strengthening of the powers of the Eastland Company in 1630, giving them the sole right to import Eastland commodities from any region was bound to excite the hostility of those Merchant Adventurers who had participated with profit in the re-export trade in these commodities from the Low Countries.[2] Further examples could be multiplied, did space permit,[3] but it must suffice to point out that the overall effect of such collisions of interest was to detract from the value of long-standing concessions and to that extent to loosen the ties of economic interest which bound the concessionaires to the Crown.

Royal fiscalism provided a no less potent source of contention. Fiscal grievances relating to the burden of taxation on foreign trade were not new to the reign of Charles I, as every student of the constitutional conflicts of the period knows. To assert that historians have paid insufficient attention to mercantile opposition to taxes *qua* taxes and not simply *qua* unconstitutional taxes is not necessarily to dispute that constitutional scruples about unparliamentary taxation held a high place among the causes of mercantile opposition to Charles I. Nevertheless, it is surely true that, *ceteris paribus*, an increased fiscal burden upon trade will always be a source of business

---

[1] P.C. 2/42/555-6, P.C. 2/44/503-4.

[2] Hinton, *op. cit.* pp. 76-7; P.C. 2/39/642, 652-4. See also P.C. 2/41/272-4, P.C. 2/42/324-5.

[3] For an interesting examination of this problem as it affected the Eastland Company, see Hinton, *op. cit.* pp. 72-3.

discontent, irrespective of whether the taxes concerned are arbitrary or constitutional. In these circumstances many business men who knew little and cared less about constitutional theory might see in the unparliamentary levy of tonnage and poundage, which precipitated something like a general strike against the payment of customs duties in 1628-9,[1] golden opportunities for refusing to pay taxes. Thus constitutional theory might well come to provide an important element in the formation of an ideology of business opposition. Alternatively, if we regard—as surely we must—the self-interest of many other merchants as being by no means unmixed with loftier motives of constitutional propriety—the unfortunate Richard Chambers is an obvious, though a somewhat extreme, example[2]—their severe losses resulting either from conscientious withdrawal from trade or from the confiscation of their goods for non-payment of duty would in turn reinforce these constitutional scruples with arguments from economic self-interest, even though the unfettered operation of self-interest might have dictated the adoption of a more pusillanimous course of action.[3] But men seldom act from motives of economic self-interest alone in such circumstances, and it is in such crucial issues as hese that we perhaps find an important point of contact between potitical and economic history, whose significance has been missed byl many historians through their tendency to concentrate unduly upon the purely constitutional aspects of royal finance.

Another cause of discontent was the diplomatic incapacity of the government. In the light of recent arguments that the rôle of the chartered companies in foreign trade was to act as a sort of substitute for, or subsidiary branch of, state power in the pursuance of the

[1] On this incident see S. R. Gardiner, *History of England... 1603-1642*, (1883-4), VII, 1-7, 28, 30-4, 82-7, 108, 167-8.

[2] On the opposition and imprisonment of Chambers, see *ibid VII*, 4-5, 37, 85-7, 114-5, 168.

[3] One member of the Merchant Adventurers Company, which played a leading part in these events, claimed that many members, pursuing 'privat ends vnder a publique shew', used the constitutional scruples of their brethren to feather their own nests, by publicly urging a cessation of trading, while privately profiting from the resultant falling off in demand for cloth by covertly purchasing cloths from the clothiers at absurdly cheap prices. [S. P. Charles I, 140/24.]

economic aims of Tudor and Stuart statecraft,[1] there may well seem
to be something distinctly incongruous in the recurrent complaints
of the companies that their struggle for privileges and commercial
supremacy abroad was inadequately backed up by the government.
The incongruity, of course, lies in the fact that, in this view, if the
state had been powerful enough to secure these ends, the *raison d'être*
of the companies would be removed. However, large considerations
of this nature would hardly placate the Eastland merchants for the
inadequate support which they received from the government
against the exactions of Poles, Swedes and Danes, nor the Merchant
Adventurers for its failure to attend to their grievances against the
Dutch in the matter of 'tareing'.[2] But the failure of royal diplomacy
to support English commercial interests was most conspicuous in the
Indies, where Dutch competition was to be found in its fiercest and
most ruthless form. At the opening of the reign the East India Company was still staggering under the traumatic experience of Amboyna,
and seemed prepared to abandon the trade altogether despite royal
and conciliar rebukes for its defeatism.[3] The king's reluctance to take
reprisals against Dutch ships in English waters in 1625-6, as recom-
mended by the company,[4] and his belated move from ineffectual
diplomacy to half-hearted force in seizing three Dutch ships in September 1627, only to release them in the following summer, on receiving a promise from the Dutch that they would expedite proceedings against the Amboyna delinquents, made the weakness of the
English Crown manifest to all.[5] The release of the ships was regarded
as an act of betrayal by many members of the company, who were

---

[1] For a concise statement of this view, see Hinton, *op. cit.* pp. 64, 164-5.
[2] On the Eastland Company, see *ibid*, pp. 66-70. On the Merchant Adventurers,
see P.C. 2/40/98-101, P.C. 2/41/53-7; E. Lipson, *The Economic History of England*
(4th edn. 1947), II, 235-6.
[3] *A.P.C. 1625-6*, pp. 122, 125-6; *Cal. S.P.E.I. 1625-9*, p. 77.
[4] *Cal. S.P.E.I. 1625-9*, pp. 77-8, 103-6, 117
[5] *Cal S.P.D. 1627-8*, pp. 351-2, 355, 360, 368, 371, 374, 377, 389; *1628-9*, pp.
136, 252; *A.P.C. 1628-9*, pp. 33-4, 95-6; *Cal. S.P.E.I. 1625-9*, pp. 413-4, 422,
424-6, 462-4, 472, 478, 491, 508, 519-20, 526-9, 532-3, 538-42. A similar attempt
to expedite a settlement by the seizure of Dutch ships in 1633 seems to have
misfired. [*Cal. S.P.E.I. and Persia 1630-4*, pp. 393-8.]

convinced that they should have been detained until the Dutch made full restitution. The fact that the company continued throughout the 1630's to complain bitterly that it was receiving inadequate support from the Crown, which it urged to press the Dutch to give satisfaction for Amboyna and subsequent outrages and to compose the differences between the Dutch and English companies, suggests that they had just grounds for complaint.[1]

Royal interference with the affairs of the chartered companies was certainly no novel phenomenon, but, when combined with other grievances might well provide an additional irritant. Such were the royal attempts to secure the election of Edward Misselden as Deputy Governor of the Merchant Adventurers at Delft and Rotterdam, which were connected with the Laudian policy—continued long after the Crown had abandoned all hope of securing Misselden's election—of reducing the overseas settlements of the company to religious conformity.[2] And when royal interference was exerted on behalf of interests at court, as was the case in the disputes between the Crown and the Levant Company over the appointment to the embassy at Constantinople and the ambassador's rights to the consulage which was paid by aliens shipping goods in English ships,[3] or Charles' decision of 1637-8 to support Lord Goring's claims to participate in the great and petty customs farms,[4] it imposed a considerable strain upon the precarious economic alliance between the court and privileged city groups. It has already been emphasized that the practice whereby many economic concessions were marketed through the court was an important medium through which the

[1] P.C. 2/51/165-7; *Cal. S.P.D. 1633-4*, pp. 259-60, 300: *Cal. S.P.E. I. and Persia 1630-4*, p. 579: *C.M.E.I.C. 1635-9*, pp. 168, 274, 284, 289, 303, 333, 336-41, 351-2, *1640-3*, p. 24.

[2] P.C. 2/42/114, P.C. 2/43/185-6, 188, 261-2, 279-81, P.C. 2/48/213, P.C. 2/50/309; *Cal. S.P D 1631-3*, pp. 445, 575; *1633-4*, pp. 74-5, 225, 364, 449; *1634-5*, p. 87; *1635*, pp. 77, 151, *1635-6*, pp. 36-7, *1637*, p. 420, *1637-8*, p. 102, *1638-9*, pp. 250-1, *1639-40*, p. 213. *Cal. S.P.D. Addenda 1625-49*, p. 500.

[3] See A. C. Wood, *History of the Levant Company*, (Oxford, 1935), pp 87-90.

[4] See my 'Revenue Farming under the Early Stuarts', *Econ Hist. Rev.* 2nd. ser. *VIII*, (1956), pp. 318, 320-1.

economic interests of courtiers were harmonized with those of a privileged section of the business world. Both stood to gain, provided that the terms demanded by the former were not extortionate, a proviso which itself suggests that extortionate terms might result in a serious collision of interest between courtly concessionaire and business sub-concessionaire. This is admirably illustrated by an episode in the history of the Merchant Adventurers. The fairly reasonable *modus vivendi* which had been worked out in the previous reign between the company and the Earl of Cumberland in respect of the latter's licence to export unfinished cloth,[1] was shattered in the 1630's, by which time the licence had come into the hands of the Duchess of Richmond and Lennox, who demanded, and for a time obtained, a greatly augmented rent for the sub-letting of the licence to the company. But in 1636, when they had held the concession for $3\frac{1}{2}$ years, the Merchant Adventurers declared that they had had enough, and indeed, they had been prevented from crying off a year earlier only by the express command of the king. The resultant dispute over terms came to a head in 1640 with the seizure of the company's cloth shipments by the Duke of Richmond and Lennox, who had now succeeded the Duchess as owner of the licence. Throughout the dispute the government made it abundantly clear that it supported the claims of the Duke, thus contributing to the breaking up of a carefully established equilibrium between court and city interests, not least in its affirmation of the Duke's right to licence exports by interlopers and aliens, if he did not reach agreement with the Merchant Adventurers.[2]

For the East India Company also, the price of royal support and the continued alignment of the company with the court proved too high. In the opening year of the reign Charles' revival of his father's request that the king should be admitted as an adventurer in the company was supported by the incredibly tactless argument that this would make him the more willing to afford to the company the

[1] See Friis, *op. cit.*, pp. 375-6.
[2] P.C. 2/46/334-5, 339, P.C. 2/50/520, 540-1, P.C. 2/51/192-3, 223, P.C. 2/52/497; *Cal. S.P.D. 1635*, p. 96; *1636-7*, p. 106; *1639*, pp. 539-40; *1639-40*, pp. 234-5, 298, 333-4, 417-8, 599; *1640* pp. 21, 163, 176; Bodleian, Bankes Mss. 5/57.

protection which it was craving from him against the Dutch. Coming so soon after Amboyna, this proposal was shocking in the extreme, and merited a sharper reply than the mild counter-argument of the company's representatives that, if the king could protect them in his capacity as adventurer, he 'may be pleased to do as much without'.[1] Moreover, once the company had rejected the royal proposals, fighting shy of undue financial entanglement with the king, the incident was bound to excite suspicions about the weakness of royal diplomatic attempts to secure restitution for Amboyna. When similar proposals for royal participation in the company's ventures were advanced in the summer of 1628,[2] the circumstances of that time were even less propitious to their success, for they were advanced by one Thomas Smethwicke, a widely mistrusted member of the company, and were inevitably associated in the minds of members with the blistering attack which Smethwicke was concurrently delivering upon the mismanagement of the company's affairs by its governing body. The publicity which his allegations received seems effectively to have hamstrung the company's efforts to raise a new joint stock. Although Smethwicke was eventually reprimanded by the Privy Council for his extravagances, there can be little doubt that his intervention helped to sow further seeds of discord between the company and the Crown.[3] Already these relations had been exacerbated by the company's outright refusal in July 1628—at the very moment when Smethwicke's proposals were under discussion—to lend £10,000 to the King. The connection between this refusal and the events which have just been recounted is underlined by the company's excuse that the royal request for a loan 'could never come more unseasonably, for they were now on a new subscription for prosecution of the trade, and, if this request should be known, it would utterly overthrow the work intended.'[4] Thus Charles' relations with the company were already badly strained before they were

---

[1] *Cal. S.P.E. I 1625-9*, p. 110.
[2] *ibid*, pp. 520, 523-4, 528-9.
[3] *ibid*, pp. 501-5, 522-3, 525, 530, 534-5, 538, 558-9, 591, 610-7, 622-4, 631, 649, 651; *A.P.C. 1628-9*, pp. 308, 322.
[4] *Cal. S.P.E. I. 1625-9*, p. 521.

brought to breaking point in the mid 1630's by the officially licensed privateering expedition of Kynaston and Bonnell,[1] and, above all, by the foundation of Courteen's association.[2] Behind both of these enterprises lurked the elegant figure of the courtier, Endymion Porter, while in the case of the latter, the king was credited with an investment of £10,000,[3] a pointed contrast with the East India Company's refusal to accept Charles as an adventurer in 1625 and 1628. The moral was clear enough: that there was now an almost irreconcilable gulf between the interests of the Crown and the Court and those of the company. Although the privileges which were granted to Courteen's association did not formally abrogate those of the East India Company, they immensely reduced their value and in a real sense the Courteen project occupies a very similar place in the history of that company's relations with the Crown as does that of Cockayne in the case of the Merchant Adventurers. Both brought in their train profound disillusionment as to the support which the chartered companies might expect from the government, although, in the case of the East India Company, the process of disenchantment had already gone a long way as a result of the frictions which had long been multiplying on all fronts of its relations with the Crown. The royal repudiation of both the privateers and the Courteen association in December 1639 made possible a uneasy rapprochement,[4] but the events of the previous four years had produced a marked deterioration in the company's affairs and had aroused a widespread

[1] The depredations of the privateers in the Red Sea resulted in the arrest of the East India Company's factors at Surat, and the subsequent protection which Kynaston and others received from Charles against the company's attempts to obtain redress provided a further source of contention [*Cal. S.P.D. 1635*, p 96; *1636-7*, pp. 342, 426, 528-9; *1638-9*, p. 46; *C.M.E.I.C. 1635-9*, pp. 211-3, 215-20, 226, 232, 240-1, 283-4, 289, 299, 337.]
[2] On Courteen's association, see B. M. Sloane MSS. 3515, passim; *C.M.E.I.C. 1635-9*, passim; G. Carew, *A Vindication of the Several Actions at Lau brought against the Heirs of Sir Peter Courten and Peter Boudaen* (1675), and *Hinc Illae Lacrimae: or an Epitome of the Life and Death of Sir William Courten and Sir Paul Pindar; A Brief Narrative of the Cases of Sir William Courteen and Sir Paul Pindar*.
[3] *C.M.E.I.C. 1635-9*, pp. 123-4, 188, 274-5. Secretary Windebank was also credited with an adventure of £1,000.
[4] *ibid*, pp. 340-2, 351-2, *C.M.E.I.C. 1640-3*, pp. 23-7; P.C. 2/51/165-8.

resentment, which a bland reassertion of the *status-quo* was hardly sufficient to dispel. Moreover, Charles' quasi-compulsory purchase of a consignment of pepper belonging to the company in the autumn of 1640, in return for tallies on the customs which were not fully honoured until after the Restoration was certainly not designed to improve matters.[1]

While it would be a mistake to generalize from the extreme case of the East India Company to that of privileged companies in general, the example could hardly have been lost upon members of the latter, most of whom had their own peculiar grievances, some of which have been mentioned above. In the circumstances of the last five years of Personal Government there can have been few members of privileged corporations who did not speculate uneasily from time to time whether their own privileges might not be next on the list for royal reconsideration. From this state of chronic uncertainty to complete lack of confidence in the continued good will of the government is but the shortest of steps, and one which must have been taken by many merchants before 1640. In the case of many of them the political events of the next two years were to facilitate the transmutation of this mere lack of confidence into a more positive and effective hostility. Thus the most powerful of the commercial interests which ultimately opposed Charles I were forced into opposition, not by their hostility to royal control as such, but by uncertainty about their future under a system of royal control, from which they formerly had everything to gain.

VII

Among the most important ties between the Crown and a section of the prominent members of the business community were those

[1] S. P. Charles I, 465/64, 473/83; *Cal. S.P.D. 1640-1*, p. 271; *1641-3*, pp. 67-8, 266-7, 275, 305, 365; A.O. 1/1948/1; *Cal. S.P. Venetian 1640-2*, p. 74; *C.M.E.I.C. 1640-3*, pp. 80-4, 242-3, 247, 256, 269, 325, 333, 343, 370. *Cal. Treasury Books 1660-7*, p. 386. I cannot agree with the interpretation of Sir William Foster ('Charles I and the East India Company' *Eng. Hist. Rev. XIX* (1904), 456-63), who treats the pepper loan as if it were an ordinary commercial transaction.

arising out of the former's needs as a borrower.[1] In an age when government securities were by no means gilt-edged, it was natural that those who indulged regularly in the hazardous business of lending their money to the Crown should attempt to make their risks worthwhile by using their loans as levers to obtain concessions. A false sense of security in its privileged position might cause the East India Company to reject outright a royal request for a loan. It was not so with Sir William Courteen, the founder of the rival association, and 'a man that deserves to be respected... in regard he so freelie and willinglie lends his money for supplie of his Majestie's instant occasions and that without interest of the old debt.'[2] In April 1635, the foundation year of the association, Courteen was still owed more than £ 27,000 on loans which he had made to the king during the first three years of the reign.[3] But these loans had yielded more spectacular returns than interest at 8 per cent. The immense loans of Sir Paul Pindar—'This Sir Paul never fails the King when he has most need'[4]— certainly helped him to regain control of the customs farms in 1640, although by that time customs farming had become a decidedly shaky investment. Thus, in so far as loans were tied up with privileges, there was a double cord of economic interest uniting lenders to the Crown. Their loans might be essential to the financial survival of the régime, while the survival of the régime was essential to their continued enjoyment of the privileges which were connected with their services as lenders, as the customs farmers quickly discovered once the Long Parliament got firmly into the saddle. Indeed the farmers provide the most striking example of the connection between loans and privileges, for from the royal point of view the making of loans

---

[1] This subject receives detailed treatment in my forthcoming book, *The Crown and the Money Market, 1603–1640*.

[2] S. P. Charles I, 4/128. The words are those of Lord Treasurer Ley, written admittedly in the first year of the reign.

[3] B.M. Harleian Mss. 3796, fo. 22.

[4] *Cal. S.P.D. 1639*, p. 3. The writer is Edmund Rossingham. Pindar lent over £80,000 in 1638-9. [S. P. Charles I, 410/108, 443/10; *Cal. S.P.D. 1639*, p. 147; *A Brief Narrative of the Cases of Sir William Courteen and Sir Paul Pindar*, p. 9.]

was the main *raison d'être* of their existence.[1] In these circumstances the community of economic interest between Crown and farmers increased with the volume of loans made by the latter. Even the royal failure to make prompt repayment might not be unwelcome to the farmers, since it facilitated the anticipation of their rents for years into the future, and thus enabled them to tighten their hold upon their privileges. However, quite the opposite is true of the loans raised through the municipal machinery of the City of London via compulsory assessemnt of citizens or companies. Here the stick was emphatically more in evidence than the carrot, and the greater the volume of loans,[2] the greater was the unpopularity of the royal borrower. Nor were matters finally settled by the large-scale repayment operation of 1628, when royal lands were conveyed to the City in satisfaction of an outstanding debt of £349,897,[3] for the repayment of the lenders out of the proceeds of the land sales was a long drawn out process and was still continuing after the Restoration. Moreover, many of the lenders found that, under the methods of selling the land which were adopted by the City, they could obtain early repayment only at a ruinous discount. This situation was bound not only to reflect discredit on the Crown, whose financial dilatoriness had been at least partially responsible for the adoption of this cumbersome and inequitable mode of debt liquidation, but also to create additional sources of contention between the Crown and the municipality, whose relations had already been exacerbated by disputes over the Ulster Plantation and other matters.

Death and, in one case, bankruptcy had disposed of most of the individual private lenders to the Crown whom Charles I had inherited from his father's reign. By the time of the opening of the Scottish War there remained only the customs farmers—now greatly

[1] See my 'Revenue Farming under the Early Stuarts.' *Econ. Hist. Rev.*, 2nd. ser. *VIII* (1956), 310-22.

[2] £190,000 was raised from this source between the accession of Charles I and 1628.

[3] Of this sum more than £158,000 represents the capital and interest of a loan of 1617, while £120,000 represents a new advance of 1627-8 made as a condition of the conveyance of lands being made.

altered in personnel—and the naval treasurer, Sir William Russell,[1] of the important regular lenders of the previous reign. The familiar pattern of the creation and subsequent alienation of a body of vested business interest in the régime is thus applicable also to the royal relations with the money market, the medium of alienation in this case being the Crown's disregard of the need to preserve its credit. There were few concessionaires whose interest in the survival of the old régime could stand the sort of shock which Charles was prepared to administer indiscriminately to institutions and persons as diverse as the corporations of small masters, the East India Company, the Merchant Adventurers, and, in the realm of finance, to a great financier like Philip Burlamachi,[2] whose bankruptcy due to his over-involvement in royal finance provided a spectacular example for all to ponder. This paper is not a plea for a resuscitation of a wholly economic interpretation of the Great Rebellion, nor even of the problem of the allegiance of business men in the conflict. Indeed, its main conclusions could be used to underline the familiar argument that, if those whose economic interests were indissolubly bound up with those of the Crown in 1640 had remained the sole source of royal support, the parliamentary cause might have been won without a battle being fought. It is often emphasized that the crucial events of 1640-2 which enabled Charles to form a party and fight a war cannot possibly be explained in exclusively, or even preponderantly, economic terms. With this judgment we readily concur, but it is surely beyond question that, in the building up of the crisis which burst with the Scottish war, economic alignments, and more particularly the royal economic concessions from which some businessmen profited at the expense of others, cannot be neglected. The exclusively economic interpretation of the Great Rebellion has long been outmoded, for the same reason that all single-dimensional inter-

---

[1] On Russell, see my 'The Disbursing Official under the Early Stuarts: The Cases of Sir William Russell and Philip Burlamachi', *Bull. Inst. Hist. Res. XXX* (1957), 162-6.

[2] On Burlamachi see A. V. Judges, 'Philip Burlamachi: A Financier of the Thirty Years War', *Economica VI* (1926), 285-300, and Ashton *Bull. Inst. Hist. Res. loc. cit.*, 167-74.

pretations of complex historical events are outmoded, a reason which also makes nonsense of the suggestions of some historians that the way ahead is to return to exclusively non-economic interpretations. To adopt this course is to neglect the need for synthesis of the various strands of historical study, whose autonomy is more apparent than real. It is to run wilfully in historical blinkers.

THE OFFICERS OF THE EXCHEQUER,
1625-1642

'I have heard many say that there are such abundance of officers belonging to that Court as it is much to your Majesty's prejudice as well to the Commonwealth, but I have heard the Lord Coventry, that was Lord Keeper of England who was both a wise man and a good lawyer and well practised in the Checker, affirme that though many went about to alter the Government and Custom of that Court, that all the wits in the world could not possibly order it better than it was, but was forced always at length to fall back to the old Government...'

(THE DUKE OF NEWCASTLE, *A Treatise on Government presented to Charles II in 1660*)[1]

UNDER the early Stuarts the Exchequer was still the main financial institution in the country. As such its importance is obvious; but the importance of the men who served in it may not be so self-evident. For if all Exchequer officials, good and bad alike, were the prisoners of a bad financial system, it may appear that their conduct and outlook as individuals could have little practical bearing on the Crown's financial position—and so on the general history of the period. In that case, antiquarian interest apart, there would be little point in troubling ourselves with these men, except to catalogue them along with the other members of a 'vast, oppressive, ever-extending apparatus of parasitic bureaucracy'. But this would be too extreme a view. Despite all that has rightly been said against the pre-Civil War financial system, certain Exchequer officers did have an appreciable effect on the state of royal finance, and so on the political strength of the regime.

---

[1] S. A. Strong (ed.), *A Catalogue of letters and other historical documents exhibited in the Library at Welbeck*, (1903). App. I, p. 194.

On the officers of the Upper Exchequer of Audit or Account depended how both revenue-collecting and spending accountants settled their transactions with the King. The rigour, accuracy and speed with which such accounts were audited could often make a difference of £1,000s either way. Almost all the major revenue and spending accounts were by this time in the hands of either the two Prest or the seven Revenue Auditors.[1]

There was no effective early Stuart equivalent of modern 'Treasury control'. But Revenue or Prest Auditors were quite often appointed to investigate and report on the internal affairs of individual spending departments.[2] The more senior and better known men in both halves of the Exchequer were also liable to be appointed to royal commissions, or—if they were M.P.s—to parliamentary committees, on improving the revenues, reducing expenditure and other financial problems.[3]

Apart from the obvious dangers to the Crown from fraud there,[4] the officers of the Lower Exchequer of Receipt had considerable influence for good or bad. On the Auditor, and to some extent his colleagues too, depended whether the Lord Treasurer was encouraged

---

[1] Even the Ship Money accounts, which were 'declared' before the Privy Council and not in the Exchequer, were handled by one of the Prest Auditors (M. D. Gordon, 'The Collection of Ship Money in the reign of Charles I', *Trans. R. Hist. Soc.*, 3rd. Ser., vol. IV (1910), p. 141). The directives of 1597 and 1637 that all accounts taken by the Auditors must eventually be lodged in duplicate in the Pipe Office, and also pass through the King's Remembrancer's Office, were victories for administrative conservatism; but they seem to have detracted little from the *de facto* importance of the Auditors (P.R.O., L.T. Remem. misc books, E 369/118, ff. 230-1; M. S. Giuseppi, *A Guide to the manuscripts preserved in the Public Record Office*, (1923-4), vol. I, pp. 118-19).

[2] E.g. Report by Auditors Sawyer and Phelips on the Household accounts, 1638 (P.R.O., State Papers Domestic Charles I, S.P. 16/385/86 Lord Steward's dept; L.S. 13/169 pp. 317-20). Compare the anonymous and undated 'Irregularities of the Ordnance Office' drawn up by order of the Lord Treasurer, *c.* 1630 (S.P. 16/179/59).

[3] For royal commissions of this type with Exchequer members, 1626-8, see *Foedera*, ed. T. Rymer and R. Sanderson (1704-35), vol. XVIII, pp. 755-8, 771-6, 806-7, 1053-7.

[4] As with Sir John Bingley, Auditor of the Receipt, 1612-18.

or restrained in the practice of 'Assignment', whereby tallies were used to obviate cash in- and out-payments. Carried to excess this led inevitably to ear-marking the revenues in advance of the current year, or—as contemporaries called it—'Anticipation', by which the King restricted his own future freedom of action. The officers of the Receipt had some influence too in the matter of priorities, or 'Preference' in out-payments when there was a shortage of ready money, or a danger of over-assignment. Likewise with the raising, repayment and conversion of loans at the Receipt, which often involved the use of tallies to enable those who were in one capacity revenue accountants owing money to the King in effect to re-pay themselves in their other capacity as royal creditors. This practice too was damaging if it got out of hand.[1] Nor could the Auditors of the Upper Exchequer do their work properly unless they received the necessary information from the Receipt, particularly the lists of out-payments and assignments provided by the Auditor there.

Despite the evidence of increasing clerical activity by the Lord Treasurer's personal staff,[2] there is no sign of any decline in the Receipt's importance before 1642. In May 1638 the Lord Treasurer wrote to the Auditor:

'I have here inclosed the Certificate of the Lords Commissioners for settling the Prince's Household, whereby you will find that besides the Wardrobe, Robes, etc. (which I intend to assign upon Sir David Cunningham, and whose receipt for the present will bear no more), there must be found some Assignments for £15,000

---

[1] Examples of such transactions: with Wentworth (Privy Seal Warrants, Auditor's, E. 403/2591, pp. 12b–13b), John Browne, the King's Gunfounder (Treasury books misc., T. 56/1, p. 32), the Earl of Holland (Original Warrants for Issue, E. 404/234, 10 July, 1630), and Sir John Jacob, a Customs Farmer (*ibid.*, 24 December, 1633). On this whole subject see R. Ashton, 'Revenue Farming under the Early Stuarts', Econ. Hist. Rev., 2nd. ser., vol. VIII (1956), pp. 310–22; 'Deficit Finance in the Reign of James I', *ibid*, vol. X (1957), pp. 15–29; 'The Disbursing Official under the Early Stuarts...', *Bull. of the Instit. of Hist. Research*, vol. XXX (1957), pp. 162–74.

[2] The 1635 Treasury Commissioners had a single minute-cum-order book; in 1637–8 no less than seven separate, and in theory distinct, sets of records were being kept for Juxon (P.R.O., T. 56/1, 4, 7–8, 9, 11, 12, 13, 14).

per annum more than the £19,000 already assigned. And this is prest, to be paid by monthly payments. What his Majesty's Revenue will afford I should willingly were primarily employed for this service. And therefore I desire you to examine where, and how this sum may be answered upon any branch of his Majesty's Revenue not already assigned. Mr. Holland, the Prince's Paymaster, shall be directed to you; he will sufficiently inform you of the haste thereof. . .[1]'

So far from being addressed to a mere mechanical functionary whose work is ossifying into formal routine, this is a letter to a tried and trusted, albeit subordinate colleague.[2] The scope afforded to the Auditor's judgment can also be seen in his comments on the lists of prest out-payments which he sent up to the other Auditors.[3] Later in the century, between the time of Pye and that of Lowndes, this influence on the conduct of financial business passed decisively from the Auditor of the Receipt to the Secretary of the Treasury.[4]

When Laud and the other Treasury Commissioners wanted to obtain a general picture of the state of royal finance in 1635, they turned first to the Auditors of the Upper Exchequer and then to the officers who accounted there. Four months after their original order, to prepare a 'Balance' of the annual 'ordinary' revenue and expenditure averaged over the last five years, they called in the two principal officers of the Receipt; four and a half months after that the Balance was ready. Together with the other documents presented to the Commissioners that year,[5] this constituted easily the

---

[1] P.R.O., T. 56/13, p. 55. Cunningham was Receiver-General of the revenues which Charles had enjoyed as Prince before 1625; Mr. Holland was Cornelius, the future republican politician.

[2] Soon after entering office Juxon gave Pye authority to hold up any warrants for issues until he had explained his objections to them (W. Knowler (ed.), *Letters and Dispatches of the Earle of Strafforde*, (1739), vol. II, p. 4).

[3] P.R.O., Prest Certificates, Auditor's, E. 403/2154, pp. 4, 11b, 55.

[4] S. B. Baxter, *The Development of the Treasury, 1660-1702* (1957), pp. 126-38.

[5] Tables of Anticipations (March and July), of gross *extraordinary* revenues, including land sales, 1625-35 (late April), of royal debts (July), and of all stipendiary fees payable from the Exchequer together with what was then owing on them (November).

most thorough survey of the King's position since Cranfield's time.[1] Even so, both fair copies of the Balance contain obvious, elementary mistakes of arithmetic:[2] something of a reflection on the 'Auditors'.

When the Long Parliament wanted a similar Balance in December 1640, they called in Sir Edward Wardour, the Clerk of the Pells, who at first offered them a copy of the 1635 Balance. Sir Robert Pye, the Auditor of the Receipt, who was himself an M.P., then asked for time for a new balance to be produced.[3] The increased prominence of the Receipt, as against the Auditors of the Upper Exchequer, is noteworthy, although the memorandum prepared for the Earl of Bedford the following spring suggested a seven- or even a ten-year Balance, to be prepared by Pye plus one Prest Auditor and one Revenue Auditor.[4] A Balance 'by a medium of five years upon Certificates from several Officers by Warrants from the Lords Commissioners [of the Treasury]' was completed in August 1641. It is less detailed than the 1635 Balance; from Pye's own copy it appears that he was more interested in the constitutional questions of which revenues were legal and certain, which illegal, and which 'Doubtful'—evidence perhaps that he had the House of Commons rather than the Treasury

---

[1] The Balance itself (Treasury misc. books, T 56/2; Exchequer of Receipt misc. E 407/78/5) appears to be more elaborate than any of the Jacobean ones; see F. C. Dietz, *English Public Finance 1558-1641* (New York, 1932), pp. 110-113, 180 n. 65, 185 n. 1; R. H. Tawney, *Business and Politics under James I* (Cambridge, 1958), pp. 297-301; Lands. Mss. 151/42 f. 49. For the nearest to a mid-sixteenth century parallel (in 1552) see W. C. Richardson, *Tudor Chamber Administration, 1485-1547* (Baton Rouge, Louisiana, 1952), pp. 394-4 and G. R. Elton, *The Tudor Revolution in Government* (Cambridge, 1953), pp. 231-4. For the fifteenth century compare J. L. Kirby 'The Issues of the Lancastrian Exchequer and Lord Cromwell's Estimates of 1433,' *Bull. Inst. Hist. Res.* Vol. XXIV (1951), pp. 121-51.

[2] Several items are added up in the wrong vertical columns on the Receipts and Issues sides; the totals for Assignations etc. are about £ 60,000 p.a. too large, and those cash handled at the Receipt about £ 60,000 too small.

[3] W. Notestein (ed.), *The Journal of Sir Simonds D'Ewes* (New Haven, 1923), pp. 191-2. Harl. Mss. 3796/30 f. 68/ (1640 copy of 1635 Balance).

[4] S.P. 16/479/89.

Commissioners in mind.[1] Again the figures cannot be accepted without question.[2]

Many officials in the Upper Exchequer spent their time on intrinsically rather unimportant work (for example those involved in the 'Ancient Course'). Likewise many of those in the Receipt spent much of theirs in keeping very detailed records designed primarily to prevent fraud and inaccuracy, and to enable them to justify themselves if they were challenged. The records of the Lower Exchequer were particularly ill-adapted for obtaining accurate totals where large sums were involved: even among the newer series of records, only the Pell's Declaration Books were in arabic numerals—and even there the Lord Treasurer's fair copies were in roman numerals—many of the older standard series, like the Receipt and Issue Rolls and Books, for these years do not even have the terminal (half-yearly) totals entered on them. This may have been due to mere *vis inertiae*, but the writing clerks may well have had a positive vested interest in resisting a general change to arabic figures.

The use of printing provides an even clearer instance of bureaucratic rigidity, involving the officials' material interests. Considering that the Puritan Edmund Grindal had used printed tax forms as Bishop of London in the early 1560's[3], remarkably little use was being made of such techniques seventy years later. James I once used printed circulars when demanding a loan, but this does not seem to have been repeated under Charles. In the 1630's one of the Receivers-General had printed receipt forms for payments of Crown land revenues.[4] But this practice only became common under the Long Parliament's war-time tax system.[5] Unless it is to be ascribed to sheer

---

[1] P.R.O. Shaftesbury Papers, P.R.O. 30/24/464 (the best version for the receipts) 463 (a copy of 464 but also has issues); Elmhirst Papers, Worsborough Bridge Yorks, Pye Mss. (1) f. 54.

[2] This time because the totals for some branches of the Customs look too high to be averages for 1636-41 and are more like the actual yield for 1639-40.

[3] P.R.O., King's Remem., Fanshawe Papers, E. 192/1, bundle 2/40-2.

[4] P.R.O. State Papers Additional (uncalendared), S.P. 46/82/81-5; John Harvey, Receiver-General of Lincolnshire, 1632.

[5] E.g. *ibid.* 201/47.

purposeless conservatism, this time-lag can only have been because the livelihood of many under-officers depended on the demand for multiple copies of handwritten documents. Many of the junior staff were indeed copying-clerks whose only expertise was their ability to write the correct 'hand'.[1]

The principle of multiple safeguards, which included the keeping of records in duplicate and even in triplicate, was deeply entrenched in the Exchequer. Traditionalists and innovators alike extolled the department precisely because so many different officers performed over-lapping functions. The whole was pictured as an intricate system of checks and balances.[2] In the Upper Exchequer, the two Remembrancers' Offices and the Pipe could in theory act as a check on the Auditors, and vice versa; within the Pipe Office, the Comptroller's duty was to act as a check on the Clerk. In the Receipt, the Auditor checked the honesty of the Tellers, and the Clerk of the Pells that of the Auditor.[3] Unhappily, admiration at the sheer complexity of the institution could blind men (like Coventry, as quoted by Newcastle) to the question of its efficiency.

Opinions may differ as to whether or not the Exchequer supports the idea of an 'ever-extending' bureaucracy in these years. The Surveyor-Generalship of Crown Lands was revived in 1625; the administration of the penal taxes on recusants was put into the hands of separate Receivers and then separate Auditors (1628 and 1637); some of the revenue farms, and the monopolies and fiscal commissions of the 1630's entailed the appointment of new Collectors. But if there was any significant numerical expansion in the Exchequer itself, it can only have been at the bottom level, among the under-officers and copying clerks. The many new types of records dating from the years *c.* 1590-1636 suggest that some expansion did take

[1] See H. Jenkinson, 'English Current Writing and Early Printing', *Trans. of the Bibliographical Society*, vol. XIII, for 1913-15 (1916).

[2] B.M. Add. Mss. 34,274 f. 132; 36,081, f. 1; C. Vernon, *Considerations for regulating the Exchequer* (1642), Dedication (to Sir John Culpepper, Chancellor of the Exchequer), p. 47 *et seq.*

[3] In the later 1620's the Clerk of the Pells can be found reporting what out-payments had been made to particular officials and patentees (S.P. 46/127/223, 242-3).

place, but this is only circumstantial evidence which is not confirmed from other sources.

The kind of men who held office in the Exchequer were in many ways representative of those in the rest of Charles I's government. They included several qualified lawyers, as well as others with some legal education, though not as many as in the other central law courts. The Exchequer's own strictly legal side had a surprisingly small staff. There were also some men of mercantile origins, though fewer than in the Customs service, and fewer than might perhaps have been expected in a financial institution. There was one peer, and—even in the middle ranks—a few men of plebeian origin. But at this level the overwhelming majority were drawn from the ranks of the gentry: in the most senior posts (which were not always the most important) sons of the greater gentry predominated, especially among those with prior family connexions in the Exchequer or elsewhere in the government; immediately below them were a great many sons of the lesser gentry. At the lower levels, among the under-officers and clerks, there were more men of non-armigerous origin; most of these were probably Londoners by birth, the others first generation immigrants from the country into the capital; they belonged to the small, but growing 'white collar' class, of which the bulk was employed in the legal profession and in the trading and financial houses of the City.

The geographical origins of the Exchequer officials were also fairly typical of the civil service in general. But the influence of family connexions and of regional patronage meant that some counties were heavily 'over-represented' and others 'under-represented' in relation to the average geographical distribution of all central office-holders. The same might well be true of other courts and departments, and only evens out by taking the members of the government as a whole. In the Upper Exchequer, Hertfordshire, Bedfordshire, Essex and Buckinghamshire were over-represented in this way; and in the Lower Exchequer, Dorset, Hampshire, Somerset and Surrey. Again, as with office-holding in general, service in the Exchequer tended to draw men nearer to London, apart from whether they owned property, rented a house, or merely lodged in the capital itself. Twelve or thirteen, out of 50-60 for whom information is available, ended their days nearer to London than where they had come from, as against only one who moved further away.

The hereditary element in Exchequer families has already been remarked on by historians.[1] Certainly it seems to have come nearer to having had an office-holding caste than any other branch of English government at this time, except possibly the Court of Wards. However only one office passed by outright hereditary succession, that of Chief Usher, which was held on Grand Sergeanty, first by the Billsbys of Lincolnshire and then by the Walkers of Somerset. Otherwise, even when the same family enjoyed the same office for three, four, and—in one case—five generations, the succession always had to be secured by a reversion obtained within the lifetime of the existing holder, and honoured at his death. In practice this may seem to amount to much the same thing as inheritance. But these successions depended on the sovereign, the Lord Treasurer, or the Chancellor of the Exchequer (according to whose gift an office was in) being prepared to grant the reversion, and on there being a son of full age when the holder died. Despite the well known case of Thomas Fanshawe in 1616, inheritance by a minor was unusual, and could indeed prove vulnerable if challenged at law.[2] Furthermore, reversions might have to be bought, or at any rate their acquisition might involve payment of a sizeable 'brokerage fee' to some intermediary, or to whoever had the gift of the office. There are even cases of families where there were sons but no effort appears to have been made to secure the father's office for any of them. Direct father to son (and elder to younger brother) descents[3] were also liable to the demographic peril of extinction: only the Chief Ushership apparently proved capable of transmission via the female line. 'Lateral' connex-

---

[1] H. R. Trevor-Roper, *The Gentry 1540-1640* (Cambridge, 1953), p. 30; Baxter, *op. cit.*, pp. 113, 139-41.

[2] See E. Coke, *Reports* (1500-59), vol. IX, 95a-99b; R. Brownlow, *Reports* (1652), vol. II, 266-8; G. Croke, *Reports* (1665), p. 880, (1683) vol. III, pp. 555-7. Whether or not a minor could take up a reversion generally depended on the kind of office involved, and on whether or not it could be executed by deputy.

[3] As in the following families: Carne, Croke, Franshawe, Hill, Knollys, Neale, Osborne, Pitt, Vernon, Walker, Wallinger, Wardour.

ions, embracing different offices, and not descending in one direct line, are equally noteworthy. These sometimes had a long span as well as a wide spread.

Among the 'vertical' connexions, in the 1630's the fourth successive Fanshawe was King's Remembrancer. The office had been in the family since 1566, and they had been connected with the Exchequer since the 1520's. The fourth Osborne was Lord Treasurer's Remembrancer, this office having been in their family since 1553. The King's Remembrancer's step-uncle was Surveyor-General of Crown Lands until his death in 1631, as well as Clerk of the Crown in King's Bench, but he only transmitted the latter office to his son, the Remembrancer's cousin. However the vacancy in the Surveyor-Generalship led to the establishment of a new succession, by a relatively self-made man, Charles Harbord (he and then his son held it until 1692). Among the Revenue Auditors, the extinction of the Neale dynasty, of which three members spanning two generations had held office since well back in Elizabeth's reign, was balanced by the emergence of other successions, such as that begun by another man of comparatively humble origins, Francis Phelips (he and then his son held office from the 1610's to the 1690's). In the Pipe Office, Sir Henry Croke had been co-Clerk since 1616, and became sole Clerk in 1632; his son and grandson between them were to hold the office until 1679 or 80.

The Darnell-Vernon-Brewster-Wallinger line in the Pipe Office was more of a lateral connexion. Christopher Vernon, Sir Henry Croke's arch-enemy, was also his second-in-command, as First Secondary. His son Francis had recently succeeded to the Comptrollership of the Pipe; Vernon's own father-in-law had been Secondary earlier in the century, and one of his sons-in-law was to hold this post later; another of his sons and another son-in-law were subsequently to be Comptrollers.

Transmission of an office to a male heir did not always entail a long tenure. Sir Henry Knollys became Receiver of Tenths and First Fruits in the 1620's, and the office passed to his son at his death in 1638; but the younger Knollys, who was a royalist in the Civil War, had lost, or parted with it by 1643 or 1644.

In the Lower Exchequer, the second Wardour was Clerk of the

Pells, and the family was not quite half-way through its 118 years tenure of that position. By contrast the second Carne was already a Teller, having just succeeded his elder brother (their father had held a reversion which he had not lived to enjoy), but the Carnes' total tenure was only about ten years.

The most striking connexion in the Receipt was that of the Freke-Swayne-Pitt-Squibb families from Dorset. Seven members of this group held office there between the 1580's and the 1670's, not counting one whose reversion was voided by the Crown on ideological grounds, or Clement Walker who married into this group but inherited his office in his own right. Apart from these two, its most interesting member was Sir William Pitt (great-great-great uncle of the first Earl of Chatham), who had done his main service in the department during James's reign, and had then—rather untypically for the period—retired in favour of his son Edward (Teller 1623-43). In the years 1617-23 William had been one of a group of 'able and conscientious officials, without whose assistance the reforms associated with the name of Cranfield could not have been planned or put in force.'[1] Then there were Arthur Squibb the elder, under-clerk in the Receipt by 1610, Teller 1623, and finally Clarenceux, King of Arms 1646-50 and Lawrence, his first cousin once removed, patentee for dice and playing cards in the later 1630's and then Secretary to the Treasury Commissioners in 1641-2 (although a reversioner in the 1630's, he only succeeded to a Tellership at the Restoration). Whereas William Pitt was knighted and—thanks partly to a prudent marriage —became a substantial property-owner, most members of this group remained on a rather lower level than the great Exchequer families— the Fanshawes, Osbornes and Crokes.

Considering the extent of direct patrimonial succession, and of wider family patronage, all this may give the impression that the Exchequer's staff did indeed constitute a closed caste; or certainly that it tended to exclude those without the right ties of blood or marriage. This was not so. As in the rest of the government, these tendencies

[1] R. H. Tawney, *Business and Politics under James I*, p. 166; on Pitt see *ibid.* pp. 83, 157. Although he held no major post in the Exchequer, Pitt served on many royal commissions connected with finance in the years 1617-30.

towards hereditary succession were counteracted by the effects of patronage exercised from above, by families dying out, and by the pressure of humbler, or anyway less well-connected men coming up from below. And where marriage appears to have helped secure men entry to office, it is particularly necessary to distinguish whether such ties were entered into before or after appointment. Intermarriage among the families of men already serving in the same department may indicate that they formed a close-knit social group, but is no evidence of nepotism, although it often leads to this in the next generation.

Nor, generally speaking, were the posts which were occupied by hereditary families the most important, as opposed to the most senior and prestigious ones. In the Upper Exchequer, neither Auditorship of the Prests and not more than one or two of the seven Revenue Auditorships were thus occupied. In the Receipt, the Auditorship, the chief under-clerkship, and the two deputy Chamberlaincies were all held by first generation incumbents. Some careers at least were open to talent, or anyway to talent plus patronage. Relatively few were open solely to wealth; for, perhaps by contrast with James's reign, it does not seem that many of the 'active' (i.e. non-sinecurist) offices were available for purchase in Charles I's time.

There are further qualifications to be made. It would be wrong to equate semi-hereditary Exchequer families with wealthy greater gentry, and first generation office-holders with middle class parvenus or genuinely self-made plebeians. Some well-entrenched families, like the Vernon-Wallinger connexion, acquired only modest wealth and rose only a short way in the social scale, while some of the new men were at least as aristocratic as the 'old Exchequer hands'. Nor can the quasi-hereditary office-holders be identified with the semi-sinecurists, whose merely routine duties were often performed by deputies, and the fresh entrants with the go-ahead careerists who filled the positions on which the efficiency of the department really depended.

Such signs of criticism as can be found within the Exchequer seem to come from first generation officials, notably Edmund Sawyer (Revenue Auditor, 1623-70), in his younger days, and Christopher

Vernon virtually throughout his career. Vernon's son Francis seems to provide about the only exception. And most of this criticism reflected little more than the direct material interest of the officials in maximising the volume of business in their own offices; the Vernons especially were extreme traditionalists, criticising only the real or alleged abuses of the existing system. In 1660 the same running battle between the Auditors of the Upper Exchequer and the upholders of the 'Ancient Course' was resumed where it had been left off in the 1630's. Other self-made careerists and first generation officers accepted the practice of the Exchequer uncritically. They simply settled down, we may surmise, to make the best of things as they found them, combining a moderate regard for the King's interest with a healthy concern for their own.

Another paradox is illustrated by the career of Sir Robert Pye, Auditor of the Receipt 1619-53 and 1660-2. When first appointed, he was described contemptuously as 'a creature of Marquis Buckingham's.'[1] At the time this was justified; Pye's sole qualification was two years or so in part charge of his patron's own finances. But here if ever was a case of 'the office making the man'. Although Pye remained loyal to the Villiers connexion—excessively so, as Wentworth thought when they clashed over the dowager Duchess's Irish customs grant in the late 1630's, he developed into a responsible public servant. Even in the late 1620's he was not afraid to tell his master the truth about the country's financial position, and ten years later Treasurer Juxon was leaning heavily on his experience. Remembering that Pye's predecessor (Bingley, a client first of the Cecils and then of the Howards) was convicted of fraud, and that the Auditors who followed his successor, Sir Robert Long (1662-73), were administratively speaking nonentities, it is perhaps also fair to say that the men made the office. This was certainly true of Thomas Falconbridge, Deputy Chamberlain in the Receipt during the 1630's, who became one of the principal financial officers under the Long Parliament and the Commonwealth before he was promoted to any technically more senior position.

[1] N. E. McClure (ed.), *The Letters of John Chamberlain*, (Philadelphia, 1939), vol. II, p. 283.

As always, at the extremes it is possible to construct a 'model' or a 'typology'. There were some semi-hereditary Exchequer office-holders in dignified semi-sinecures, the two Chamberlains being the most extreme instance, with deputies in both Upper and Lower Exchequers. Whether inherited or newly acquired,[1] such men regarded their offices as 'estates', from which some (like Sir Thomas Fanshawe, the King's Remembrancer), hoped for the steady income of a rentier, others (like Sir Henry Croke of the Pipe) for what a man of enterprise could make of them. At the other extreme were the self-made, hard working careerists: Justinian Povey, Francis Phelips, and Sawyer among the Revenue Auditors, Harbord the Surveyor, Christopher Vernon, Falconbridge, and George Bingley (no relation of Sir John·) and John Worfield the Prest Auditors. But in between, with men like Sir Robert Pye, Arthur Squibb the elder, or Robert Long (younger son of a knightly family but himself an administrative careerist), it is virtually impossible to make a meaningful classification.

Even so, one or two safe generalizations are helpful in assessing how far the officers of the Exchequer were responsible for the Crown's financial difficulties. The method of payment in fees and gratuities by the users of the department is one obvious way in which all—good and bad—were the prisoners of a thoroughly bad system. And, although despite the strong hereditary element the more important offices were largely open to new entrants, they would not necessarily stand for improvement of existing methods, still less for any more fundamental changes in financial administration. Occasionally the need for radical reform was implied in the course of criticising the abuses of the existing system, but this was bound to trench on the vested interests of their colleagues, and not merely of those involved in such abuses. Real reform could only be effected by determined action on the part of the King and his ministers, or in the 1640's of the House of Commons.

Political and administrative attitudes were also likely to depend on the degree of men's commitment to their offices. Most Exchequer posts were held on life tenure, their holders thus being removable

[1] One of the Chamberlains had bought his office, with family help, in 1611 and the other in 1625.

only for a few very serious offences. A reforming Lord Treasurer, like a lax one, must for most purposes make do with the human as well as the mechanical materials that he found to hand. In some respects a distinction can be drawn between those full-time professionals whose social and financial position depended wholly on possession of their offices, and the part-time semi-amateur landed gentlemen who happened to have posts in the Exchequer. But as has already been explained, these classifications only cover the extreme cases. Thus in the mid-1630's the Revenue Auditors were certainly serious and hard-working, but all them were property-owners on a varying scale, and at least one was a considerable moneylender.[1] Many medium-ranking officials had inherited property (out of 42 whose place in their family is known, 28 were eldest sons), though several of these added to it in the course of their careers. Altogether a minimum of fourteen were enlarging their estates, for only one or two (the brothers Carne) who were going downhill. Financially speaking few above the lowest ranks can have been entirely dependent on the profits of office; but all would have been in some measure impoverished by its loss, as many were to be in the years 1642-60. The extent of this dependence varied very widely: by the 1620's the senior line of the Fanshawe family almost certainly enjoyed a larger income from land than from the King's Remembrancership. In the mid-1630's Povey's fees and pensions as Auditor seem to have comparable to the interest which he was receiving on loans. Sir Robert Pye's £1,500 a year as Auditor certainly exceeded the yield of his estates; the same was emphatically true of Sir Henry Croke's Clerkship of the Pipe before, and probably still after he had acquired the Chequers estate through his wife. Among the major office-holders the situation of the Fanshawes of Ware was the exception rather than the rule.

[1] P.R.O. Exchequer, King's Remem. misc., E. 163/18/27, Justinian Povey's personal account book for 1634-6, shows the extent of his money-lending activities. It is anonymous, but it can be identified by payments to him in his capacity, as Revenue Auditor, Auditor to the Queen, and recipient of a pension from James I, and by some of the borrowers' names, which can be cross-checked with Lord Chamberlain's dept. Recognisance Books, L.C. 4/201.

The annual value of all offices in the Exchequer from fees and gratuities was probably within a suggested range £38,000-45,000. But this total was very unevenly distributed:

Holders of the top 11 positions (Lord Treasurer, Chancellor and Under-Treasurer, Chief, Puisne and Cursitor Barons, King's and Lord Treasurer's Remembrancers, Clerk of the Pipe, Auditor of the Receipt)   Total £22,100-26,600

Average *per capita* £2,009-2,418

The next 83 officers and under-officers in the Upper Exchequer, and the next 27 in the Receipt   £16,000-18,000

Average *per capita*   £145-164

Apart from the quarrels about excessive fees (especially the Vernons' attack on Croke), only one man was accused of misusing his office for private gain in these years. This was the other Sir Thomas Fanshawe, of Jenkins, Essex, (Surveyor-General 1625-31) who was said to have grossly under-valued the royal manor of Barking, then to have bought it, and finally to have only paid half of what he had undertaken. His tenants there had other grievances against him and his son, and the case was never proved, though on the surface it looks bad.[1] Otherwise, as far as actual corruption was concerned, the fall and punishment of Lord Treasurer Suffolk and Auditor Bingley in 1618-19 may have had a salutary effect. If the charges against Cranfield's financial probity in 1624 were largely fabricated, or at least no worse than could have been brought against almost any statesman from the fifteenth to eighteenth centuries,[2] the offences of Suffolk and Bingley were all too real. Nor can we tell how many eyebrows were raised when, in the last year of his life, Lord Treasurer Portland secured the King's pardon for having recouped himself to the tune of £44,500 out of money which might, and perhaps ought, to have gone to the King.[3] These pickings were certainly very much the kind of thing for which Cranfield had ostensibly been attacked ten years before.

[1] S.P. 46/80/279; 127/233-4; Fanshawe Mss. (Bratton Fleming, Devon).
[2] See Tawney, *op. cit.*, pp. 231-74.
[3] R. Scrope and T. Monkhouse (ed.), *Clarendon State Papers* (1767), vol. I, pp. 158-9.

Consideration of how far the state of royal finance depended on the officers of the Exchequer also raises the question of their attitude towards royal policy in general. Positive evidence is very slight. But the papers presented by Pye and others to the Treasury Commissioners in 1635 do suggest a feeling that with Portland's death an anti-reforming influence had been removed. If they had a candidate to succeed him, it may be assumed that they were too prudent to commit a name to paper. Some must have been Cottington supporters, having themselves risen with the Chancellor, knowing his ways, and preferring his promotion to the entry of any new and unknown force. However, when he was disappointed of his hopes, Cottington seems to have transferred his energies to the Court of Wards, of which he had become Master in March 1635.[1] Whether or not the Exchequer officers would as a whole have preferred Cottington to Juxon, it is a safe guess that several of them heaved a sigh of relief on learning that it was not to be Wentworth. Some of them (e.g. Sir Henry Croke) had already had a taste of 'Thorough' through the Lord Deputy's membership of the Commission on Fees. His forceful views on the officials of the spending departments may well have been spread around; and it may have seemed all too likely that, given the chance, he would develop a similar attitude towards the revenue-raising side of government, as had already happened in Ireland.[2]

It would be unwise to infer too much about their attitude under Charles I in the years 1625-40 from what the Exchequer officers did or did not do after 1642. But some deductions can safely be made. The fear of impeachment or other punishments for collaboration in the fiscal policies of the Crown before 1640 must have weighed heavily on some of them during the first session of the Long Parliament. One of the Auditors (Sawyer) had already experienced the Commons' wrath back in 1628. The relatively small proportion

[1] See *Strafford Letters*, vol. II, p. 5. I am grateful to Mr. M. J. Hawkins of Wadham College, Oxford, and Edinburgh University for further information about Cottington's active concern with the Court of Wards.
[2] For Wentworth as a fee commissioner see *Bull. Inst. Hist. Res.* vol. XXXI (1958), pp. 61-2; on his undertaking reform of the Irish Exchequer and Court of Wards see *Strafford Letters*, vol. I, pp. 190-1; for his views on the officers of the spending departments in England and Ireland, *ibid.*, pp. 247, 280, 391.

of positive royalists among the pre-1641 Exchequer officials cannot of course be used as proof that they were against royal policy in the previous decade; but it is suggestive of something less than full support of the King, or enthusiasm for his undertakings. In an age of a 'political', or at least a 'not non-political' civil service, this may not be surprising. But it should at any rate remind us that the interactions between a government and its servants in such an epoch involved several factors, of which the conditions of official service (e.g. payment in fees, and life tenure) were not the least.

To some extent this survey points to negative conclusions. The Exchequer officers could certainly help or hinder a reforming Lord Treasurer. But, actual fraud apart, they could make little difference for either better or worse under an inadequate one. Unless Parliament was sitting and they were also M.P.s, their influence on financial policy as opposed to its execution seems to have been slight, notwithstanding that some of them were inveterate petitioners and submitters of memoranda. This appears to be equally true in terms of increasing the revenues, reducing expenditure, or simply improving the machinery and the sources of information needed to formulate policy and carry it out. While they could undoubtedly affect the existing system for better or worse, its inherently bad features meant that the price of virtue was likely to be high. As for more fundamental change, the real question is not how the Exchequer officers would have reacted to it, but how it could have happened at all until there had been a decisive shift in the balance of the constitution, either towards absolutism or towards parliamentary government. In deciding the outcome of this conflict the early Stuart Exchequer and its personnel were important only in that archaic systems both of 'public' finance and of office-holding were contributory causes of the Crown's defeat. It is significant that these systems were largely superseded under the Long Parliament and the Commonwealth (c. 1643-53), but partially restored under the Protectorate, and almost completely so in 1660. Circumstances such as Parliament's substitution of the Excise for the old feudal dues, more than deliberate royal policy, were to differentiate the financial institutions and methods of the Restoration era from those of the Personal Rule.

THE ACCOUNTS OF THE KINGDOM
1642-1649

THE Civil War was won by Committees. Behind the victory of the Parliamentary armies was the cumbersome, ill-tempered machinery, functioning in the chambers of the Palace of Westminster, the halls of the City Companies, manor-houses and inn parlours, that directed the resources of the towns and the country-side into the service of the cause. The work of some of the committees is well-known from their calendared records—especially that of the big money-raising departments and of the Committee of Safety and the Committee of Both Kingdoms. We are concerned here with a less august body, created in February 1643/4 under the uninspiring title of the Committee for Taking the Accounts of the Kingdom. The large and chaotic heap of documents it left behind[1] will not be considered as a source of statistical information on the finances of the Parliamentary side. Though they leave a vivid and detailed impression of the burden borne by the English people as a whole, they do not readily tell us the total of any major items of income or expenditure. But the activities and aspirations of the main Committee in London and its Sub-committees in the counties provide instances of what was happening at every level of government. The committeemen were amateurs, doing a job badly but seldom failing to do it at all. They were also minor and unsuccessful competitors in the struggles for administrative power that arose when the old sovereignty and pa-tronage had been removed.

The declaration of war in August 1642, a crucial moment in the eyes of the political theorist and the bewildered citizen, did not mark

---

[1] Mainly in the misleadingly-named *Commonwealth Exchequer Papers*, P.R.O. S.P. 28.

as sharp a break in the actual working of central government as might be assumed. The King summoned his loyal subjects to fulfil their duty of defending him against treason and rebellion. The Lords and Commons in Parliament—or some of them—took steps to save His Majesty from his evil counsellors. But while these rival myths were shouted from press and pulpit, the real change was the transfer of the work of governing from the King's establishment to that of the Parliament. This process had begun, in the broad historical sense, under James I, or for that matter under Elizabeth, and in the narrower immediate sense with the meeting of the Long Parliament. In the summer of 1642 the King deserted his post in the mixed constitution and raised the standard of rebellion. Parliament had to replace the royal administration by one of its own—and one capable of winning a civil war.

In finance there was no sudden break. Wartime accounts begin with the subsidies and poll-tax of 1641. The Exchequer in London was not dissolved: it merely ceased to matter. During the Scots Wars large government funds had passed instead through the hands of Sir William Uvedale, Treasurer to the Armies in the North, who had skilfully exaggerated his needs and arranged his own loans.[1] MPs and the servants of the king had been equally concerned about the cost: detailed proposals for reform of the revenue were put forward by Lawrence Squibb, Secretary to the Commissioners of the Treasury, in November 1641, when the Commons and its Committees had long been devoting themselves to the same problems.[2] Barons of the Exchequer continued to exercise occasional functions throughout the Civil War, and Trials of the Pyx were held from 1643;[3] but generally the Exchequer officials who ignored Charles's summons to

---

[1] *Cal. S.P. Dom. 1640-1*, pp. 273, 431, 545, 553, etc.
[2] *Cal. S.P. Dom. 1641-3*, pp. 173-7.
[3] *H. of C. Journals* III, pp. 69, 390; *Acts and Ordinances of the Interregnum* ed. C. H. Firth and R. S. Rait (1911) I, pp. 299-303. There are occasional references in S.P. 28/252(1) to dealings of the Accounts Committee with the Barons. Sheriffs were still accounting in the Exchequer in 1643 (*H. of C. Journals III*, p. 333). Two of the Tellers were compensated for the loss of their office in 1645. (*H. of C. Journals*, IV, p. 161).

Oxford did little in their old posts. In December 1642 Parliamentary committees were ordered to search the office of Mr. Pitt, one of the Tellers, and to break open hampers in the hope of finding money and plate.[1] Presumably the place was deserted.

Control of revenue and expenditure did not in practice fall to Parliament alone. How close was the City to the financial service of the crown we have been shown in the career of Lionel Cranfield; and one of the many ironies of the Civil War was that the Parliamentary side, whose protest against the power of monopolists had been so long and bitter, should rely more firmly than the King ever had on the merchant community of London. In the first weeks of the Long Parliament the six subsidies voted to the King had been heavily pledged in advance to Customer Harrison and to the Aldermen of London. Long negotiations through Thomas Soame and Isaac Pennington had made it clear that in return for their support the financial magnates expected to have both a strong voice in the making of policy and the direct handling of the receipt of money. Accordingly collectors of the subsidies had paid their cash into the office of Robert Bateman, Chamberlain of the City, at Guildhall. And it was at Guildhall, in August 1642, that Gilbert Gerrard established his office as Treasurer for the Army,[2] into which came the receipts from most of the direct taxes, gifts, and loans that reached central funds.

From then until the Restoration, through all the quarrels of Army and Parliament, and all the political revolutions of the fifties, the grip of the London magnates on the main revenues did not relax. When the New Model Army was created, the price of a further City loan of £80,000 was that Gerrard, relinquishing his post a little before the Self-Denying Ordinance, was succeeded by Sir John Wollaston— the goldsmith who had long been the leading figure in the engineering of Parliament's borrowing—and seven other aldermen and merchants.[3] The City had no longer to go to the Bar of the House to receive the commands of Parliament: it virtually summoned Par-

---

[1] *H of C. Journals II*, p. 882; H.M.C. 5th Report, p. 87.
[2] *Acts and Ordinances* I, pp. 20-22.
[3] *Acts and Ordinances* I, p. 656.

liament to attend in the City.[1] For much of the day-to-day administration however, City financiers and MPs worked side by side: in
the application of the main revenue ordinances of the spring of
1642/3[2] they formed together the managing committees of departments of state.

The House of Commons had by this time found among its
members a number of recognised financial experts, from whom the
nucleus of many committees was drawn. The City MPs, Thomas
Soame, Isaac Pennington, Samuel Vassall, and John Venn, were
among them almost of right. John Rolle was a London merchant
whose family had lands in the south-west. Others were holders of
financial office under the royal government: Sir Robert Pye, Auditor
of the Exchequer of Receipt, and William Wheeler, who besides the
distinction of being husband of the King's laundress[3] had held office
as Comptroller of the Mint. Gerrard and Uvedale were both officials
from families with traditions of service to the crown; though Gerrard
was one of the Providence Island group and Uvedale a courtier who
returned to Parliament after joining the King at the outbreak of war.
Perhaps the ablest of them all was Robert Scawen, another figure to
contrast with the familiar image of the Parliamentarian. He had been
a receiver-general in Hampshire, Wiltshire and Gloucestershire, a
servant of the Earl of Northumberland, and a Straffordian. Then as
chairman of the Army Committee he became one of the most powerful figures in the management of the war. Not all the merchants who
became regular committeemen were Londoners. William Cage of
Ipswich and Richard Rose of Lyme Regis were provincial townsmen
who came into the accounting committee of 1643. Denis Bond,
former mayor of Dorchester, probably sat on more committees than
any other member; Giles Green of Weymouth became the leading
figure in Naval finance, and a rival of the younger Vane. But the

---

[1] In March 1645 the Commons adjourned for six days so that they could meet
at Grocers' Hall to discuss with the Common Council and others the raising
of money. (*H. of C. Journals* IV, p. 71.)

[2] *Acts and Ordinances* I, pp. 85-100, 106-117, 145-155.

[3] The accounts of Elizabeth Wheeler for this office, ending 30 January 1648/9,
are in P.R.O. E 407/50.

most prominent of the many Dorset men in the House's financial groups was John Trenchard, who belonged to the county gentry rather than to the commercial community. Finally there were the lawyers: Edmund Prideaux (another Dorset member) and Oliver St. John's cousin, Samuel Browne, were two men of widely differing temperament and politics who took on financial tasks.[1]

The importance of keeping and auditing accounts was deeply ingrained in the thoughts of MPs, office-holders, and merchants alike. The early Stuart parliaments had grown accustomed to hearing statements of the national revenue and expenditure.[2] As the debts and the needs increased with the progress of the war, so too did the necessity for detailed information about past and future income. But accounting was even more vital to the individual. Everyone through whose hands public money passed regarded himself in the natural order of things as being charged with the receipt of it and only discharged from the liability and the risk to his own estate by possession of an authoritative acquittance.[3] Everyone to whom it was owing wanted the most specific recognition of the debt, and if possible the assignment of it to a particular fund. 'Taking accounts' meant therefore two, possibly conflicting, things: furthering the interests of the state, and fulfilling the just demands of individuals.

In its first three years the Long Parliament tried repeatedly to devise means of surveying its finances. Parliamentary committees were its inevitable answer. There was the committee set up in March 1641/2 to take account of the Poll Money 'and all other monies that have been borrowed and raised by the Kingdom, and how and to whom the monies have been paid.' John Trenchard was its chairman, and the fifteen members included Bond, Rolle, and Scawen.[4] There was the committee of four—Pye, Wheeler, Rolle, and Vassall, for

---

[1] For all these MPs see M. F. Keeler, *The Long Parliament, a Biographical Dictionary* (1954), The Dorset members are discussed in D. Brunton and D. H. Pennington, *Members of the Long Parliament* (1954), pp. 153-175.

[2] F. C. Dietz, *English Public Finance 1558-1641* (1932), Part I.

[3] One of the tasks of Trenchard's Committee (see below) was to 'think of some discharge' to be given to the Treasurers of some of James I's subsidies. (*H. of C. Journals*, II, p. 566.)

[4] *H. of C. Journals* II, pp. 474, 499, 795.

the scrutiny of some specific accounts.[1] There was the big committee of March 1642/3, in which some front-rank politicians—Holles, Selden, Harbottle Grimston, and the younger Vane—were added to the finance specialists.[2] But in June the House accepted that 'all or most' of the Acts for bringing in money remained fruitless, 'chiefly for want of a select committee for accounts.'[3] Trenchard was again chairman of the body set up to remedy this, with two lawyers— Prideaux and Glynne—and three provincial merchants. The new committee seems to have failed to satisfy the Lords, who were sometimes eager to share in the business of taking accounts.[4] Its creation had met with opposition,[5] perhaps supported by those who thought that any accounting machinery ought to be on the City side of Temple Bar. Trenchard and Wheeler already had a foothold there when they were given the task of scrutinising and recording the acquittances for the Weekly Pay from Guildhall.[6]

In November 1643 the House at last considered what proved to be the effective procedure for taking accounts.[7] Two features distinguished this from all earlier attempts. It was not to be a parliamentary committee, or even a combination of MPs and outsiders. In an early self-denying clause, Lords and Commons excluded themselves from membership. Secondly, it was to be the centre of a system of county Sub-committees comparable to those set up by the money-raising departments. At the centre the Committee for Taking the Accounts of the Kingdom consisted mainly of merchants below the level of the leading Aldermen.[8] There were also lawyers, who as chairmen of the Committee and its divisions, and as its spokemen at the bar of the House, were its main champions in the struggle for survival and prestige. They included John Glover of Lincolns Inn;

---

[1] *H. of C. Journals* II, p. 780.

[2] *H. of C. Journals* III, pp. 9, 32.

[3] *H. of C. Journals* III, p. 115.

[4] *H. of L. Journals* VI, p. 161.

[5] *H. of C. Journals* III, p.p 142, 236, 280.

[6] *Acts and Ordinances* I, 98.

[7] *D'Ewes' Journal* (B.M. Harleian Mss 165, ff. 200-201); *H. of C. Journals* III, p. 301.

[8] *Acts and Ordinances* I, pp. 387-391.

John Stephens, who later moved to the Goldsmiths Hall Committee and to the Commons; and, among later additions, Peter Warburton from Cheshire. Another lawyer was the one outstanding Parliamentary figure who happened to be neither in the House nor in military command. William Prynne was now rather less active than at most stages of his career. His talents were being devoted largely to preparing evidence against Laud and to denouncing Nathaniel Fiennes for the surrender of Bristol.[1] The latter enterprise was, he claimed, the reason for opposition in the Lords to his nomination to the Accounts Committee, presumably on the initiative of Fiennes's father. Was it just, Prynne demanded, 'that Accountants should have a negative voice in the election of their auditors?'[2] At a Painted Chamber conference the Lords gave way.[3]

The original ordinance, and the usual supplementary one that filled the omissions in drafting,[4] gave the Committee abundant powers on paper. It could demand accounts from anyone at ten days' notice, take monthly muster-rolls from the army, break locks and doors to get access to information, control its officers and its local Sub-committees. In March 1644 the Committee established its headquarters at a house in Cornhill formerly belonging to Alderman Ralph Freeman, bought some books, vellum, and rulers, and started on tasks whose magnitude it had not weighed very carefully.[5] Warrants went out forthwith demanding the accounts of the Sequestration Committees; of the prominent City financiers; of the

[1] E. W. Kirby, *William Prynne*, p. 61. 'Let it be delivered when Mr. Prynne is present' was a request attached to one communication to the Committee. (*Cal. S.P. Dom.* 1645-7, p. 471.)

[2] W. Prynne, *A Check to Britannicus*, p. 7.

[3] *H. of L. Journals* VI, p. 437.

[4] *Acts and Ordinances* I, p. 468-470.

[5] The main sources for the Committee's work at this stage are the 'Copies and Abstracts of Warrants and Letters', March 1643/4 to March 1645/6, and the book of 'Warrants issued and Accounts Received', March 1643/6 to September 1649, both in P.R.O. SP 28/252(i). A 'Journal containing several Orders, Warrants, and Appearances' March 1643/4 to April 1646 is in SP 28/252(ii). A second letter-book from April 1646 to January 1648/9 is in SP 28/253(B), and a day-book of 'Orders and Votes of the Committee' from March 1645/6 to March 1649 in SP 28/252(i).

Committee for Advance of Monies at Haberdashers Hall; of the Army's own auditors, Broade and Wilcox; and of the Treasurers of the various Irish funds. The response was not enthusiastic. The big finance committees ignored repeated requests; the London Militia Committee denied having anything that concerned accounting.[1] The Excise Committee resisted so firmly that county Sub-committees had to be told to desist from enquiries in this field.[2] Papers from Ireland were always inaccessible.

The attitude of individuals naturally varied. Some appeared promptly enough: the monopolist Sir John Jacob gave ready assistance with the pre-war customs accounts; and Lord Goring when temporarily a prisoner offered, for the 'vindication of his credit', full information about the £3,000 paid for the Portsmouth garrison he had betrayed to the King. But from beginning to end of the Committee's work, the recalcitrance of 'great accountants' occupied much of its time. Alderman Fowke and Samuel Warner in the City, officials of the army's finances such as Uvedale and Commissary-General Lionel Copley, and—most notorious of all—Sir John Clotworthy with his multiplicity of Irish accounts fought long battles against Prynne and his colleagues. Their defence often took the form of appeals to the Commons. Fowke was rescued from imprisonment by the intercession at the Bar of a delegation from the Common Council; Uvedale initiated a move to have a committee of the Commons to investigate the accounts presented by Prynne and Glover; and in 1648 another Commons committee spent long hours in the Exchequer Chamber enquiring into Copley's business.[3]

In contrast to the great men who resisted investigation, large numbers of officers were eager to have their accounts take and their arrears certified. From the Commons Committee for Petitions, or by

[1] 'Copies and Abstracts' in SP 28/252(i) *passim*. B. M. Harleian Mss 166, f. 197.
[2] Letter-book in SP 28/253(B), ff 17, 33.
[3] *Book of Certificates to the House of Commons* in SP 28/253(B); *H. of C. Journals* IV, pp. 116, 215, 223, 229, 301, 431, 508; V, pp. 291, 298; *Cal. S.P. Dom. 1644*, p. 24; 'Warrants and Accounts' in SP 28/252(i) 9 Mar. 1645/6, pp. 121-3.
For the charges against Clotworthy see *Cobbett's Parliamentary History of England* (1808), III, cols. 671, 696-8. Abstracts of the depositions on abuses in his accounts are in SP 28/253A.

direct resolution of the House itself, a queue of names was steadily brought before the Committee at Cornhill, which broke up into several divisions for these tedious enquiries. Some of the higher commanders were rewarded by Parliament with specific sums charged on a particular fund;[1] but for most it was a long step from having arrears certified to having them paid.[2] Some officers, such as Philip Stapleton, were commended by the Committee for presenting accounts that were 'very fair and just'; others, including Lieutenant-Colonel Robert Lilburne, were accused of trying to conceal the arrears they had already received.[3] The Committee's constant grievance was that the burden of this routine clerical work diminished its status. Men who felt it their job to assess and protect the economic position of the state spent their time adding up the daily pay of captains. The way to greater power lay through more control over revenue. In April 1645 they brought to the House a new ordinance ('drawn as I guess by Glover and Prynne', says D'Ewes). Their requests for enhanced powers met with strong right-wing opposition, particularly in connection with Sequestrations. D'Ewes himself protested extravagantly. It 'concerned not their business of accounts'; it gave them power to imprison anyone they regarded as a defaulter, with no right of appeal until he had paid; and he claims that, with Glynn, Selden and others, he 'did so lay open the shamelessness of these men to desire such a vast power to themselves as I believe most men abominated the thing.[4] Clearly those who feared to 'see the ancient families of the nobility and gentry wholly ruined' opposed proceedings which they believed would accelerate the work of the sequestrators.[5] Nevertheless the Ordinance as passed in July did provide for drastic penalties.[6] It also tried to deal with the complaint that the Committee had no funds to pay its officials. This was a

[1] e.g. *H. of C. Journals* IV, pp. 265, 331.
[2] Papers from the Committee of Petitions are in SP 28/265. Books of certificates to the House of Commons are in SP 28/252(i) and SP 28/253(B).
[3] *H. of C. Journals* V, pp. 54, 61-2.
[4] B.M. *Harleian Mss.*, 166f. 205.
[5] B.M. *Harleian Mss.* 166, f. 102. For later complaints of failure to bring the sequestrators to account see B.M. *Add. Mss.*, 5491.
[6] *Acts and Ordinances* I, pp. 717-722.

revealing problem. Even when powers were given to collect and use the arrears the Committee discovered, difficulties arose because other ordinances had allocated them elsewhere. Officers found that fees were being charged for making up their accounts, and there were allegations of bribery. Members of the Committee—unpaid themselves—claimed that they had to pay their clerks and under-officers out of their own pockets. £1,500 for this purpose was charged on the Excise; but at the end of 1647 it had still not been paid.[1]

Legislation did not help much. In August 1645, when the Commons in one of their periodic efforts to rescue their finances from disaster called on the Committee to give a summary of the general state and condition of the accounts of the Kingdom, Prynne and Glover were quite unable to do so. It was Scawen and the Army Committee who kept track of the state of the Guildhall treasury and some others. The Accounts Committee may have felt at this period that its struggles were hopeless. Of its original members, 'some were dead, others taken off with other employment'[2] and meetings of the whole body were infrequent. But it acquired in October a dozen new members, again drawn mainly from the trading community;[3] and they found plenty to do. Much of their time was now occupied with the Committee's great source of business, and of irritation, the county Sub-committees.

London provides less than half the picture of Parliamentary finances. When the great revenue ordinances demanded that all money should be sent to Guildhall they were utterly unrealistic. In the first months of the war the loans and contributions raised in the capital provided the bulk of Parliament's resources, and a good deal came in, on the new taxes or as arrears on the old, from the south-eastern counties.[4] But an increasing proportion was raised in the country and spent there, both for local forces and for the great armies during their unpredictable passage.

In the winter of 1642-3 there came into existence in most of the

---

[1] Day-book in SP 28/252(i) p. 24. *H. of C. Journals* V, p. 196.
[2] Order-book in SP 28/252(ii), p. 33.
[3] *H. of C. Journals* IV, pp. 269, 306, 331-2.
[4] Gilbert Gerrard's Accounts in SP 28/350 and E 101/676/52.

Parliamentary area County Committees, for assessment, recruiting, or the general conduct of the war. Some owed their existence to special ordinances; some simply evolved from the meetings of deputy-lieutenants or JPs, or through the authority given for committees in all counties to raise victuals, horses, and money.[1] Whatever their origin, they consisted of those established leaders of county affairs who were thought (sometimes wrongly) to be on the Parliamentary side, together with a few who had risen by military activity. The more royalist a county was, the further down the scale it might be necessary to go.[2] A few months later the national and local finance ordinances began to name other committees in the counties for their specific purposes. But membership of the various committees theoretically established side by side in each county tended naturally to be much the same. In Warwickshire for instance all but two of those named for the committee to assess the 'Weekly Pay'—the main direct tax—were members of the county 'militia' committee, and one of the two was the brother of a member. The committee for the 'Propositions'—the forced loan of 1643—was the same as that for the Weekly Pay; and the sequestration committee had one additional name. It is not surprising that at their meetings these bodies showed little concern about which committee they were supposed to be.

The Sub-committees for taking accounts were a very different matter. The same principles were applied in the selection of names locally as centrally: those liable to account, whether through holding military command or through membership of a money-raising committee were excluded. So, like the MPs, were members of the main county committee. But restrictions which at the centre had kept the Accounts Committee one stage removed from the politics of the Commons, were in the counties the source of endless bitterness and obstruction. Beside the committeemen who were striving to get their power in the county accepted, and the officials burdened

---

[1] *Acts and Ordinances* I, 41-2, 49-63 etc.; A. M. Everitt, *The County Committee of Kent in the Civil War* (1957), p. 10.

[2] Surrey, for instance, had nine knights out of twenty names for its assessment committee; Herefordshire had only Sir Robert Harley and five other names. See also Everitt, *The County Committee of Kent*, chapter I.

with inflated administrative duties,[1] there now arose bodies of men with no other apparent object than to pry into the shortcomings of their betters. Since the new committeemen were qualified for the job by not having served prominently in other capacities, it was natural to ask why. Either they had less zeal for the cause, or they were for some other reason unacceptable to those already in power. Repeatedly the accusation was heard that these unwelcome representatives of a London authority were royalists.

Not that they were intendants sent in as foreigners to the county. The central Accounts Committee was well aware of the dangers, and tried hard to make them acceptable. The establishment of the Sub-committee sometimes began, as in Kent, with an enquiry to the county committee about whether one would now be desirable.[2] From Norfolk, the county committee sent a list of names for the accounts sub-committee which was accepted in full. But a similar list from Staffordshire proved to emanate from one faction of the county committee without the knowledge of the rest; Prynne's Committee was obviously anxious to avoid being drawn into the dispute.[3] Often there was great difficulty in getting people to serve, and the rules excluding those liable to account had in practice to be relaxed. The Hereford Sub-committee, for instance, was invited to find a way round it by having the accounts of prospective new members passed in London before they sat.[4] Members who 'dwelt remote' were often bad attenders; yet it was desirable to recruit 'men of worth' from all parts of the county.[5] On the whole the accounts Sub-committees had fewer county gentry and more townsmen and lesser freeholders than the county committees; but there was no wide social gulf between them. Committeemen of all kinds were, in general, unpaid. The Earl of

---

[1] I have quoted some of their complaints in 'The Cost of the English Civil War', *History Today*, VIII, pp. 127-8, (Feb. 1958.)

[2] 'Copies and Abstracts' in SP 28/252(i), p. 27; Letter-book of the Committee at Canterbury in SP 28/255; Everitt, *The County Committee of Kent*, p. 43.

[3] 'Copies and Abstracts' in SP 28/252(i), p. 134.

[4] Letter-book in SP 28/253(B), 5 Dec., 1646. f. 27.

[5] Richard Goldsmith, chairman of the Sub-committee in Staffordshire, stressed this in a letter to Cornhill (SP 28/255), where he listed the disqualifications of over thirty proposed members.

Manchester personally authorised fees for attendance at some Committees in the Eastern Association, but this seems to be exceptional.[1] As in London the absence of any reliable provision for administrative expenses meant that members of Sub-committees were threatened with personal loss. Unauthorised use for such purposes of arrears discovered and collected by the Sub-committees had to be discouraged. 'We doubt not but that the Parliament will remember us hereafter' was the cold comfort on this question that went from Cornhill to the Yorkshire Subcommittee when it was set up in 1646. And to reduce the work of each of its members a list of names was drawn up long enough to enable them to take turns at their duties.[2]

In some counties the Sub-committees got to work fairly smoothly in 1644. They found a meeting-place, usually in the county-town, or the best in Parliamentary hands, though some were from the beginning divided to cover different parts of the county. In August a typical inaugural meeting was held at the Bell in Hertford, with Edward Atkyns, Sergeant-at-Law, as chairman.[3] The Sub-committee was soon at work sending warrants to the High Constables to call the Petty Constables and two or three persons in each parish to meet and consider how to compile accounts for the advances on the Propositions and the loan to the Scots. When returns from the parishes began to come in the Sub-committee split into four divisions for groups of hundreds, and by 1646 there was a general meeting only about once a fortnight.

At Northampton the Sub-committee first met in September 1645, when it received from Cornhill detailed orders on how to do its job. It was to get the accounts first, then summon the parties themselves. Nothing was to be allowed unless provided for by an Ordinance; all accounts were to be fairly written in books; the validity of every voucher was to be determined. Certainly the Sub-committee proved a stern schoolmaster to parochial accountants. 'The said book is not perfect but full of blots and queries'—and was to be brought back

---

[1] William Hickman's accounts in SP 28/155.

[2] Letter-book in SP 28/253(B) Dec. 1646, f. 30.

[3] Day-book of the Hertfordshire Sub-committee in SP 28/254. The Hertfordshire accounts (SP 28/154-5 and SP 28/129-30) are among the fullest.

'fairly written' on the first of October without fail. Such rebukes were not always well-received: on October 6th the Sub-committee appealed to the central Committee to spare one of its members to help them, since 'for us to reprove may be harsh, being our neighbours, and [they] may conceive the business more for their prejudice than the benefit of the state.'[1]

In many places the county committee put every possible obstacle in the way of the interlopers, objecting to the lists of names, refusing to send in their own accounts and papers, questioning the validity of every action. Such obstructions in Lincolnshire and Rutland were brought to the notice of the Commons in 1645.[2] 'We understand', wrote the central Committee to the Leicestershire Sub-committee in 1646, 'that Colonel Hacker hath arrested divers of you, at which we desire you not to be discouraged.'[3] But the most complex story of bickering and jealously comes from Warwickshire. Behind it was the Earl of Denbigh, a commander identified with the 'peace party' and mistrusted by every militant Parliamentarian. Among his officers, and between them and the various civilian groups, were many tangled threads of hostility. In the autumn of 1644 charges and counter-charges between the Earl and his enemies on the Committees were before both Houses and a joint committee: the 'unauthorised raising of monies' was a prominent issue. The Lords, in a resolution clearing Denbigh, ordered that a Commission be sent down to appoint a Sub-committee in Warwickshire and Coventry for taking accounts.[4] It looked like revenge on the County Committee for their accusations against the Earl, though in fact the Accounts Sub-committee had been chosen shortly before the vote.

It met under the presidency of the antiquary Sir Simon Archer in St. Mary's Hall Coventry, from which the main County Committee had moved to Warwick. But Coventry, as a City and County, had nominally a separate Committee. Like London it had gone

---

[1] Day-book of the Northamptonshire Sub-committee in SP 28/254. Instructions to the Northamptonshire Sub-committee in SP 28/252(i), p. 51.

[2] 'Copies and Abstracts' in SP 28/252(i), p. 56; *H. of C. Journals* IV, 98.

[3] Letter-book in SP 28/253(B), 31 Dec. 1646, f. 33.

[4] *H. of L. Journals* VII, p. 51.

through a minor civil war of its own between two parties among the Aldermen. Its military governor, Alderman and now Colonel Barker, was an active Independent MP, an enemy of Denbigh and associate of the County Treasurer, Alderman Thomas Basnett. He had been the leader of resistance by the City to the proportion of ship-money assessments imposed on it by the County. The committeemen who remained there exercised some authority over the garrison and the neighbouring hundreds. A more shadowy unit was the Association of Warwickshire, Staffordshire, and later Shropshire, whose sole civilian official appears to have been the Treasurer Rowland Wilson. The Warwickshire Committee had also made him its 'Mustermaster and Auditor-General'; and one of the first acts of the Accounts Sub-committee was to call for his papers and those of the Treasurer for Sequestrations. But the County Committee was not disposed to co-operate: it ordered the officials to 'make no account to the present Sub-committee, nor take any oath that shall be administered.' To do so would be dangerous to many well-affected persons, and many members of the Sub-committee ought not to be in office.' The Sub-committee thereupon arrested the defaulters, whose case eventually came before the Commons, where the allegations of delinquency against the Sub-committee were aired.[1] Coventry proved a disagreeable place for the Sub-committee to sit. At one time the committee-men, few of them normally resident there, found themselves heavily assessed for the City's taxes. In 1645 Archer and the main body of the Sub-committee moved to Warwick; but they too left behind a contingent in Coventry; so that for a time there were two committees in each town involved in the wrangles. Peace party against War party; County against City; Committee against Committee—all these helped to produce and align the personal acrimonies. The road between Coventry and Warwick was sometimes said to be threatened by royalist forces. Archer remarked that if that were really so his Sub-committee would not use it, 'for we do value the safety of our persons a thousand times more than these things.'

The official grievance of the two Sub-committees was the refusal of the County Committees to give the help they needed for their auditing; but this became submerged in a flood of mutual spite. The

County Committee was said to have appointed members of the accounts Sub-committees as officers to make them ineligible to sit; it released men committed to prison by the Sub-committees; it arrested their messenger—merely 'for summoning accountants to appear', said one side; because he 'contemptuously came into the Committee parlour during their sitting and served Mr. Basnett with a warrant', said the other. But relations between the two Sub-committees for Accounts were not much better. In September 1645 they ceased to be on corresponding terms, after the members at Coventry had insulted those at Warwick by sending copies of various documents instead of the originals. In all this the Cornhill Committee did its best to keep the peace. It had of course to support and encourage its colleagues. The allegations against them were of no weight; they were to continue with 'cheerfulness and alacrity'; and their power was equal to that of the main Committee. It even gave permission for the Sub-committee to refuse to pass the personal accounts of members of the County Committee who had money due to them until it proved more amenable, and threatened to bring the matter before the House. But when Wilson agreed to send his accounts to Cornhill but not to Coventry, the central Committee made every effort at appeasement. Having pleaded with the Coventry Committee to commute Wilson's imprisonment to a fine, it now asked that this too should be remitted, and hoped—perhaps without much confidence—that the business would 'be a means to reconcile all the differences between you and the Militia Committee.' The quarrel between the two accounts Subcommittees it naturally regarded as a disastrous complication. 'Nothing can be more fatal to your proceedings', and all private considerations should be laid aside to heal the differences. By 1647 the Cornhill Committee was working fairly smoothly with both. But for one reason or another it was long an unhappy fate for a committeeman or officer from the principal committees of the county at Warwick to be sent to Coventry.[1]

---

[1] This account is derived mainly from the letters of the Coventry and War-wickshire Sub-committees in SP 28/246 and SP 28/248, and of the Committee for Taking Accounts of the Kingdom in SP 28/252(i) and SP 28/253(B). For the disputes between Denbigh and the Warwickshire committees see also D. H.

To dip into the petty quarrels, the grudges, and the excuses for failure that fill the correspondence of the central and local Committees leaves an impression of chaotic ineptitude. Certainly no tidy abstracts of the income and expenditure of Parliamentary government or even of major parts of it emerged from their sittings. Yet despite all the 'obstructions' vast amounts of paper did find their way to the Sub-committees and thence to Alderman Freeman's house. Nothing could illustrate better than these accounts the fragmentation through which Parliament somehow groped to victory. The centralising machinery of the Ordinances, the London treasuries, the great commanders was for the most part beyond the reach of the Cornhill Committee. Its successful investigations concerned instead the Civil War of counties, hundreds, and parishes drained of their wealth through multiple channels; of colonels and captains supplying their forces as opportunity allowed; of garrisons living like robber-barons on the countryside within their reach. Yet all of them struggled to keep within the framework of law and administrative acceptance: behind the musket that extracted money came the voucher that established responsibility for it.

While the Committees fought their private battles, they managed with surprising success to accumulate the records of the cost of the war in Parliamentarian counties. In time it became clear that separate enquiries into each tax were less feasible than general enquiries into what each locality paid. At various times from 1646 onwards, Sub-committees were directed to send their warrants, as the order to Stafford put it, 'to two or three honest and able men' of each parish to write out details of *all* the money received there.[1] Usually lists were provided of the local and national contributions that were supposed to have been received. The Buckinghamshire Sub-committee in the summer of 1646 circulated a printed list of 29 levies on the county or parts of it, and asked for the amounts collected for each. Those responsible for the returns ranged from Sir John Lawrence Bt., collector in the Hundred of Stoke, to the 'illiterate and timorous'

Pennington and I. A. Roots (ed), *The Committee at Stafford 1643-1645* (1956), pp. lxxiv-lxxxiii, and sources there cited.
[1] Letter-book in SP 28/253(B), June 1646.

constable of Chenies, who 'could not nor durst not keep any papers.'[1]
In the Eastern Association 47 separate questions were supposed to be
answered;[2] but in counties more remote from London or less safely
Parliamentarian there were often no more than a dozen taxes to list.
The passing of this type of account usually involved the examination
on oath of the constables and collectors, together with some of the
parishioners, and the scrutiny of all the papers they had managed to
preserve. Sometimes the mere certificate of a few inhabitants was
accepted as adequate. ('They must have a care that they certify nothing
but what they can produce receipts for', the Hertforshire Sub-
committee warned them).[3] Sometimes an effort was made to check
the returns with the accounts of the various Treasurers. Often those
questioned hoped to rely on any information the Sub-committee had
rather than risk being contradicted. The inhabitants of Milverton in
Warwickshire could not 'certainly remember' what they had paid
for any of the early taxes, and referred themselves to accounts returned to the Exchequer. But they remembered in great detail what
they had lost through freequarter, and the exact amounts assessed for
Weekly Pay.[4] Since for many levies no prior assessment was made, a
little harmless juggling was usually possible. 'The gross sum is true,
though if you cast up the particulars they do in some of them differ a
little' was an admission from Herefordshire that could be applied
to many accounts.[5] Gradually abandoning the quest for perfection,
the Sub-committees managed by 1649 to discharge a great many
constables and collectors and leave them to the less complex tasks
imposed by Commonwealth taxation.

Military commanders were more interested in the Accounts Committees when their personal pay was concerned than when information
was demanded from them for more general purposes. Ireton, in
August 1644, attributed a demand for his accounts to the 'malicious
and divillish practices' of people he had himself called to account

[1] SP 28/148.
[2] SP 28/152(b).
[3] Order-book of the Hertfordshire Sub-committee, SP 28/254, p. 10.
[4] Milverton accounts in SP 28/183.
[5] Accounts of Thomas Blaney in SP 28/129, p. 85.

for sequestration monies. Nor were the treasurers employed by county committees always helpful. While men like Rowland Wilson ignored the Sub-committees, more compliant types such as Thomas Blaney of Herefordshire pleaded their inability to resist pressure from the armies. 'Being but a ministerial officer', he wrote, when asked to explain arrears of over £3,000, he could not withstand the power of the soldiery to enforce irregular payments; and he hoped his small estate would not suffer.[1] Robert Willmott at Stafford was another pitiful character whose accounts would never quite come right.[2] But despite their sorrows and excuses these and many other county treasurers did in the end produce some informative figures.

By no means all wartime accounts came to Cornhill. The Committee of the Northern Association determined those of its own counties;[3] and though Vane brought his own accounts to the central Committee in 1648 few details of naval expenditure seen to have been examined.[4] Most important of all, the Committee was not at first concerned with the pay of the common soldier.[5] When this became in 1647 a great national issue, the task of examining and certifying did not fall to any one authority. The Army and its parliamentary committee had little use for the Accounts Committee, now a firm ally of the Presbyterians. (Prynne and Glover were appointed as counsel for the defence of the Eleven Members.)[6] But administrative necessity sometimes counted for more then politics. While a Parliament with alternating Independent and Presbyterian majorities was producing contradictory and often hopelessly unrealistic legislation,[7] soldiers were in fact receiving certificates from their officers with varying regard to strict accountancy.[8] According to the Declaration attached

---

[1] Letter to the Commissioners of Assessments, 1653/2, in SP 28/229.
[2] *The Committee at Stafford*, pp. 333-4.
[3] *H. of C. Journals* V, pp. 141, 570.
[4] *H. of C. Journals* VI, p. 11. Customs Revenue was however constantly before the Committee: see especially SP 28/252(ii).
[5] *Cal. S.P. Dom. 1645-7*, p. 553; Letter-book in SP 28/253(B), Dec. 1646.
[6] *H. of C. Journals* V, p. 243.
[7] e.g. *H. of C. Journals* V, pp. 307-8; *Acts and Ordinances* I, pp. 940-7, 1051, 1053.
[8] The main facts about the pay and debentures of the New Model Army are in C. H. Firth, *Cromwell's Army* (1903) Chapter 8.

to the Ordinance of May 28th 1647, the Committee for Taking the Accounts of the Kingdom was to determine the accounts of all officers and soldiers—for which a new committee seems at first to have been contemplated. But the Instructions that followed recognised that for most claimants confirmation from a superior officer was all that could be expected. The final authority over many such accounts was exercised by the salaried professional auditors of the Army, Broade, Wilcox, and three new colleagues, Prince, Richardson, and Nicholas Bond. To them, in July 1647, fell the task that looked like the nadir of parliamentary control over finance: they were to attend the House every morning to deal with the 'clamorous women' who brought their husbands' demands for pay to the door.[1] A year later the auditors had acquired the status of a 'committee' with sole responsibility for the accounts of those soldiers who belonged neither to the great armies nor to the counties, and they were given Worcester House as their headquarters.[2] For Fairfax's army, which alone was able to back its claims by the threat of violence against Parliament, the Army Committee was given in the autumn undisputed control of accounting.[3] It claimed also to supervise the county committees, who were required to provide the money for disbanding as well as the accounts. In December yet another authority appeared: the Commissioners for the Monthly Assessment in the counties were to take the accounts of the local forces about to be disbanded.[4]

Despite these rival concerns, the Committee in Alderman Freeman's House had plenty to do. The county Sub-committees were still handling a great variety of accounts, military and civil, and were directed, encouraged, and reprimanded in long correspondence with Cornhill. Sequestration business increased in 1648, when the Commons sought to bring in to Guildhall money remaining in the hands of local committees.[5] But it was clear that a body so closely identified

---

[1] *H. of C. Journals* V, p. 629.
[2] *Acts and Ordinances* I, p. 1170. *H. of C. Journals* V, p. 696.
[3] *H. of L. Journals* IX, p. 446; *H. of C. Journals* V, pp. 340-1.
[4] *Acts and Ordinances* I, p. 1053.
[5] *Acts and Ordinances* I, p. 1187.

with political presbyterianism and the old hands in the City was unlikely to survive the devastations of 1649.[1] Even in its friends in the House its cause had seldom aroused enthusiasm: opponents of the Army tended also to be opponents of bureaucracy and upholders of parliamentary privilege, and hence not particularly well-disposed towards a non-parliamentary committee. The disbanding of most of the local forces and the decline of county government left the Sub-committees also in a weak position. In May 1649 a Commons committee was named to 'present somewhat fit to pass for taking the accounts of the Commonwealth'. In October the Act was passed that repealed the Ordinance of 1642/3, discharged the Committee for Taking the Accounts of the Kingdom, and put in its place a much smaller body the nucleus of which was the group of professional auditors who had risen to prominence in the determining of the soldiers' pay. No one from the old Committee served on the new.[2] Though its powers extended to all persons in any way accountable since November 1640, there was one notable reservation: they were not to take any accounts 'which by law are to be taken and passed in the Court of the Public Exchequer.' Long before Cromwell's reforms, the ancient administrative system was re-appearing amid the shifting improvisations of the new.[3]

Political conflicts necessarily dominate the history of the Parliamentary cause and the struggles to govern the country without the king. The divisions between Army and Parliament, Independent and Presbyterian, were deep and comprehensive enough to align a multitude of quarrels that sprang from individual or collective greed, ambition, or habit. In the unspectacular careers of the Accounts Committees the confusion of motives and pressures was much the same as on more exalted levels. Committees liked to have power, preferred important jobs to seemingly unimportant ones, complained of their burdens but hated to surrender them, bristled at every slight

---

[1] One of the first acts of the Rump was to set up its own committee to view the Treasuries and estimate the arrears due. *H. of C. Journals* VI, p. 101.

[2] *Acts and Ordinances* II, pp. 277-281.

[3] For duties given to the Barons of the Exchequer in 1649 see *Acts and Ordinances* II, pp. 5, 62-3, 207 etc.

to their privilege and dignity. They and their members made friends and enemies, and knew which side they were on in every game. Social, economic, ideological differences are the foundations for any understanding of the period. But before we build too much on them it is worth remembering that men will fight for their team, whether it is the King in Parliament or the committee in the inn parlour.

SIR JOHN BANKS, FINANCIER: AN ESSAY ON GOVERNMENT BORROWING UNDER THE LATER STUARTS

'... it seems to me very important for you... not to throw your freedom of action away any more, and to prefer commercial operations proper, where the profit is reduced but certain, to the more lucrative but more perilous role of money-lender to the government.'

ALFRED ANDRÉ to Edouard Dervieu, 22 October 1864.[1]

'Din'd with Sir Jo: Banks at his house in Lincolns Inn fields... This Sir Jo: Banks was a Merchant, of small beginnings, but by usurie etc. amassed an Estate of 100,000 pounds.'

JOHN EVELYN, 25 August 1676.[2]

I

THE ancient but unloved activity of lending money has seemingly benefited from the therapeutic effects of a long historical voyage. Our customary reaction to the banker of today is not always that of instinctive suspicion; and even the nebulous comprehensiveness of the name of financier covers a multitude of doings not all of which are necessarily regarded as sinful. The transformation is patently a product neither of a mere change of name nor of a massive change of heart, but rather of the evolution of new economic and financial organisations in the modern industrialized state. Though many areas of the world still know well the extortions of the moneylender, such exactions are not typically a subject of complaint in the advanced societies of today; and André's cautionary comment to his friend Dervieu, then banker to Ismail Pasha, Khedive

[1] Quoted in D. Landes, *Bankers and Pashas* (London, 1958), p. 219.
[2] *The Diary of John Evelyn* (Ed. E. S. de Beer, Oxford, 1955) IV, p. 96.

of Egypt, has lost at least some of its relevance to the modern world of
public finance. But its relevance to those centuries of history which
saw the urgent aspirations of the national state caught in the fiscal
mire of the pre-industrialized economy is unmistakeable. At the same
time, over the great bankers and financiers of medieval and Re-
naissance Europe there hung the shadow of usury; and many generations later, after the seeming chasm of the Reformation, Defoe
was warning his fledgling English tradesman against the 'Procurer or
Scrivener or Banker', against 'Usurers [and] Money-Lenders.'[1]

The vast and intricate web of credit which stretched through all
ranks of society, making money-lending a by-employment for many
and a rich racket for a few, formed an integral element of the economic
order and provided the rationale of the hatred of usury. Professor
Tawney has written of Tudor England: 'If the first impression of the
student accustomed to the centralised financial organisation of modern
societies is surprise at the small use made of credit, the second is
likely to be surprise at its ubiquity.'[2] It is a lesson which still needs
to be repeatedly learnt, for the full historial consequences of that
credit economy which prevailed long before our modern world of
hire purchase have not been much explored. Certainly in later Stuart
times the credit network was not less ubiquitous nor the financial
demands of the government less pressing than they had been a
century earlier.

All transactions have two faces: the monetary and the real. The
gaps between sowing and reaping, between buying the wool and
selling the cloth: these were real enough and not only in the econo-
mist's sense of the word. Their implications were also monetary.
Expanding the markets and lengthening the channels of trade,
pushing out the range of commercial agriculture and widening the
scope of industrial activity: such movements of economic life—and
17th century England knew them all—meant a greater number of
transactions. How were they to be financed? How was the increased
liquidity which they demanded to be found?

[1] D. Defoe, *The Complete English Tradesman* (Ed. 1727), suppl. p. 15.
[2] R. H. Tawney, Introduction to Thomas Wilson, *A Discourse upon Usury*
(London, 1925), p. 19.

To complain today that one is short of money is not, save presumably for the very rich, to testify to a unique woe. Complaints of a persistent scarcity of money, on the other hand, would strike an odd note in our modern economy. Such complaints were far from odd in 17th century England, nor indeed were they limited to this country and that century. Any changes in the relative valuations of gold and silver which resulted in an outflow of the silver coin which was widely used for ordinary transactions 'could and did reduce supplies of *effective money*'.[1] Although the phrase 'scarcity of money' was ambiguously used, contemporaries sometimes meant what they said. In addition to this important bimetallic source of monetary scarcity, there was the problem of the relation between the mint output of coin and the transaction demand for cash. Can it reasonably be assumed that as the number of transactions increased—be it through the expansion of private economic activity or the growing range of State demands—so also did the monetary liquidity of the economy? The well-known shortage of coin in 18th century England suggests the very opposite. And it seems probable that a persistent tendency— let us put it no more strongly than that—towards a shortage of cash in the economy had been making itself apparent long before then. 'Cash' must also include the next best thing, i.e. first-class short-dated bills. The often disturbed financial, commercial and monetary circumstances of the time could readily produce periodic shortages of these nearly liquid means of payment. There is much that points in the general direction of inadequate liquidity: the sundry comments of contemporaries not all of which are simply products of passing crises with their attendant acute shortages; the evidence of much petty borrowing and lending of cash in circumstances which preclude the 'real' needs of poverty; the laments of governments that shortage of coin hindered the payments of taxes; the increase in credit transactions

---

[1] B. E. Supple, 'Currency and Commerce in the Early Seventeenth Century', *Econ. Hist. Rev.*, 2nd ser., X (1957), p. 255; see also J. D. Gould, 'The Royal Mint in the Early Seventeenth Century', *Econ. Hist. Rev.*, 2nd ser., V (1952) and 'The Trade Depression in the early 1620's, *Econ. Hist. Rev.*, 2nd ser., VII (1954); and Sir John Craig, *The Mint* (Cambridge, 1953).

and the appearance of new types of paper instruments, despite which the complaints of shortages do not disappear.[1]

Dudley North observed that 'there is required for carrying on the Trade of the Nation, a determinate sum of Specifick Money, which varies, and is sometimes more, sometimes less, as the Circumstances we are in require.'[2] His statement illustrates both current awareness of the need for varying amounts and the contemporary idea of fixity, the essentially static viewpoint which virtually precluded, in this case, any awareness of the need for a long-term increase. His corollary that the problem could confidently be left to the operations of the Mint which, actuated by economic laws, would automatically match the supply of money to the demand for it, has all the dogmatic optimism of pure-bred economic laissez-faire. Five years after he wrote the country's economy was throttled by a monetary crisis of exceptional severity. Although this particular crisis had its roots in the bimetallic problem of gold and silver values and the current extremely bad state of the silver coinage, it was exacerbated by the circumstances of war.

Government demand for money played then, as it does today, an important role in determining what the authors of the Radcliffe

---

[1] As well as Supple, op cit., see E. F. Heckscher, *Mercantilism* (2nd Ed., London 1955) II, pp. 217-24; J. Child, *A Discourse about Trade* (1690), esp. Preface; Pepys, *Diary* (Ed. H. B. Wheatley). 19 May 1663, 7 April, 9 and 31 December 1665, etc.; Evelyn, *Diary*, 26 July and 3 August 1669, and letter from J. Evelyn to, G. Evelyn quoted in W. G. Hiscock, *John Evelyn and his family circle* (London, 1954), pp. 188-9; there is a mass of evidence on the accute shortage of 1696 in *Commons Journals* XI. For examples of small-scale lending and borrowing, see the diary in W. D. Christie, *Life of Anthony Ashley Cooper, 1st Earl of Shaftesbury* (London, 1871), I, Appx II; the journals of John Locke, particularly the later volumes, also contain many records of every-day minor transactions of this sort (Bodleian: Locke Mss f. 1-10); for evidence of a mass of petty borrowing in humble rural circles, see Lord Leconfield, *Petworth Manor in the 17th Century* (London, 1954). For similar liquidity problems in France, see J. Meuvret, 'Comment les Français voyaient l'impôt', in *Comment les Français voyaient la France au XVIIe siècle* (Paris, 1955), pp. 63 ff. and 'Circulation monétaire et utilisation économique de la monnaie dans la France du XVIe et XVIIe siècles', *Études d'histoire moderne et contemporaine* I, 1947, 15-28; also F. C. Spooner, *L'Économie Mondiale et les Frappes Monétaires en France*, 1493-1680 (Paris, 1956), pp. 208 ff and *passim*.

[2] Dudley North, *Discourses upon Trade* (1691), pp. 24-5.

Report have recently called the 'general structure of liquidity in the economy'.[1] Few consecutive years of the 17th century passed by during which the major powers of Europe were not engaged in wars which grew more costly, demanded more money, more goods and services, in effect more transactions and more liquidity. Superimpose this habitual belligerency upon economies suffering from the inherent difficulties of bimetallism, inadequate Mint output, clipped coinages, a slackening of the influx of precious metals from the New World and an increase in the outflow of bullion to the East, as well as a gradually rising long-term level of economic activity, and it is hardly surprising that in the 17th century complaints of a shortage of money are to be heard even though the general level of prices did not markedly rise after the middle of that century.

War also gave extra power to the forces which otherwise tended to attract money towards the capital. In France, Colbert lamented the absence of money in the provinces because it hindered the collection of taxes;[2] authors as far apart as J. J. Becher and Sir William Petty remarked on the difficulties of the poor in finding money to pay taxes.[3] In England the heavy involvement of the London bankers in State finance conduced to the same end. Sir Josiah Child commented sourly in 1690 about:

'... the Trade of Bankering, which obstructs circulation, advanceth Usury, and renders it so easie, that most Men as soon as they can make up a sum of £50 or a £100 send it unto the Gold-smith; which doth, and will occasion while it lasts, that fatal pressing necessity for Money, so visible throughout the whole Kingdom, both to Prince and People.' Moreover, 'the Trade of Bankers being only in London it doth very much drain the ready money from other parts of the Kingdom.'[4]

Sixteen years earlier, Shaftesbury wrote, apropos the Third Dutch War and the Stop of the Exchequer:

[1] *Report of the Committee on the Working of the Monetary System* (1959: Cmd. 827), p. 132.
[2] *Lettres, Instructions et Mémoires de Colbert* (Ed. P. Clément), VII, pp. 233-6.
[3] Heckscher, *op. cit.*, II, pp. 220-1.
[4] J. Child, *op. cit.*, Preface; and *Trade and Interest of Money Considered*, p. 18.

'... the bankers were grown destructive to the nation especially to the country gentleman and farmers, and their interest: that under the pretence, and by the advantage of lending the King money upon very great use, they got all the ready money of the kingdom into their hands so that no gentleman, farmer or merchant, could, without great difficulty, compass money for their occasions, unless at almost double the rate the law allowed to be taken; ... as to the King's affairs... twelve in the hundred did not content them, but they bought up all the King's assignments at 20 or 30 per cent profit.'[1]

There was, in short, a premium upon liquidity. This had a variety of effects. It meant an extension of credit dealing of all sorts, thus reinforcing those 'real', as distinct from monetary, factors which, as mentioned above, made the credit network ubiquitous. It is not perhaps easy for us today to imagine the implications of the pay of sailors or dockyard workers being 12 to 18 months in arrears; but that it could have reached that stage is not only a comment on the government but a tribute to the pre-existence and acceptance of far-reaching credit arrangements. It meant, too, that governments already grappling with the task of making an inelastic and archaic revenue system match the formidable demands put upon it, were also faced by a tendency towards a shortage of money being turned into an acute scarcity of it. This in turn meant, as Shaftesbury indicated, a widening range of interest and discount rates; and they were not simply a product of the government's poor credit, but of the premium on liquidity. Evelyn's observation in 1696 that 'there was so little money in the nation' that it was impossible to borrow money 'under 14 or 15% on bills or on Exchequer Tallies under 30%,'[2] provides something of this double reflection.

A sharper reflection of the problem as it affected government borrowing and the price of liquidity is provided by a letter which Pepys wrote to Sir William Coventry in November 1665 when the Navy's needs for the second Dutch War were growing urgent.

[1] Shaftesbury to Locke, 23 Nov. 1674, quoted Christie, *op. cit.*, II, p. 63. See also below, p. 230 n. 1.
[2] *Diary*, 26 July and 3 August, 1696.

Coventry had made a proposal that government creditors should be asked to advance £100 in money for every £200 owing to them, the whole debt to be secured on the supply recently voted by Parliament, interest to be at 6%. Pepys then explains the facts of financial life. Most of the Navy's stores have been supplied on credit, but it is one thing to supply goods in this way and quite another to advance money. Moreover, he doubts whether many of even the bigger suppliers are capable of doing so, because-:

'... they having already trusted us further than they are able by their own stocks, but are forced to borrow money to do it, which if lent by the goldsmiths (and few else are able to do it) comes not to them at less than 8 per cent or 9 per cent, and therefore it would be hard for them to borrow at 8 per cent at least, to lend at 6. Besides, though this of borrowing money may not be the case of all, yet I am apt to think they all are helped by the credit they have for provisions, of which one tradesman can be supplied by another to £1000 value when he can't be trusted nor will think it fit to be known to borrow £500 in money.'

Of the bigger traders with whom the Navy dealt, Pepys thought that the Navy owed some of them twice as much as they were worth, and all of them four times as much as they could raise in ready money. Even Sir William Warren, in view of the credit or money which he had to find, would, Pepys thought, be 'as unfit for the advancing £100 or £200 is actually due to him as some of his neighbours'. If 'our great dealers' could not help, how much less could the small men. Furthermore, most of the Navy bills had already been sold to the goldsmiths:

'... half (if not 2/3) of all the bills signed by this Office are paid in Lombard Street by such as will never advance you anything upon 6 per cent today when out of the next sum payable to the Navy they can hook in all those bills at 10 per cent with consideration for forbearance past, as well as 8 or 9 per cent given them by the poor merchants for their present advancing their money.'

What is to be done? Pepys does not know: 'for unless this or some other proposition extraordinary be set on foot... I know not in the world what will be the issue, for I have reason from all hands to despair of the City's doing much for our relief.'[1]

Pepys was right. And he was soon to add experience to knowledge: a few months later he made an agreeable little profit for himself by buying from Sir William Warren a piece of government paper and then selling it to a goldsmith.[2] The premium on liquidity offered glittering opportunities for all who could lay their hands on cash and knew how to exploit it. At about the same time as he wrote the letter to Coventry Pepys' acquaintance with the merchant Sir John Banks was ripening into friendship; he was later to become intimate with Banks' family. And Banks, though not a goldsmith, nor a banker, nor a scrivener, nor a revenue farmer was to become a very successful exploiter of the government's need for money.[3]

II

John Banks was born in 1627. His father prospered as tradesman and woollen draper in the small but growing Kentish market town of Maidstone, attained the dignity of 'gent.', and on his death in 1669

[1] *Further Correspondence of Samuel Pepys 1662-79* (ed. J. R. Tanner, London, 1929), pp. 70-72.

[2] see below, p. 223.

[3] Much of the remainder of this article is derived from the ledgers, journals and other account books and business papers of Sir John Banks, most of which are deposited in the Aylesford Mss at the Kent County Archives, Maidstone. Of the surviving ledgers—B, C and D—and their corresponding journals, covering the years 1657-99, ledger C has strayed and is to be found in the Library at the Guildhall, London. Unless other or specific references are given the sourcee used in the account which follows are these six ledgers and journals. Dates throughout have been put in the New Style; quotations taken directly from contemporary Ms sources have been modernized in spelling and punctuation.

For some years I have been working intermittently on Banks' papers and related sources, and hope soon to publish the results in the form of a biography; I will then discharge the many and various debts of gratitude which I have incurred in the course of these enquiries. For the present however I wish to thank for particular advice or specific references used here my colleagues Professors F. J. Fisher and B. S. Yamey as well as Messrs. D. G. Allan, Basil Henning, Master of Saybrook College, Yale, and H. Roseveare of King's College, London.

left lands and property which brought a net accretion of some £28,000 to his son's estate. John Banks did not start at the bottom. That son, meanwhile, was himself prospering in the wider and more dignified world of foreign trade, and had cemented his interests there by marrying, in 1654, the daughter of John Dethick, merchant, member of the Mercers Company of London, and shortly to be knighted as Lord Mayor. In 1661 John Banks was made a baronet, and his career as an East India merchant—which is not the concern of this article—was well set on its successful path. Suffice to say that he combined trading to India with participation in trading ventures to and from the Mediterranean and Levant; that his ascent in the hierarcy of the East India Company took him to the Governorship in 1672-4 and again in 1683; that he also became a member of the Royal African Company, and its Sub-Governor in 1674-5. At the same time as he was advancing his career as a merchant he was also building up a substantial landed estate, the centre of which was his seat, Aylesford Priory, secularized in name to 'The Fryers', and acquired from Sir Peter Ricaut, a Delinquent, in 1657. It passed, together with the bulk of his property, to his eldest daughter and co-heir who in 1678 married Heneage Finch (second son of Heneage Finch, 1st Earl of Nottingham), created Earl of Aylesford in 1714. When that improbably named gossip, Narcissus Luttrell, recorded in October 1699 the death of Sir John Banks who "'tis said, has left behind him, in money and land, to the value of £200,000', his information was not much in excess of the truth.[1]

[1] Narcissus Luttrell, *A Brief Historical Relation of State Affairs, 1678-1714* (Oxford, 1857), IV, p. 573; see also, as well as Aylesford Mss the Journal of Sir Roger Twisden (in Maidstone Museum) f. 79; Edward Hasted, *History of Kent* (Ed. 1798), IV. pp. 427-9; *D.N.B. sub.* Finch; *Calendar of the Court Minutes of the East India Co.* (Ed. E. B. Sainsbury), esp. the volume for 1671-3; K. G. Davies, *The Royal African Company* (London, 1957), pp. 68, 337, 338; A. B. Beaven, *The Aldermen of the City of London* (London, 1908), pp. 125, 124, 257; G.E.C., *Complete Baronetage*, etc.

I would like to take this opportunity of correcting the slip in my article 'London Scriveners and the Estate Market in the Later Seventeenth Century', *Econ. Hist. Rev.* 2nd. ser., IV (1951), p. 225, where I spoke of Banks' daughter marrying 'Heneage Finch, subsequently Earl of Nottingham and of Aylesford'. This is of course wrong and, as the above text shows, a confusion between two Heneages, father and son.

So much, in broad outline, is a career of familiar shape. It may serve to give some hint of the measure and status of the man. But this bare chronicle of mercantile success, the acquisition of titular and landed dignity, the socially successful marriage of a daughter, omits an important element in the story. Evelyn's comment, quoted at the beginning of this article, though describing Banks as a merchant, attributed his gains to 'usurie, etc.' Faintly sanctimonious and smug as it may seem, like so much of Evelyn's comment, it contains a good deal of truth. Banks was a royal moneylender—to Charles II, James II, and William III; at the Stop of the Exchequer he was the largest single government creditor aside from the biggest of the goldsmith bankers; he emerged from that financial fracas with notable success. How was it done?

Banks' performances in the 'lucrative but more perilous role' as André was later to describe it, fall into four phases. The first runs to 1665; during this period, although his direct lending to the government was trifling in amount, he was building up useful commercial and financial connections with the Navy. The second phase extends over the war-ridden decade from 1665 to 1675 and resounds with a crescendo of furious activity which comes to a fairly sudden stop. In the third phase, from 1676 to 1688, Banks' performances in the perilous role were meagre; in the fourth and final phase he emerged from this seeming retirement to a new round of energetic money-lending. Only the first two phases will be considered here. But as a rough indicator of the magnitude and timing of these activities, the following table gives the sums annually passing through royal accounts in his ledgers, accounts dignified by such names as 'Charles King of England', 'King James, his Majesties Exchequer', and, most ponderously, 'King William and Queen Mary, their Majesties Exchequer.'

D. C. Coleman

Sums annually passing through royal accounts in Banks' Ledgers, 1657-99[1]

£s

1657	—	1671	87,224	1685	8,583
8	—	2	77,580	6	
9	—	3	15,612	7	—
1660	5,421	4	—	8	—
1	—	5	—	9	31,781
2	—	6	—	1690	34,460
3	—	7	—	1	36,549
4	—	8	—	2	84,430
5	—	9		3	31,631
6	40,565	1680	2,456	4	38,200
7	26,200	1		5	42,387
8	50,405	2		6	3,500
9	11,120	3	—	7	17,570
1670	29,384	4	—	8	34,199
				9	14,652

These figures, it must be emphasised, offer only an approximate guide. Inconsistencies and irregularities of Banks' accounting are one reason for this caveat; another is that these royal accounts omit some loans made in effect to the government but recorded under the names of specific officials. These include some £34,000 which went through the account of Sir George Cartaret, Treasurer of the Navy, in 1665-6; about £30,000 recorded under the name of Lord Clifford, Lord Treasurer, in 1673-4; some £27,000 in 1674-5, to his successor Lord Latimer; and, the biggest and most important exception during the first and second phases of lending, Sir Denis Gawden, victualler of the Navy from 1660 to 1671, through whose account with Banks there passed an annual average of over £6,000 for the two years 1658-60, over £13,000 a year fro the period 1661-4 inclusive, and an average of nearly £38,000 per annum from 1665 until 1671 when Banks' arrangements with Gawden ceased more or less abruptly.[2] These

[1] The totals are the amounts entered on the debit side of the accounts, minus the balances carried forward.

[2] Although Gawden was effectively the main victualler of the Navy from 1660 to 1671 he was not formally the sole victualler throughout the period. Pepys was

large amounts in Gawden's account are, however, swollen by the entry there of assignments, by Gawden to Banks, of government paper also included in the royal accounts.

The item of £5,421 which marks the entry of 'Charles King of England' into Banks' ledgers is curious and significant. The debt apparently originated in a bill of Charles II for money lent him in Holland in 1648 and which in 1660 was worth £ 2,736. 12s. 6d. It seems unlikely that Banks provided the money in the first place— the then 21 year-old son of a Maidstone tradesman sounds an improbable lender to Charles Stuart in Holland in 1648—but he was evidently willing to accept the bill. Negotiations for settling the debt apparently produced the familiar demand for the advance of more cash. Although that money was provided by Banks, the arrangements for the whole deal were furthered by two other persons: Giles Lytcott and Thomas Killigrew. The outcome was that Banks paid Lytcott £2,684. 13s. 4d. (which, added to the bill value of £2,736. 12s. 6d. makes up the total debt of £5,421. 5s. 10d.) and Lytcott secured in his own name, but in trust for Banks, Charles' seal for repayment of the total in 6 months. The seal was then assigned to Banks who allowed Lytcott 'for Mr. Tho. Killigrew and himself', the sum of £985. 8s. 10d 'being so much I do allow for his assistance in this business', to be paid only 'after I have received (and not otherwise) the sum of £4,435. 17s. 0d' (i.e. the balance of the total). And for himself? He credits his profit and loss account with £1,751. 3s. 8d, 'being so much allowed by his Majesty upon a bill under his hand...' £1,751. 3s. 8d + £985. 8s. 10d = £2,736. 12s. 6d, i.e. the whole value of the bill was shared between them. The return was not to be scorned; support of Charles' cause had its rewards for some; and Banks seems eager to be aboard the band-wagon. The money was

surveyor-general of victuals from 1665 to 1667 and in 1668 Gawden was joined by his son, Benjamin, and Sir William Penn, who died in 1670. In January 1672 a new victualling contract started, with a syndicate consisting of Gawden, his son, Josiah Child, Sir Thomas Littleton, and Thomas Papillon. *Catalogue of the Naval Mss in the Pepysian Library* (Ed. J. R. Tanner, *Navy Records Society*, 1903), I, pp. 152-160.

duly paid in July 1661; and in the official records the whole deal is hidden behind the blank formality of 'money warrant for £ 5,421. 5s.10d to Giles Lytcott for moneys lent to the King.'[1]

In November 1657 Banks recorded that his 'present stock, God be praised' was £13,493.14s.2d. Less than six years later, in June 1663, it had more than doubled, at nearly £29,000. This is solid prosperity and a very acceptable rate of advance, but it hardly put Banks in the top flight of big merchants or gave him scope for large-scale transactions. His links with the Navy during these years were fairly modest. Some £31,000 passed through his account with Richard Hutchinson, then Treasurer of the Navy, in the years 1657-60, in the course of which Banks figures as a supplier of such wares as canvas and that explosive Indian contribution to English might—saltpetre. Dennis Gawden had been a member of the Navy victualling syndicate of 1650 headed by Thomas Pride,[2] and Banks had some small dealings with that body and its successors. After Gawden took on himself the frightening task of victualling the Navy, those dealings grew and so did Banks' profits therefrom. Until the end of 1665, the dealings were of three main types. Banks lent money to Gawden on bond or against the security of tallies; he sold him agricultural produce; and he rented land to him in Kent.

The second and third of these categories testify to the use which Banks made of the favourable geographical position of his growing Kentish estate. His riparian seat at Aylesford, with its substantial home farm, was some three miles downstream from Maidstone and less than ten miles upstream from the great naval dockyards at Chatham, all on the navigable Medway, and all within 30 miles not only of London but also of the other Naval yards at Deptford and Woolwich. His sales of produce, though never on a large scale,

---

[1] Aylesford Mss. ledger B. f. 76, journal B, f. 80; *Calendar of Treasury Books* (ed. W. A. Shaw), *1660-67*, pp. 84, 252. Giles Lytcott later figures frequently in Banks' accounts as a factor at Leghorn; Thomas Killigrew was probably the actor, Court jester, favourite and Groom of the Bedchamber to Charles II, with whom Banks also had a number of business dealings.

[2] M. Oppenheim, *History of the Administration of the Royal Navy* (London, 1896), p. 324 and n.

continued right up to 1671, with even a trickle thereafter. Peas, wheat, bullocks, and hops, sometimes from his own farm, sometimes bought from tenants or local dealers—all were traded to Gawden for the ultimate and doubtful delectation of English sailors. The returns varied. In February 1664, for example, he bought 24 bags of hops at £3.2s per bag and sold them to Gawden at £3.5s—no great rate of profit; between March and May 1666, however, he sold Gawden 1,562 quarters of peas and 136 quarters of wheat for £3,052, having bought them for £2,646, allowed Gawden £76.15s.2d, and was thus able to put away £329.14s.3d to the credit side of his profit and loss account, a gross return of 12%. The leasing of land to Gawden started in December 1662. It was at Aylesford, part of his home farm, and the annual rent paid was £76 until March 1664; then Gawden presumably took over more land for the rent jumped to £350, stayed at this level until March 1671 when it rose to £425, and then ceased entirely after September of that year when the new victualling syndicate took over. Not knowing how much land was rented, it is impossible to estimate Banks' net profits. But profit apart, the purpose was probably to fatten cattle; Banks' lands by the Medway included some good pastures and his sales of agricultural produce from his own land, before and after this period, included cattle.

The first category of activity—the lending of money—did not assume very large proportions before the 2nd Dutch War, though loans gradually mounted and multiplied, and in 1664 Gawden owed over £1,000 for interest. Thereafter cash advances and indeed all Banks' dealings with Gawden were soon to be complicated by a rising spate of assigned government orders. Such orders were assignable by endorsement, bore interest, were secured on specific branches of the revenue, were registered, numbered, and payable 'in course', i.e. in sequence after a given amount of the revenue on which they were secured had been received. Their proliferation owed much to the financial policy of Sir George Downing, to its embodiment in the terms of the Additional Aid, granted by Parliament in October 1665,[1] and to the growing monetary scarcity made worse by the demands of the Navy. 'Unless the King can get

[1] 17 Car. II c.1.

some noblemen or rich money-gentlemen to lend him money, or to get the City to do it, it is impossible to find money.'[1] The orders multiplied because they became, by reason of their ready assignability,[2] and still further by dint of over-issue, a device for raising cash. They were of three sorts: for the repayment of cash loans (when the order was accompanied by a 'tally of loan'); for the advance of goods; and for cash issues to departments. The last of these were in effect imprests from the Exchequer to departmental officers; and in their desperate search for cash the latter assigned them to bankers and financiers who advanced cash against them—at an increasingly heavy discount. The total issue of orders, not only anticipating but exceeding the yield of the revenues on which they were secured, eventually led, as is well-known, to the Stop in January 1672.[3]

This brings us to the second and active phase of Banks' lending. During that period many of these orders came into his hands. The following table sets out the annual value of those assigned to him by Gawden:

TABLE II

Assignments of Orders by Gawden to Banks

£s

18 March 1666	10,000		25 June 1668	14,150
25 May 1666	10,000		25 June 1668	15,000
30 Nov. 1666	10,000		30 Dec. 1668	20,955
10 Dec. 1666	10,000		31 Aug. 1670	7,000
27 March 1667	6,000		12 June 1671	17,286
16 April 1667	7,000		30 July 1671	16,068
31 Oct. 1667	12,000			

(The dates are those on which the entries were made in Banks' ledger; they are debited to the Royal accounts and credited to Gawden's account).

[1] Pepys, *Diary*, 7 April 1665.
[2] Assignability was statutorily facilitated by 19 & 20 Car. II c. 4.
[3] On government borrowing and the proliferation of Exchequer orders, see D. Ogg, *England in the Reign of Charles II* (Oxford, 1934), II, esp. pp. 442 ff; Shaw's Introduction to the *C.T.B.* for Charles II's reign (these introductions have their uses but should be accepted with caution, not to say suspicion); and for the most detailed and valuable account, C. D. Chandaman; *The English Public Revenue, 1660-88* (unpublished Ph. D. thesis, London, 1954), esp. I, pp. 23 ff., 42 ff.

In addition to lending money to Gawden against the assigned orders, Banks was also lending direct to the Exchequer: not much in the '60s but, as a comparison of Tables I and II will show, increasingly in the '70s. In February 1671, for example, he lent £25,000 (£10,000 for the Treasurer of the Navy, £10,000 for the Victualler, and £5,000 for the Duke of York); in July of the same year he took over £10,000 of orders on the Customs and Excise from Pepys. Then came the Stop and the onset of the Third Dutch War.

In September 1671 the Treasurership of the Navy passed to Sir Thomas Osborne.[1] The outbreak of war in March 1672 put the usual slippery ball of naval finance at his feet. On 2 June 1672 he recorded in his Journal that 'the King sought several ways for the borrowing of money.'[2] And well he might. The bigger goldsmith bankers, though not ruined by the Stop, were unwilling or unable to lend. On the 10th Osborne wrote that he had 'solicited his Majesty for money upon our last demands and acquainted him with the then state and that we could have the whole fleet ready to sail in ten days if provided with money.'[3] Cash was urgently needed for victuallers and for the pay of the sailors. Relief came from three sources: from direct cash assignments by the Treasury; from the group of merchant financiers under the titular leadership of Lord St. John who had bid for the abortive customs farm of 1671; and from Banks. 'I attended the King at my Lord Arlingtons with the victualler where it was agreed I should receive £35,000 of Sir John Banks and £20,000 thereof was ordered to be paid to the victuallers.' Thus wrote Osborne on the 15th June. His entry for the 20th clarifies the position further: 'I was at the office where I acquainted the board with Sir John Banks' ... promise to me of £15,000 within a week, and the Lords of the

There were certain novel elements in these Restoration developments but amongst their antecedents was the earlier practice of assigning and discounting tallies directed at the Customs farmers: see R. Ashton, 'Revenue Farming under the Early Stuarts', *Econ. Hist. Rev.*, 2nd ser. VIII (1956).

[1] A man of many names: shortly afterwards he became the Lord Treasurer Latimer referred to earlier; he finished life as the Duke of Leeds, and is best known to history as the Earl of Danby.

[2] B.M. Add. Mss 28,040, f. 24.

[3] *ibid.*, f. 25.

Treasury promise to assign us £10,000 on Saturday out of the Exchequer; and my Lord St. John's promise to pay £20,000 to me and £10,000 to the office of the Ordnance in 3 weeks...' Taken in conjunction with the foregoing, the immediately following entries provide as illuminating a comment on the shoestring economics of England's navy as could be wished:

'1672. 22 June. I went with his Majesty to the fleet and carried £10,000 with me.

26 June. The fleet sailed...'[1]

Banks, in short, provided urgent relief. He also provided it on time, which the St. John syndicate did not. The full amount he supplied was in fact not £35,000 but £36,500 which was received by Osborne in 8 instalments between 17 June—£14,500 of it on the 17 and 21 June—and 21 July when a final £9,000 came 'in full of £36,500 payable by him.'[2] In his account of receipts of money for the Navy, Osborne also records at various dates from 5 to 28 October 1672 the receipt in five instalments of £47,512.7s.9d 'from Sir John Banks for payment of ships.' This, however, came not from Banks' personal resources but from those of the East India Company, and was delivered by him in his capacity as Governor.[3]

So both directly and indirectly, Banks made important contributions to naval finance in the third Dutch War. His direct, personal contribution was contingent upon a settlement of his outstanding claims upon the government after the Stop. Settlement hinged as usual upon the further loans which were so urgently needed. Towards the end of May 1672 the Treasury ordered that a statement of the government's outstanding indebtedness to Banks should be prepared. Duly certified by the Auditor of the Receipt on 20 June 1672 it recorded, to the last farthing, the existence of a debt of

---

[1] *ibid.*, f. 25.

[2] *ibid.*, ff. 28-31. Osborne did not receive the final instalment from Lord St. John's syndicate until 26 Aug: 'in full of the £20,000 from Lord St. John which they promised to have paid the 16th July.'

[3] *ibid.*, and *C.T.B.*, *1669-72*, 1324, 1325. The sum consisted of two elements: a £20,000 loan and £27,512.7s.9d. advanced out of the Customs payable by the company on their own imports.

£60,202.6s.8¼d, principal and interest.[1] It consisted chiefly of orders on the Hearth Tax, Customs, Excise, and the Wine Act,[2] many of them assignments from Gawden, with overdue interest, some of it dating from June of the previous year. The settlement was worked out in June and put into effect on 2 July 1672. Banks agreed to make further loans totalling £51,500, and advanced £17,500 thereof in June. The £36,500 which Osborne received from Banks came out of the total and his early receipts out of the advance. Because Banks had already produced this and was 'speedily to furnish us with a greater sum', the £17,500 was added to his £60,202.6s.8¼d, making £77,702.6s.8¼d and arrangements were made for this entire debt to be transferred to Banks in the form of fee-farm rents.[3]

These were fixed annual rents payable out of former Crown lands, mainly Tudor confiscations from the Church which had been alienated in perpetuity. An Act for the sale of these rents went through Parliament in 1670.[4] The rents to be sold were those in the King's possession and those in the jointure of the Queen; the former were offered at 16-18 years purchase, for immediate possession; the latter at 8 years purchase for possession in reversion after the Queen's death. Between 1670 and 1682 total sales realised approximately £800,000 but over £550,000 accrued in 1671-2.[5] The Act had stated that preference was to be given in purchase to the immediate tenants

---

[1] *C.T.B., 1669-72*, 1076, 1082, 1243, 1266-7. For a note on the interest see below p. 225 n.

[2] 19 & 20 Car. II, c. 6: an act designed (unsuccessfully) to raise £310,000 by duties on wine imports.

[3] Of the £51,500 the £17,500 advance was first secured against tallies of loan and then placed on the fee farms, £20,000 were secured on the sale of prize goods, and the remaining £14,000 on the East India customs See ledger C. f. 3 and *C.T.B.*, 1669-72, 1258, 1267 Formally Banks was 'admitted to purchase' fee-farms to the total of £77,702.6.s.81.d. but the instructions givne to the Exchequer officials and to the trustees for the sale of the fee-farm rents indicate that in reality his debt was to be satisfied by their transfer to him. It is clear that he was given preferential treatment in the whole affair. See *C.T.B., 1669-72*, 1090, 1092, 1100, 1106, 1252, 1267, 1276, 1278, 1781, 1289, 1463, etc., and B.M. Add. Mss. 28,073.

[4] 22 Car. II, c. 60.

[5] Chandaman, *op. cit.*, pp. 323-9.

liable for payment. It seems clear, however, that substantial blocks of rents were used, especially in 1671-2, to satisfy important creditors.[1] Banks' grant was apparently the largest amount transferred to a single person in this manner. Certainly, as the Chancellor of the Exchequer remarked in 1674, 'Lord St. John (for himself and his partners in the late intended farm of the Customs) and Sir John Banks (for his own debt) made the first breach into the fee farms.'[2]

Leaving aside a few relatively minor transactions, two main concluding items end this phase of Banks' lending. Between January 1673 and March 1674 he made the loans mentioned above which he recorded under the account of Lord Treasurer Clifford: they were mainly short-term advances, for example, £2,000 lent on 10 January to be repaid on 10 February, and they were duly repaid. In March 1674 he advanced, to Lord Treasurer Latimer, £20,000 against the Dutch indemnity totalling 800,000 patacoons,[3] payable under the terms of the Treaty of Westminster; by June of the following year Banks had been repaid in full. This brings us nearly to the date of Evelyn's comment of August 1676. Like Luttrell's his figure for Banks' estate, £100,000, was not far from the truth. Perhaps it was common gossip; perhaps Banks boasted about it. If the latter he may have kept to the side of modesty or safety, for his books show that his capital of a mere £29,000 in 1663 had grown to over £124,000 in 1676.

Banks' profits in the 'perilous role' are difficult to calculate at all accurately and it is impossible here to isolate their particular contributions to his growing wealth. For convenience they will be examined under two main heads: the discounting of orders, and the collection of interest. The former may be approached, as a matter of

---

[1] Apart from Banks' £77,702 repayments of this type included part of a government debt of £60,000 to the City of London, much of the £200,000 owing to Lord St. John's syndicate for an advance on the abortive Customs farm of 1671, and £61,700 towards the debt owing to the goldsmith, John Lyndsey C.T.B., *1669-72*, 1330, 1332, 1334, 1339-40, etc.; Chandaman, *op. cit.*, p. 327 n; Add. Mss. 28,073.

[2] C.T.B., *1672-5*, 226.

[3] A patacoon was worth about 4s. 8d.

comparison and illustration, via Pepys' transaction, referred to earlier. In this, at the instigation of Sir William Warren, Pepys put a cautious finger into the financial pie and pulled out a modest plum. With much trepidation and preliminary research, he advanced £1,900 to Warren in cash and took his assignment of an order for £2,602.2s.7d. Of the £700.2s.7d difference he records that £300 was a gift from Warren, the remainder interest. Four months later he sold the assignment to John Colvill, the goldsmith, for £2,432.2s.7d, thus allowing Colvill £170 'for the forbearance till (when ever it shall be) he shall be paid.' So in this transaction Warren got his cash at a discount on the face value of the order of about 15% (excluding the gift). Colvill's acquisition of the order was at a discount of $6\frac{1}{2}$% at a time when, according to Pepys, it had about three months to run before becoming due for payment. Thus on the whole transaction, and excluding the gift, Pepys made a net profit of £230 on his original venture of £1,900, i.e. about 12%, and all in four months (with the gift included, it would be £530 and about 27%).[1]

Pepys being the man he was has kindly left the historian a precise record. Banks presumably had no need then to provide himself with such careful information, and his methods of entering transactions of this type in his ledgers are so oblique as to seem discreet. But occasionally in his journals he is obligingly detailed. In August 1670, for instance, he settled a debt of £8,456 to the goldsmith Joseph Horneby with orders on the Wine Act, received from Gawden, to a total value of £11,500, the surplus £3,044 'being for his consideration and hazard till said orders are received which is supposed to be about 3 years.' This works out at a crude discount on the face value of nearly 27%. And this same rate was immediately applied in the opposite direction to another batch of orders for £7,000 received from Gawden: '£1,852 allowed me in consideration of the... orders for £7,000 upon the Wine Act being about 3 or 4 years to come, being the same as I allowed unto Mr. Horneby.'[2] Nearly a year later, either the same or another £11,500's worth of orders on the Wine Acts were again

---

[1] Details of the transaction will be found in Bodleian: Rawlinson Mss. A. 174, f. 436 and *Diary*, 1, 2 & 3 April 1666 and 11 & 13 Aug 1666.
[2] Journal, B. f. 273.

being peddled between Banks and Horneby, and this time Banks bought them for £9,448, 'not being expected to come to be received these 2 years and a half', the balance of £ 2,052 'in allowance for time till paid',[1] representing a discount of 18% which, in proportion to the differing periods before payment was expected, seems to be about the same rate as in the earlier deal. In July 1671 he took £2,637 on Hearth Tax orders from Gawden to the value of £17,286, a discount of about 15%.

Rates of discount varied according to the branch of the revenue on which the orders were secured and the expected (and it was no more than that) time they became due for payment, as well as sometimes including imprecise elements of gifts and considerations. The premium on liquidity remained and whoever could afford to wait stood a good chance of reaping his reward in the long run. Meanwhile he collected interest. The legal maximum rate of 6% was formally payable on government orders and Banks' accounts provide plenty of evidence that he collected sums both large and small in this way. This was the rate received by the ordinary investors who were induced to lend on the security of the Aid of 1665, but it was not enough to attract the large cash loans which the government increasingly needed. For this it had to pay an extra 2% or 4%. Banks, in common with other financiers of his status, frequently received the extra 4%, variously called 'over interest', 'reward' or 'gratuity'. In 1668, for example, he had orders on the Hearth Tax, 'as Meynell's [i.e. the goldsmith banker] with interest at 6% and 4%'; in February 1671 he received principal and interest on two orders on the Wine Act totalling £9,611.2s.2d, the interest being £444.6s.0d plus, as he put it, 'given in allowance for pains, etc.,' £296.3s.6d, i.e. 6% + 4% for 9 months; and, for a final example his advance of £20,000 on the Dutch indemnity of 1674 brought him interest 'at the rate of 6% interest and 4% gratuity' in the wording of the official order of repayment.[2]

[1] *ibid* , f 289.
[2] *C.T.B.*, *1667-8*, 385; Journal B. f. 283; *C.T.B.*, *1672-7*, 719 and Journal C. f. 28 and Waste Book (where there is a copy of the repayment order); for some other examples of gratuities and rewards paid to Banks, see *C.T.B.*, *1669-72*, 781, 787,

Interest and discount together could provide an ample return. But there were other advantages which accrued to such men as Banks. His status as a merchant baronet and financier, and his position in the hierarchy of the East India Company had their special and devious rewards; use and profit likewise flowed from political connections and influential friends. None of these can be examined here. For the present it must suffice to indicate that although he sat intermittently in Parliament from 1654 to 1697 in an interest which seems to be describable as Tory, and although his connections with the East India Company and the Navy also linked him to the Court and its party, he nevertheless numbered Locke and Shaftesbury amongst his friends; and it may not be wholly irrelevant that Shaftesbury, who in 1677 referred to Banks as his 'intimate good friend', was variously Chancellor of the Exchequer, one of the Commissioners of the Treasury, Treasurer of Prizes, and finally Lord Chancellor, between 1661 and 1673.[1]

It was probably influence, as well as the promise of more cash, which brought the fee-farm settlement of 1672. The settlement had potential disadvantages, of course: it could reduce Banks' own liquidity; the many and scattered rents could prove irksome to collect. In the long run, however, it was not unsatisfactory, and Banks could probably count himself fortunate to be one of the favoured few. He got the rents at the 10% discount which, by the terms of the Act for their sale, was allowed for cash payment; and the possession rents were all valued at the minimum figure of 16 years purchase. Of the £77,702's worth he thus received, he rapidly disposed of rents to the value of some £42,000, mainly to Horneby; and in the following decade sold more, mainly possession rents at 17 and 18 years purchase, and a few reversions at 8½. By 1682 he had succeeded in selling all the possession rents not in his own county of Kent, retaining those 799, 807, 856, etc.

Although the interest shown in the statement of his claims in June 1672 (above pp. 220-1) was calculated at 6 per cent, it is clear from entries elsewhere that he received the extra 4% on at least some of the major items included therein, e.g. on £16,068 of orders on the Customs and Excise assigned him by Gawden (see *C.T.B., 1669-72*, 1159).

[1] Christie, *op. cit.*, II, p. 235 and *passim*.

there to the annual value of £380. In the '90s he continued to sell, and at values which nearly, though not quite, justified the optimistic book values to which he had appreciated the rents by 1694: 21 years purchase for possession, and 18 for reversion. The latter proved a poorer bet for Banks in his lifetime, for the Queen obstinately lived on to 1705, thus leaving Banks at his own death saddled with a reversionary asset which he was then valuing at over £19,000.

Bargaining power and influence, from whatever source, also brought two other valuable but not precisely quantifiable rewards. One of these was the ability to arrange for orders registered on one branch of the revenue to be shifted to another, either more secure or more likely to produce earlier repayment. Banks procured a number of such transfers: his orders on the Poll Bill were shifted at his request to the Hearth Tax in July 1668; so also in 1670, were various orders of his (and Viner's) originally registered on the over-burdened Additional Aid; a number of orders secured on the inadequately yielding Wine Act were transferred to the Excise. He also arranged similarly advantageous shifts on behalf of the East India Company, for example in 1672 the £40,000 owed to the company by the Crown was moved from the Hearth Tax to the Customs payable by the company itself.[1] The other and closely related reward of this power and influence was the ability to secure repayment promptly or before the current position 'in course'. Sometimes this was secured by shifting the security. But a new and better replacement 'in course' of existing orders to the value of £25,000 secured on the Wine Act was part of the price demanded, and obtained, by Banks in February 1671 for the further £25,000 cash which he then agreed to lend. And it is clear from sundry instructions issued that as his value as a supplier of cash grew in 1671 and 1672, so was extra care and promptitude exercised in the payment of money due to him.[2]

The procedure by which the government's thirst for liquidity was assuaged and Banks' profits were multiplied was akin to that in which a juggler balances a number of balls and also rotates them faster

[1] *C.T.B.*, *1667-8*, 379, 385; *C.T.B.*, *1669-72*, 445, 503, 506, 774, 1105.
[2] *C.T.B.*, *1669-72*, 731, 774, 844, 897, 974, 1049, etc.

and faster. Both cash and credit were made to work harder: the demand for liquid funds increased the velocity of circulation of cash and brought it higher returns in the process. Where, then, did Banks' cash come from?

Before trying to answer this question it must be made clear that in his accounts Banks does not regularly indicate the precise nature of what he enters as cash payments or receipts. In other words we cannot determine how much he received or supplied money in the form of specie or in the form of good short-dated bills or other readily acceptable commercial paper. The 'cash', with this reservation, came from sundry sources, be they differing forms of income or variations in the structure of his assets: from profits on his trading ventures, from dividends on East India stock, from rents, and interest. None can be considered in detail here, but certain points may be noted. First, it is clear that an important role was played by the goldsmiths with whom he banked: Viner, Backwell, and then increasingly after the middle of 1671, Joseph and Nathaniel Horneby who were not themselves major lenders to the government. Second, during this period Banks held many of his assets in fairly liquid form: money lent on demand at 5% to the East India Company, a variety of small loans to neighbours, relatives or friends at a similar rate; he also seems to have had a few deposits from such sources. Third, and perhaps most important, there were cash repayments by the government. In the sometimes over-dramatized picture of later Stuart finances—the violence of the Stop, the inadequate and reluctant Parliamentary grants, Charles II's soliciting of Louis XIV's aid, the unpaid sailors—it is sometimes forgotten that, for all its woes, the Exchequer long continued to make cash payments and that even the Stop did not affect all government issues of money. Given adequate resources, credit and influence, and the financial judgment, or luck, to know when to lend and when not, it was possible so to juggle payment, waiting, and repayment in such a manner as not to impair one's own liquidity.

Throughout this period, Banks received large cash sums in repayment of earlier loans, plus interest, and it is clear from his accounts that they were never allowed to stand idle. Nor were they much used during this period for buying illiquid assets. Although some land was bought, it was mainly obtained before or after these years of high lending, and much of his biggest expenditure on household and domestic matters, marriage portions, travel and education for his son, and the like, was incurred after this phase was over. As soon as cash came in, it was sent out again to earn its fat reward. Table III may help to illustrate this:

TABLE III

Cash receipts, net surplus and stock, 1657–84

Period	Av. ann. receipts in Cash a/c. £s	Av. ann. net surplus to Stock a/c. £s	Stock at beginning of each period £s
Nov. 1657—June 1663	46,160	2,723	13,494
June 1663—May 1665	32,250	1,942	28,993
May 1665—Mar. 1667	70,935 ⎰	3,862	32,715
Mar. 1667—Dec. 1669	68,900 ⎱		
Dec. 1669—July 1671	105,600 ⎰	10,180*	50,416
July 1671—Apr. 1672	41,300 ⎱		
Apr. 1672—Oct. 1674	140,800 ⎰	5,388	101,960†
Oct. 1674—June 1676	77,230 ⎱		
June 1676—May 1679	60,560	3,064	124,411†
May 1679—June 1684	81,980	3,305	133,349†

* excludes inheritance from his father in 1669 of £28,637
† includes inheritance from his father in 1669 of £28,637

The irregularity of the periods in this table arises from the irregularity with which Banks made up and balanced his accounts: convenience, whim, space on a page, or the end of a volume seem to have been the main determinants. It should be added that the cash balance at the end of each period was always very small; the figures for average annual receipts may therefore be used as a reasonable indicator of cash turnover. The table thus reveals how the ratio of cash turnover to stock changed after the years of vigorous lending were over; how his liquidity was sharply reduced in the period during which the Stop occurred; and how his greatest net surpluses were achieved during years of war or preparation for war. Dudley North spoke of goldsmiths and scriveners depending 'upon a course of Trade, whereby

Money comes in as fast as it is taken out; wherefore I conclude, that the specifick Money of this Nation is far less than the Common Opinion makes.'[1] The first part of the observation equally holds good for Banks' financial activities; and the second part, as a comment on the general tendency towards a scarcity of money is as valid for the 1660s and '70s as for 1691 when it was written.

III

To stress the importance of monetary scarcity and the government's demand for cash is not to depreciate the familiar bogeys. This essay is an apology neither for government behaviour nor for the financial machinations of a rich tycoon. The unpaid sailors were still there; the rich creditors did better than the poor. They usually do. And liquidity is no explanation of that. My aim has been rather to present these particular activities of a particular man as reactions to problems posed by a set of economic and financial circumstances.

Banks may have been more grasping or shrewd or lucky or ruthless than the mythically average man; with this, for present purposes, I am not concerned. Suffice that he acted logically, skilfully and profitably in reaction to given stimuli. And he did what he did for practical reasons and not because he was moved by mystic forces. He ploughed back his cash into more lending now or bought land and status later because these actions were in the logic of economic exigencies and contemporary conventions, not because of a nebulous Protestant Ethic urging frugality and mysteriously favouring the reinvestment of gain, and not because the Spirit of Capitalism had spectrally alighted to shed its money-grubbing aura over the former priory of Aylesford. Nevertheless, in these conventional, though perceptive, economic reactions to the premium on liquidity he committed what had once been a sin, was in his time only a crime, and has always been regarded as morally invidious. And so in August 1672, four years before Evelyn's comment, two months after he had brought cash to Osborne to help pay the English fleet and set it to sea, Sir John Banks thought

[1] North, *op. cit.*, 21.

fit to take out a personal insurance: he secured from the King a grant of pardon for all usurious contracts.[1]

[1] *Calendar of State Papers Domestic, 1672*, p. 492. Banks was again one of the favoured few. Bakwell got his pardon in June 1672. Viner, Horneby, Meynell, and certain other goldsmiths in August, and the St. John syndicate in September. The particular concern of these pardons was the taking of interest of more than 6%, thus contravening 12 Car. II, c. 13 and 14; *ibid.*, pp. 245, 515, 550, and *C.T.B.*, *1669-72*, 1314, 1318, 1331.

Viner's pardon *(Cal. S. P. Dom., 1672*, pp. 515-6)* specifies that he had 'taken a higher rate of interest than 6 per cent, he having since the restoration advanced sums amounting to several millions to the King and having for that purpose borrowed and kept by him unemployed great sums, and for such services payments above the usual interest having been made to him by way of reward'— an interesting comment on Child's and Shaftesbury's observations quoted above pp. 208-9.

INDEX